THE CRYPTICS

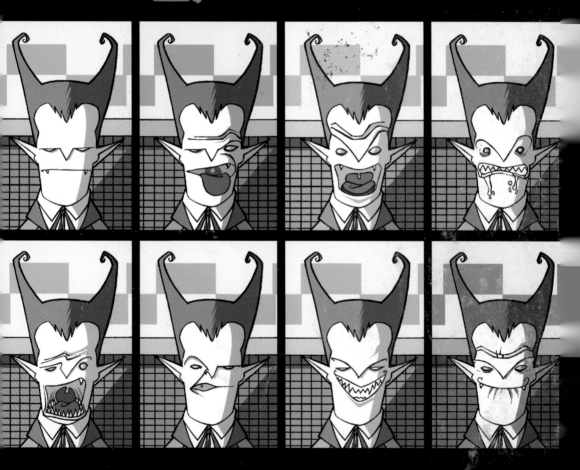

Issue #1

Written by Steve Niles
Illustrated by Benjamin Roman
Lettered by Jason Hanley

"Big Black Cat"
Colors by Paulo Henrique S.B.

"Dem da Rules"
Colors by Fabian "Monk" Schlaga

"Gone Fish'n"
Colors by Benjamin Roman

"Milkbones and Biscuts"
Colors by Nicolas Chapuis

"Mirror Mirror"
Colors by Benjamin Roman

"Murky Waters"
Colors by Chuck Pires

"Scary Wolfman"
Colors by Jorge Molina Manzanero

"Test"
Colors by Jorge Molina Manzanero

"X Massacre"
Colors by Benjamin Roman

Issue #2

Written by Steve Niles
and Benjamin Roman
Illustrated by Benjamin Roman
Lettered by Jason Hanley

Issue #3

"Frontline"
Written by Steve Niles
and Benjamin Roman
Art by Billy Martin

"Identity Crisis"
Written by Benjamin Roman
Art by Benjamin Roman, Robert Iza,
Dylan McCrae, Kris Anka,
Vidar Cornelius, Shane Long,
Fabian "Monk" Schlaga, and David Igo

"Old Debts"
Written by Benjamin Roman
Art by Benjamin Roman
Colors by Kyle Foster
Letters and Layout by Jason Hanley

Collection Designed by Neil Uyetake
Collection Edited by Justin Eisinger

IDW Publishi
Operatio
Moshe Berger, Chairm
Ted Adams, Preside
Matthew Ruzicka, CPA, Control
Alan Payne, VP of Sa
Lorelei Bunjes, Dir. of Digital Servi
Marci Hubbard, Executive Assista
Alonzo Simon, Shipping Manag

Editori
Chris Ryall, Publisher/Editor-in-Ch
Scott Dunbier, Editor, Special Proje
Andy Schmidt, Senior Edit
Justin Eisinger, Edit
Kris Oprisko, Editor/Foreign L.
Denton J. Tipton, Edit
Tom Waltz, Edi
Mariah Huehner, Assistant Edi

Desig
Robbie Robbins, EVP/Sr. Graphic Art
Ben Templesmith, Artist/Design
Neil Uyetake, Art Direct
Chris Mowry, Graphic Arti
Amauri Osorio, Graphic Arti

ISBN: 978-1-60010-254-7
11 10 09 08   1 2 3 4
www.IDWpublishing.com

THE CRYPTICS

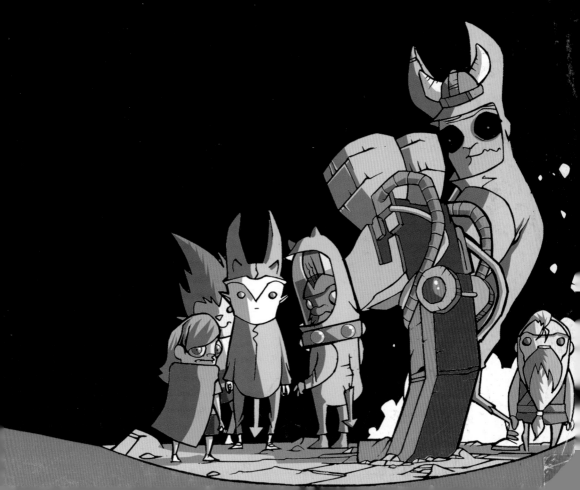

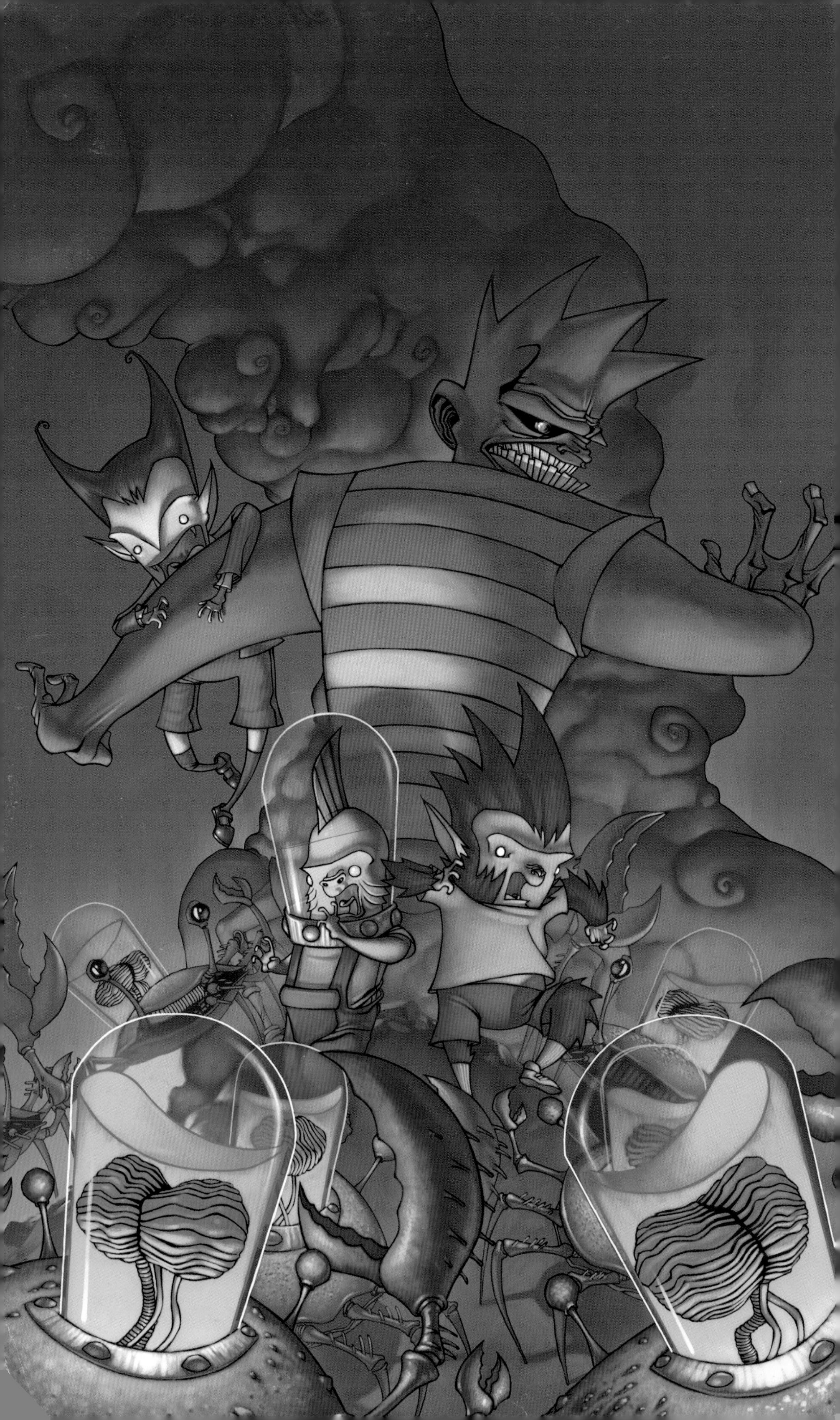

THE CRYPTICS
IN:
BIG BLACK CAT

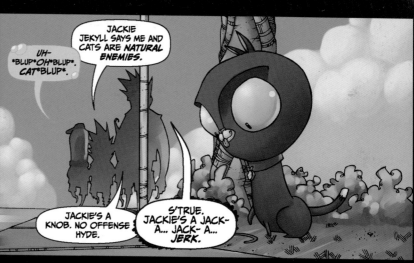

UH— *BLUP* OH *BLUP*. CAT *BLUP*.

JACKIE JEKYLL SAYS ME AND CATS ARE *NATURAL* ENEMIES.

JACKIE'S A KNOB. NO OFFENSE HYDE.

S'TRUE. JACKIE'S A JACK- A... JACK- A... *JERK*.

WUZ THE MATTER, WOLFY? YOU AFRAID OF CATS?

I DUNNO. WHAT IF JACKIE'S RIGHT AND CATS AND WOLVES *ARE* NATURAL ENEMIES? WHAT IF WE HAVE TO FIGHT TO THE BLOODY DEATH?

purr!

SO MUCH FOR NATURE.

fin.

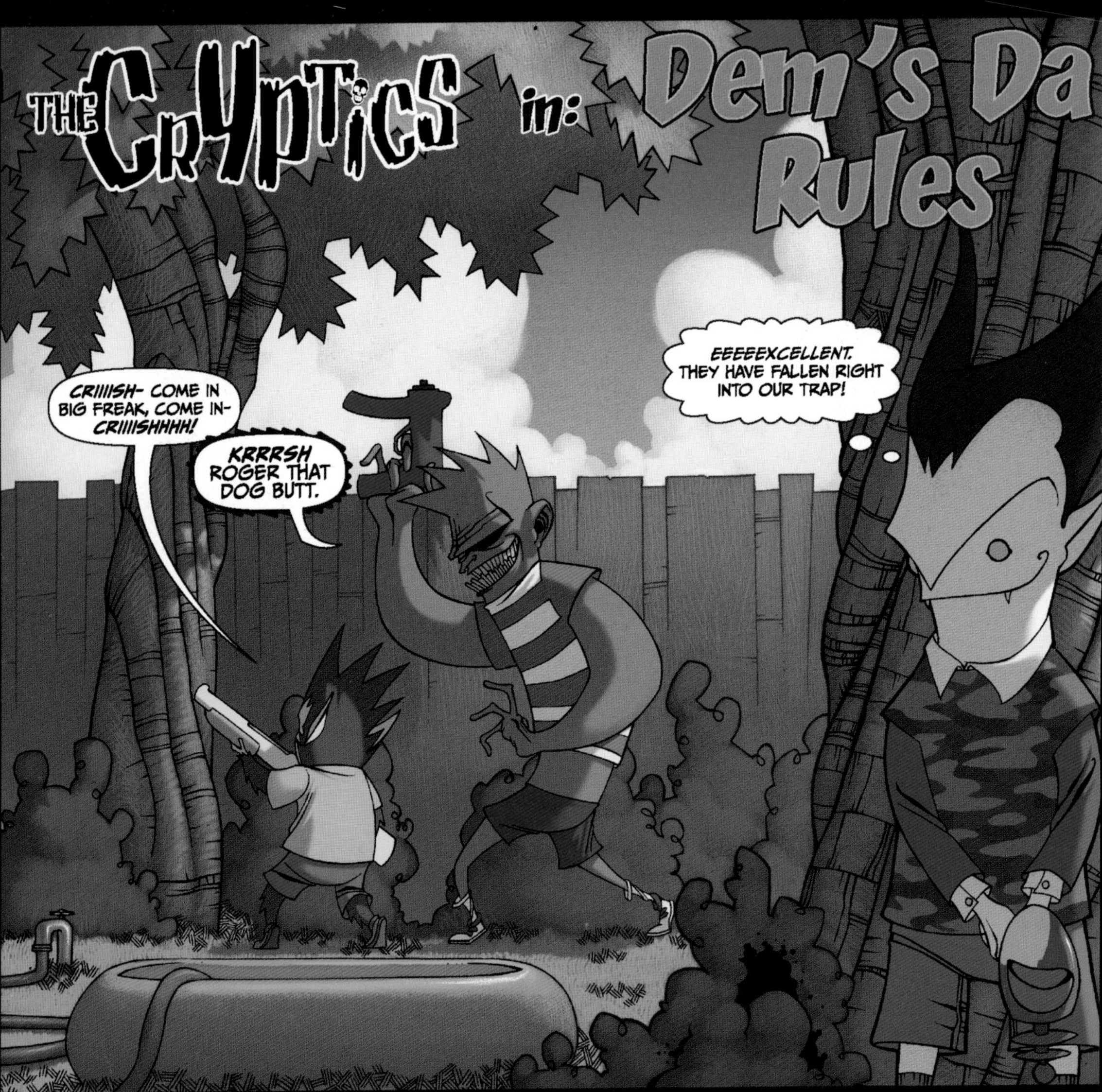
THE CRYPTICS in: Dem's Da Rules
CRIIIISH- COME IN BIG FREAK, COME IN- CRIIIISHHHH!
KRRRSH ROGER THAT DOG BUTT.
EEEEEXCELLENT. THEY HAVE FALLEN RIGHT INTO OUR TRAP!

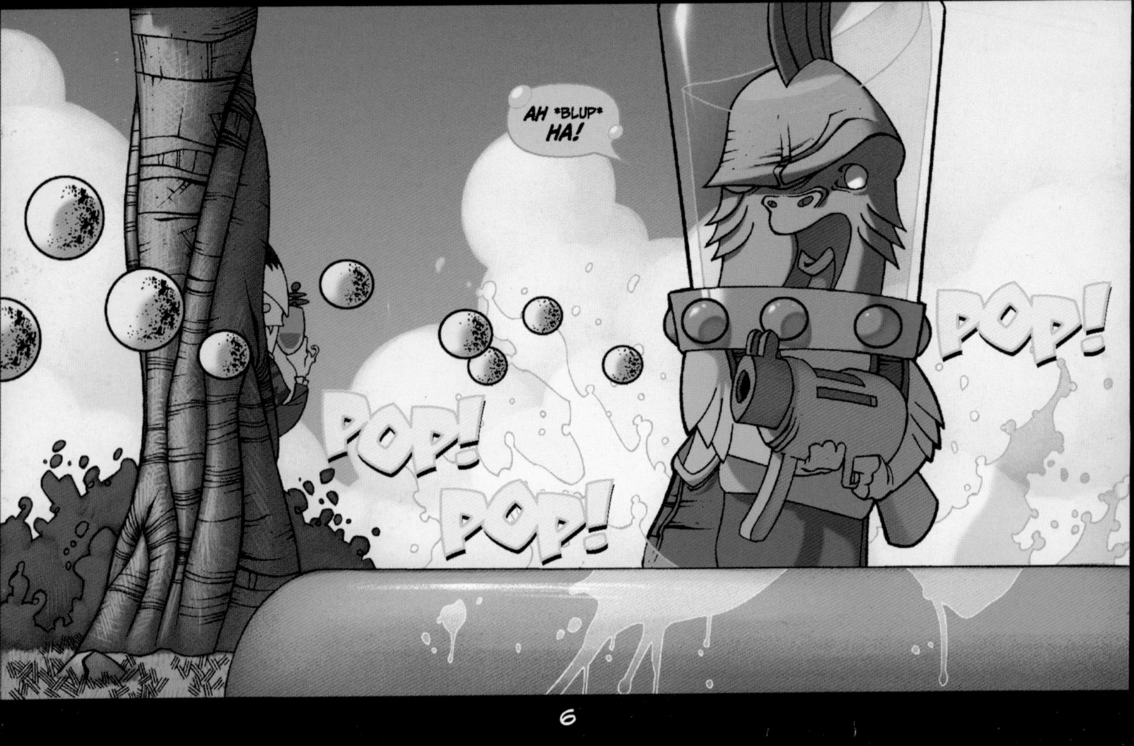
AH *BLUP* HA!
POP!
POP!
POP!

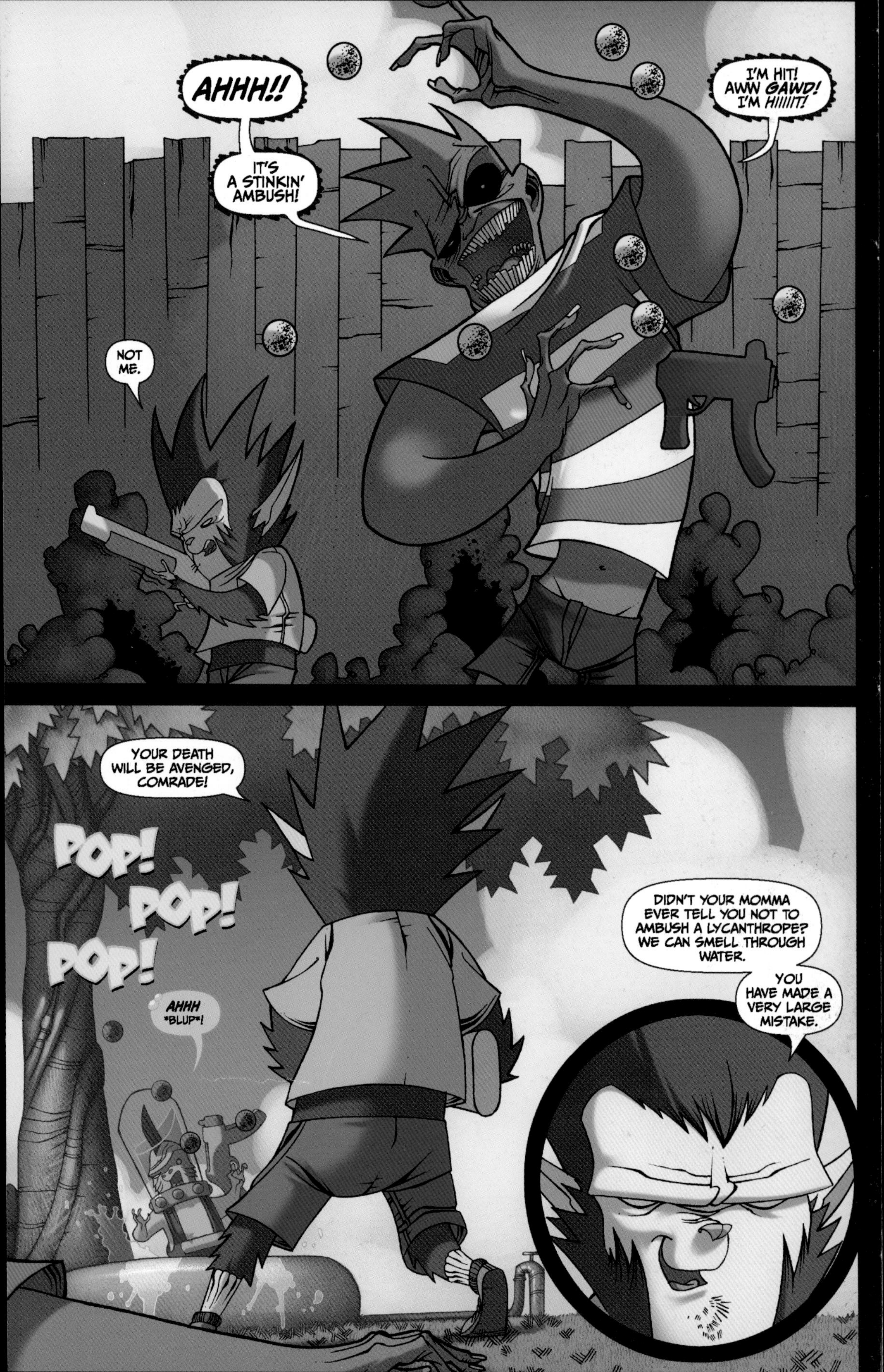
AHHH!!
IT'S A STINKIN' AMBUSH!
I'M HIT! AWW GAWD! I'M HIIIIIT!
NOT ME.
YOUR DEATH WILL BE AVENGED, COMRADE!
POP! POP! POP!
AHHH *BLUP*!
DIDN'T YOUR MOMMA EVER TELL YOU NOT TO AMBUSH A LYCANTHROPE? WE CAN SMELL THROUGH WATER.
YOU HAVE MADE A VERY LARGE MISTAKE.

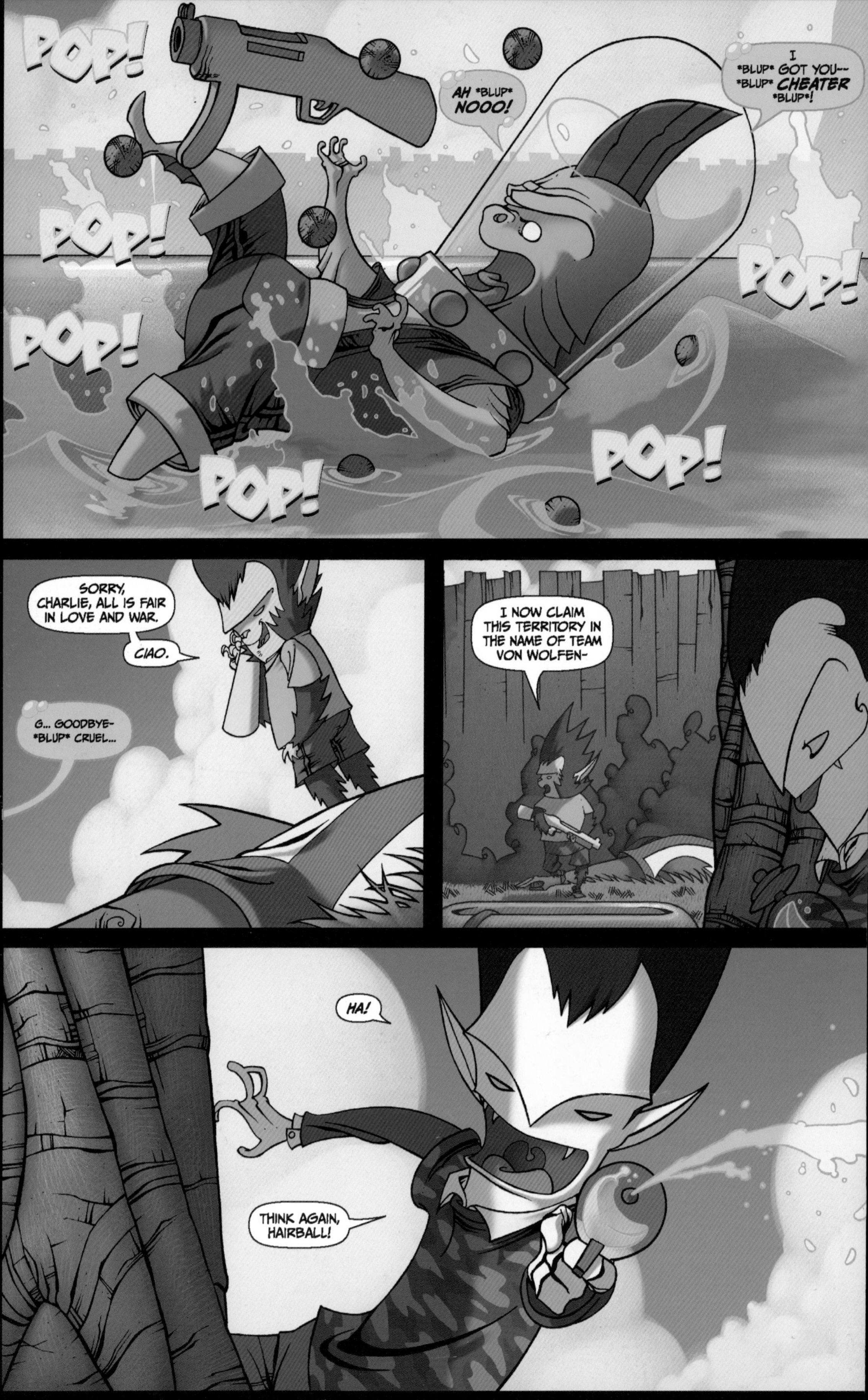
POP!
AH *BLUP* NOOO!
I *BLUP* GOT YOU-- *BLUP* CHEATER *BLUP*!
POP!
POP!
POP!
POP!
POP!
SORRY, CHARLIE, ALL IS FAIR IN LOVE AND WAR.
CIAO.
G... GOODBYE- *BLUP* CRUEL...
I NOW CLAIM THIS TERRITORY IN THE NAME OF TEAM VON WOLFEN-
HA!
THINK AGAIN, HAIRBALL!

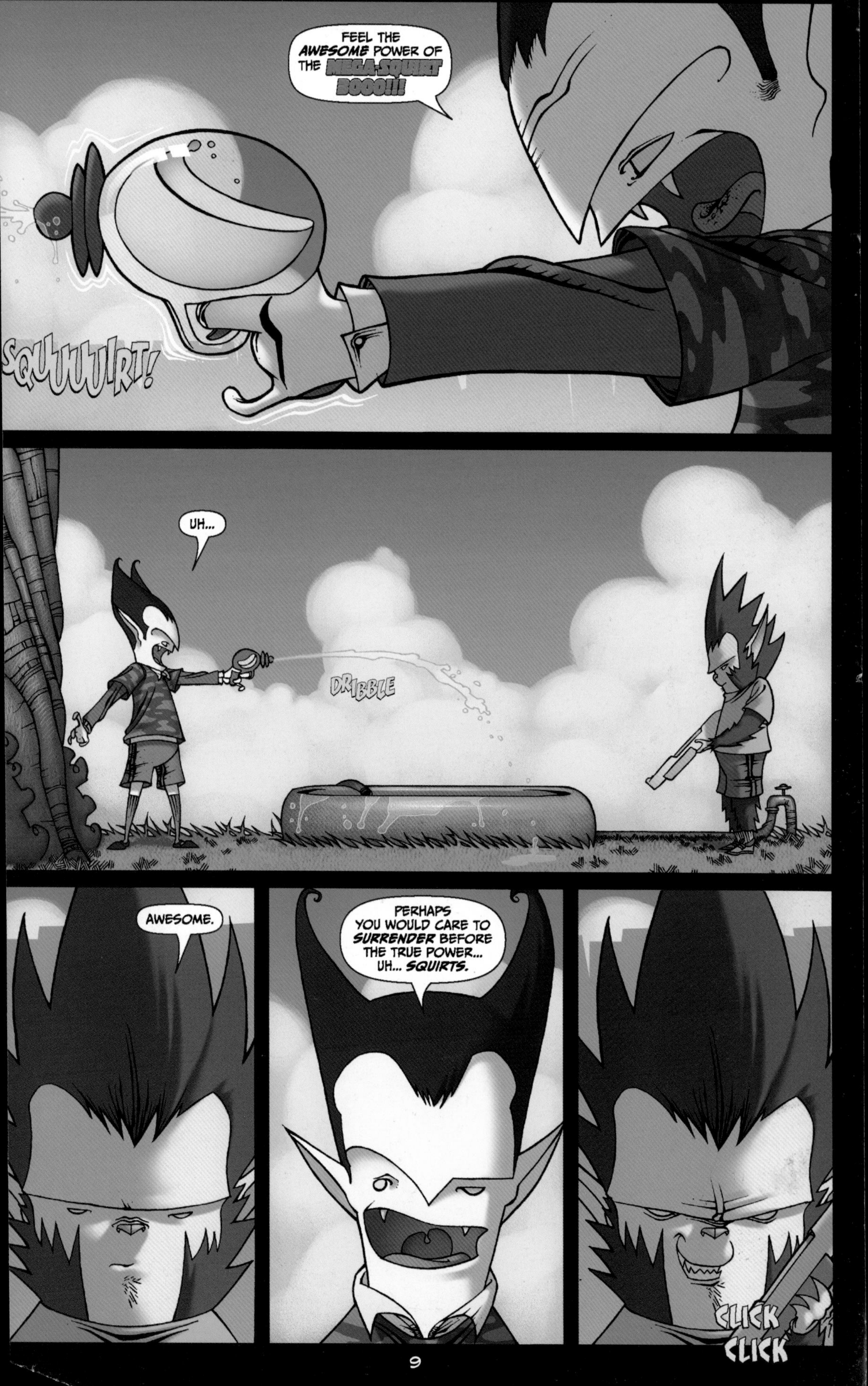
FEEL THE AWESOME POWER OF THE MEGA-SQUIRT 3000!!!
SQUUUUIRT!
UH...
DRIBBLE
AWESOME.
PERHAPS YOU WOULD CARE TO SURRENDER BEFORE THE TRUE POWER... UH... SQUIRTS.
CLICK
CLICK

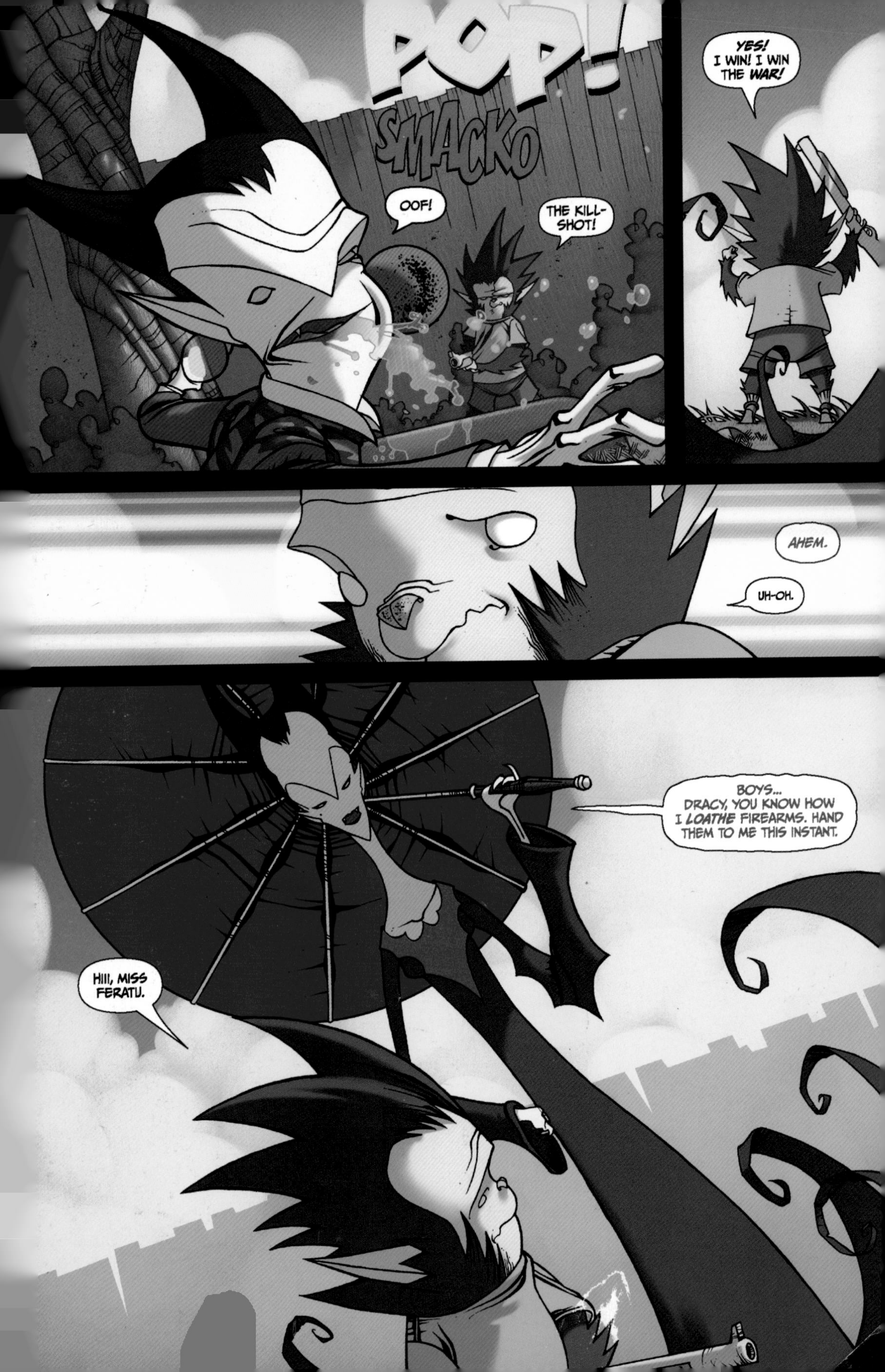
POP!
SMACKO
OOF!
THE KILL-SHOT!
YES! I WIN! I WIN THE WAR!
AHEM.
UH-OH.
BOYS... DRACY, YOU KNOW HOW I LOATHE FIREARMS. HAND THEM TO ME THIS INSTANT.
HIII, MISS FERATU.

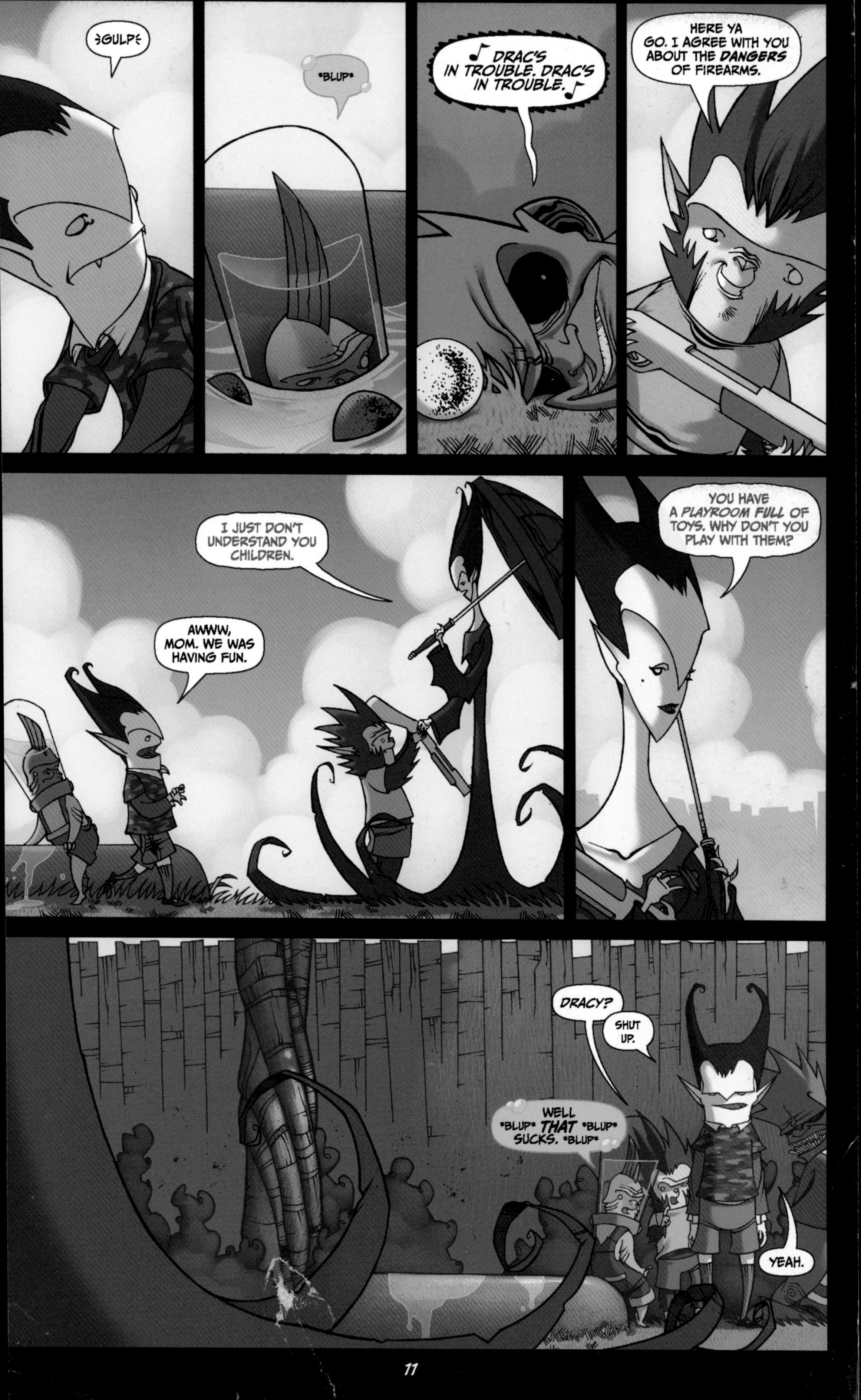

GULP
BLUP
DRAC'S IN TROUBLE. DRAC'S IN TROUBLE.
HERE YA GO. I AGREE WITH YOU ABOUT THE DANGERS OF FIREARMS.
I JUST DON'T UNDERSTAND YOU CHILDREN.
AWWW, MOM. WE WAS HAVING FUN.
YOU HAVE A PLAYROOM FULL OF TOYS. WHY DON'T YOU PLAY WITH THEM?
DRACY?
SHUT UP.
WELL *BLUP* THAT *BLUP* SUCKS. *BLUP*
YEAH.

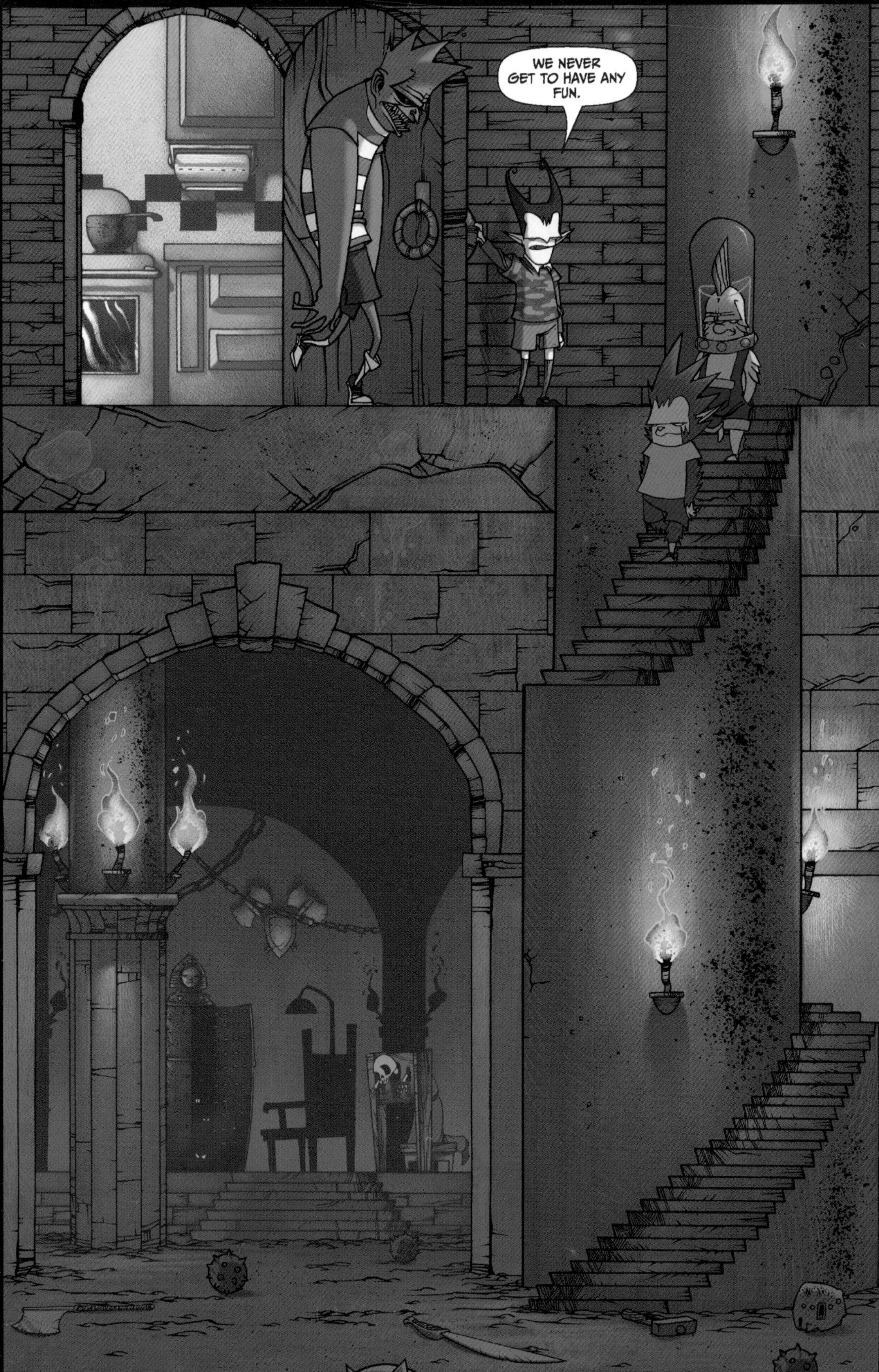
WE NEVER GET TO HAVE ANY FUN.

FIN

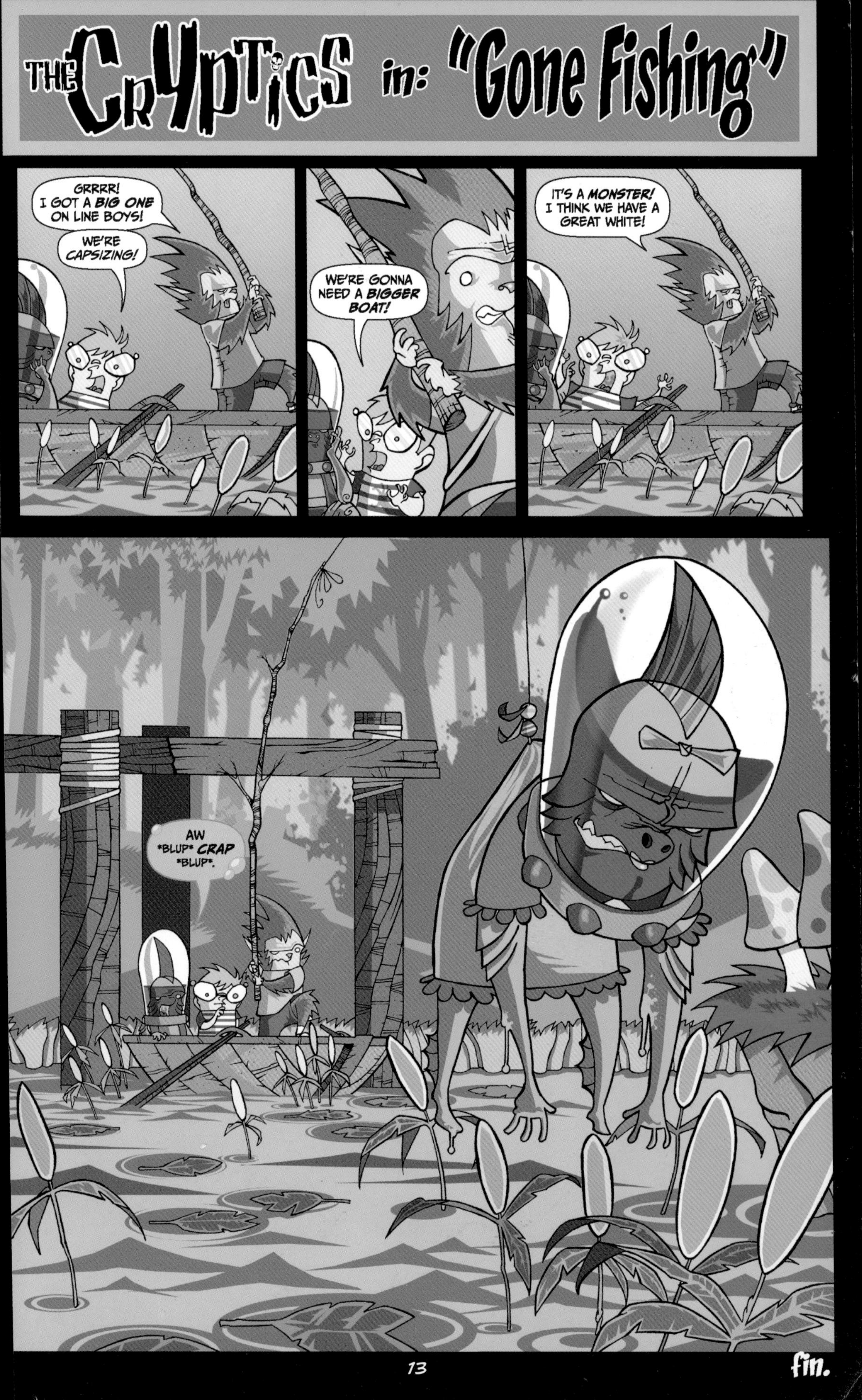
THE CRYPTICS in: "Gone Fishing"
GRRRR! I GOT A BIG ONE ON LINE BOYS!
WE'RE CAPSIZING!
WE'RE GONNA NEED A BIGGER BOAT!
IT'S A MONSTER! I THINK WE HAVE A GREAT WHITE!
AW *BLUP* CRAP *BLUP*.
fin.

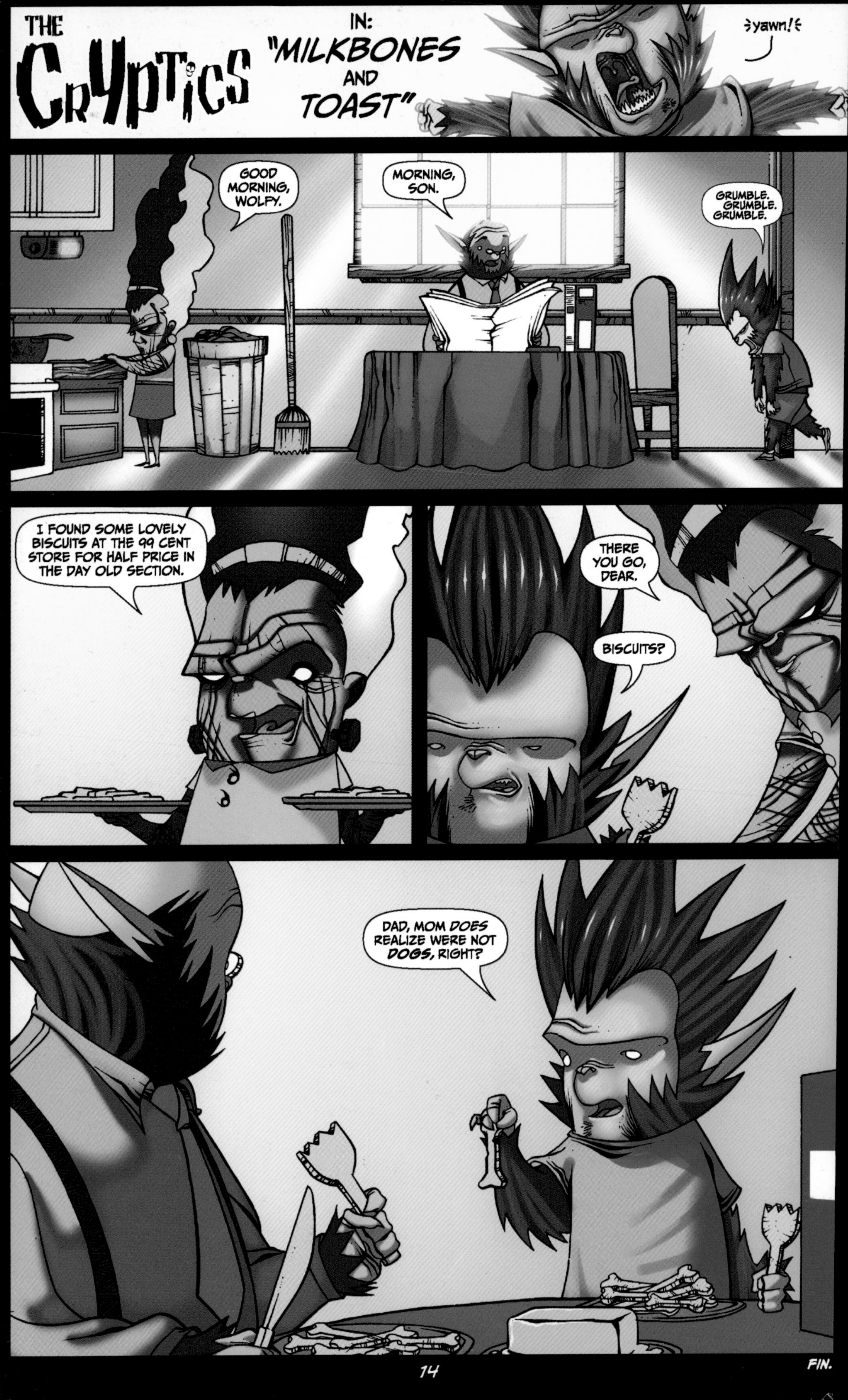
THE CRYPTICS
IN: "MILKBONES AND TOAST"
yawn!
GOOD MORNING, WOLFY.
MORNING, SON.
GRUMBLE. GRUMBLE. GRUMBLE.
I FOUND SOME LOVELY BISCUITS AT THE 99 CENT STORE FOR HALF PRICE IN THE DAY OLD SECTION.
THERE YOU GO, DEAR.
BISCUITS?
DAD, MOM DOES REALIZE WERE NOT DOGS, RIGHT?
FIN.

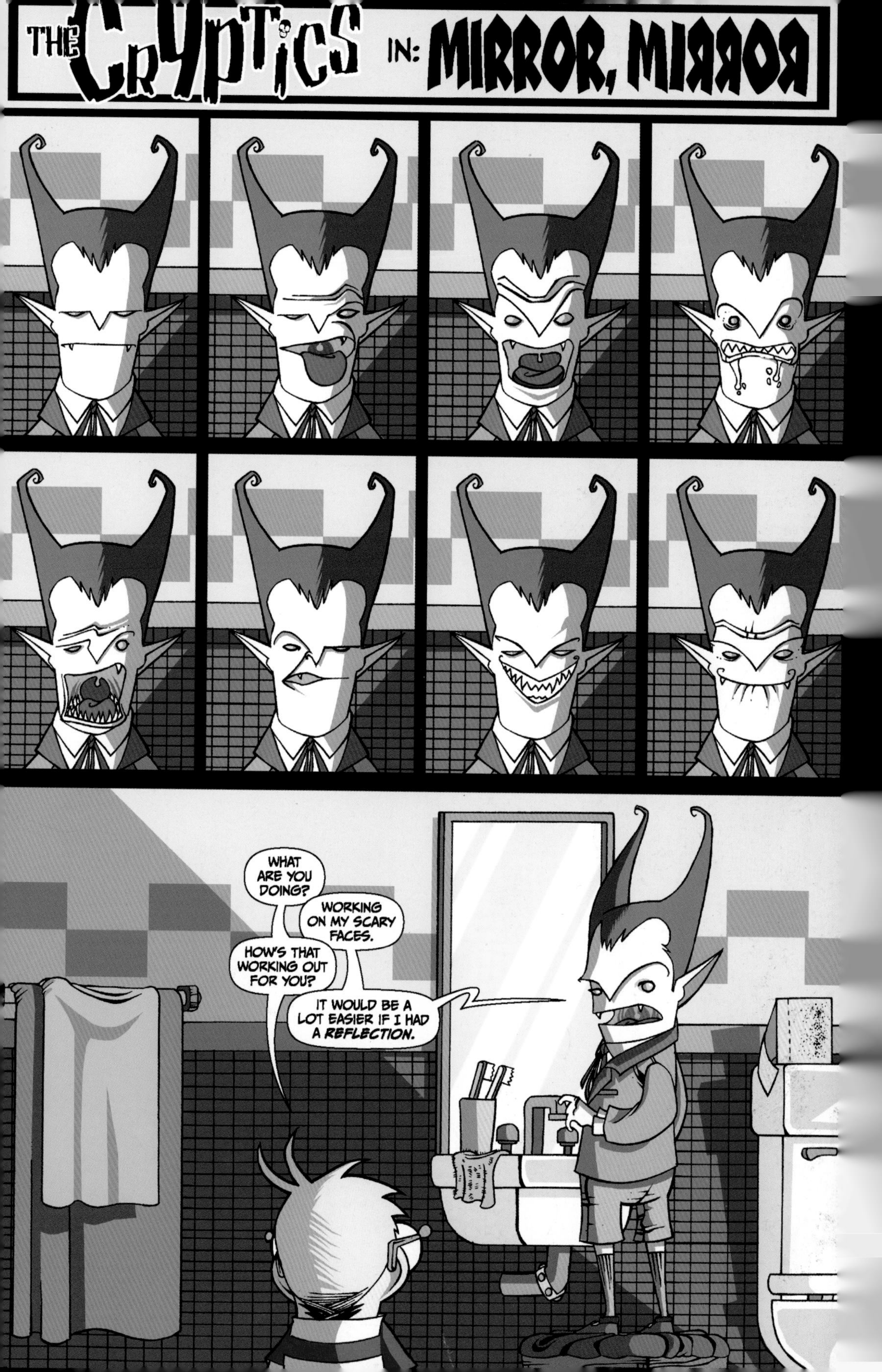
THE CRYPTICS IN: MIRROR, MIRROR
WHAT ARE YOU DOING?
WORKING ON MY SCARY FACES.
HOW'S THAT WORKING OUT FOR YOU?
IT WOULD BE A LOT EASIER IF I HAD A *REFLECTION*.

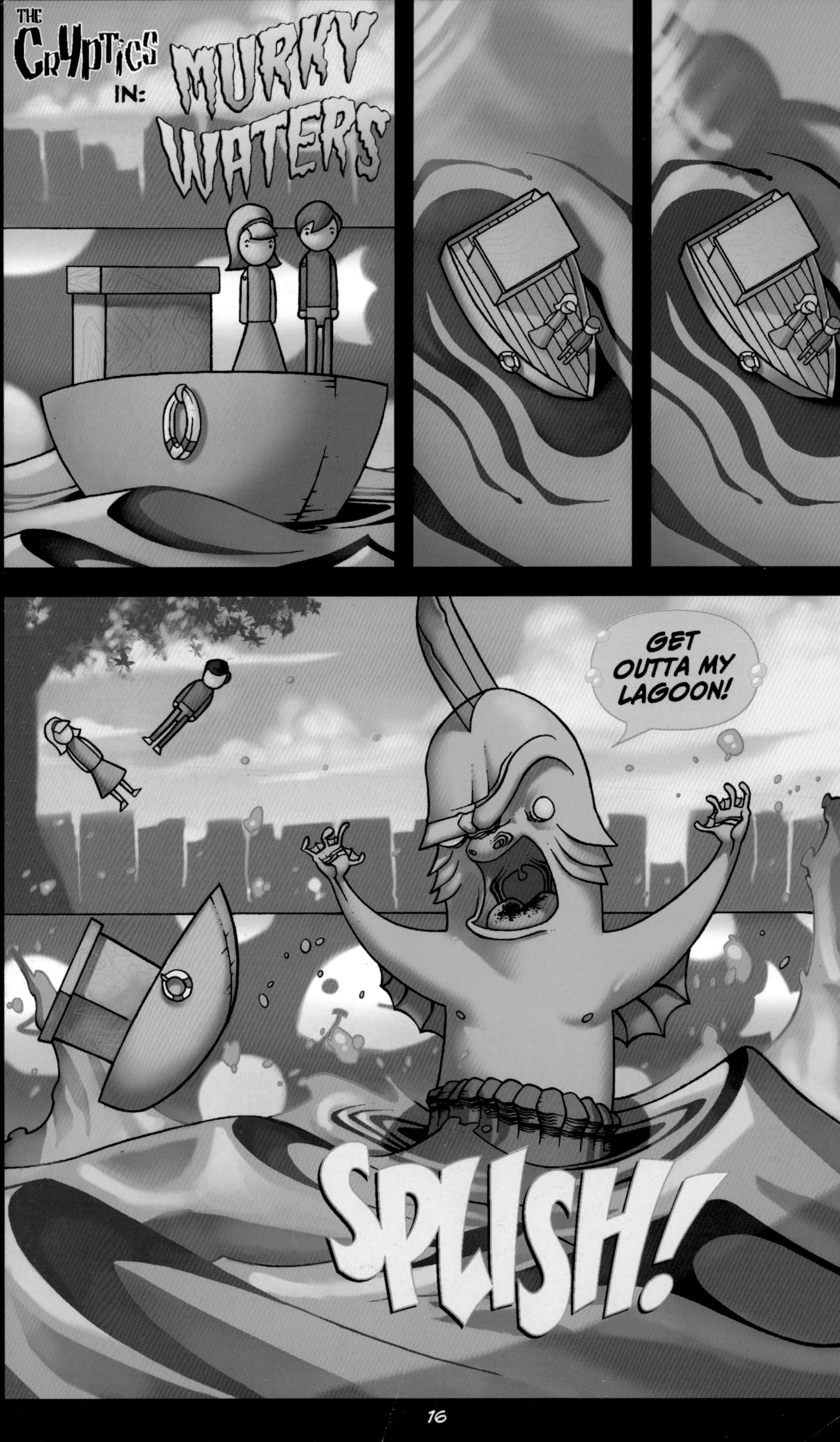
THE CRYPTICS IN: MURKY WATERS
GET OUTTA MY LAGOON!
SPLISH!

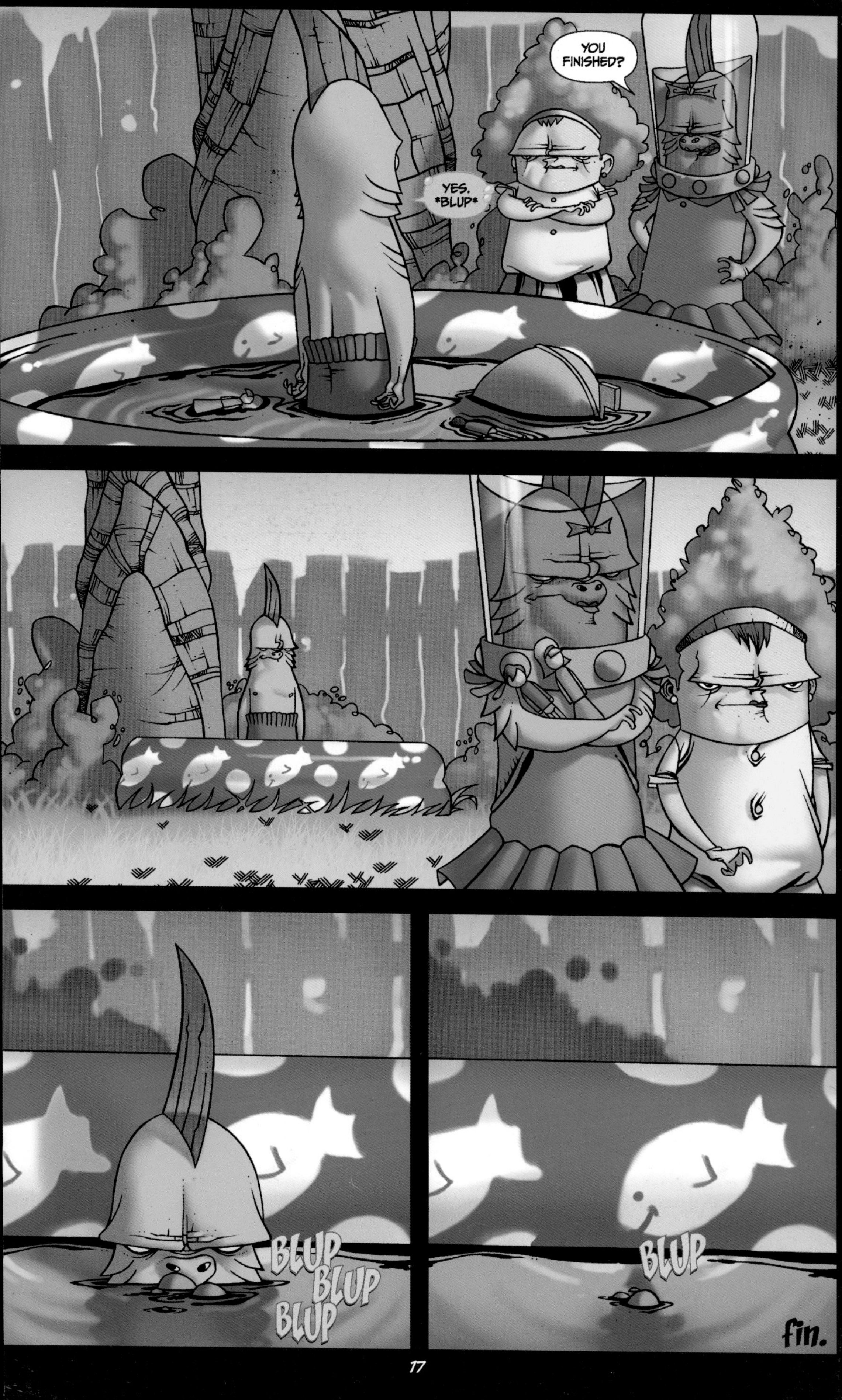
YOU FINISHED?
YES. *BLUP*
BLUP BLUP BLUP
BLUP
fin.

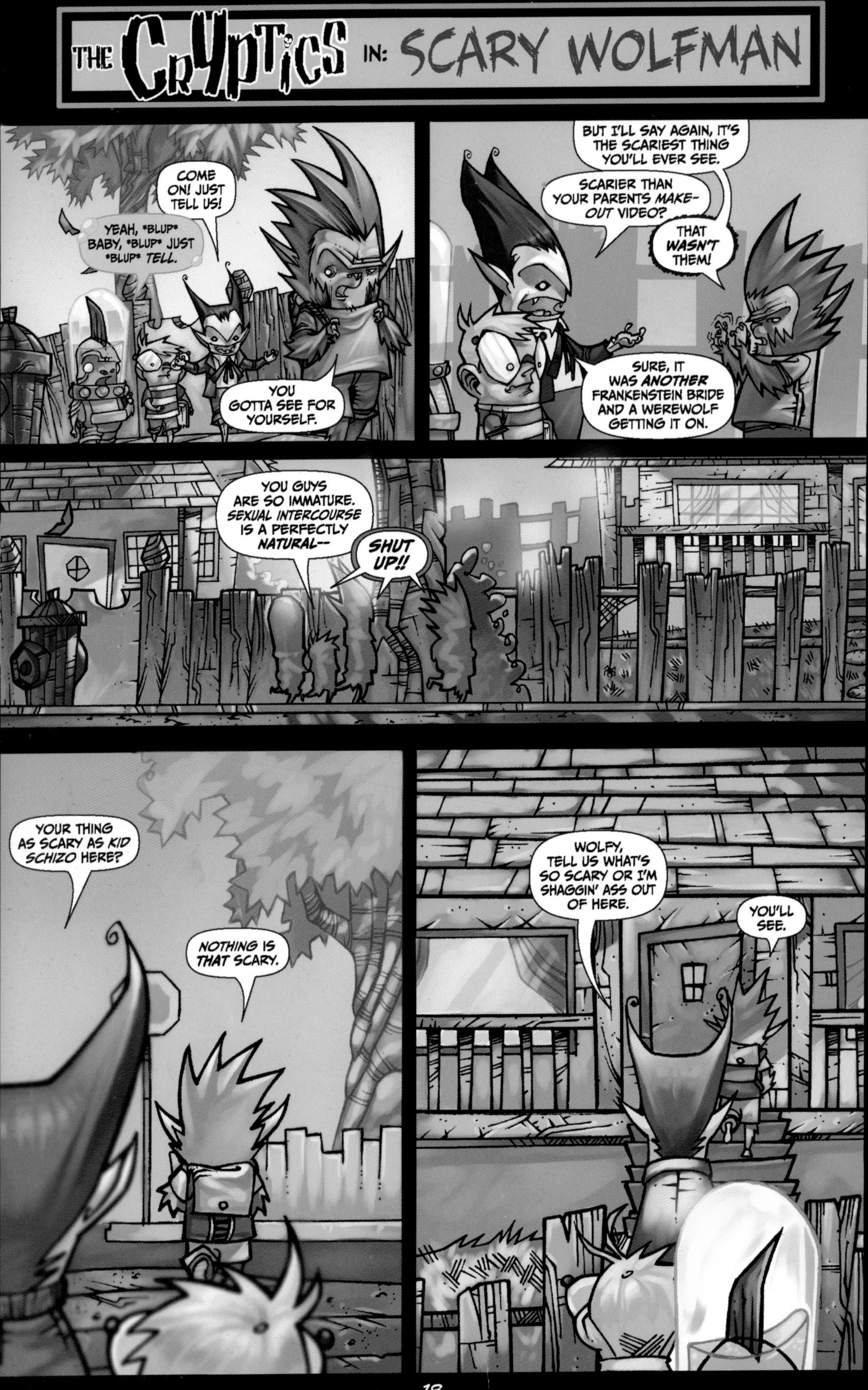
THE CRYPTICS IN: SCARY WOLFMAN
COME ON! JUST TELL US!
YEAH, *BLUP* BABY, *BLUP* JUST *BLUP* TELL.
YOU GOTTA SEE FOR YOURSELF.
BUT I'LL SAY AGAIN, IT'S THE SCARIEST THING YOU'LL EVER SEE.
SCARIER THAN YOUR PARENTS MAKE-OUT VIDEO?
THAT WASN'T THEM!
SURE, IT WAS ANOTHER FRANKENSTEIN BRIDE AND A WEREWOLF GETTING IT ON.
YOU GUYS ARE SO IMMATURE. SEXUAL INTERCOURSE IS A PERFECTLY NATURAL--
SHUT UP!!
YOUR THING AS SCARY AS KID SCHIZO HERE?
NOTHING IS THAT SCARY.
WOLFY, TELL US WHAT'S SO SCARY OR I'M SHAGGIN' ASS OUT OF HERE.
YOU'LL SEE.

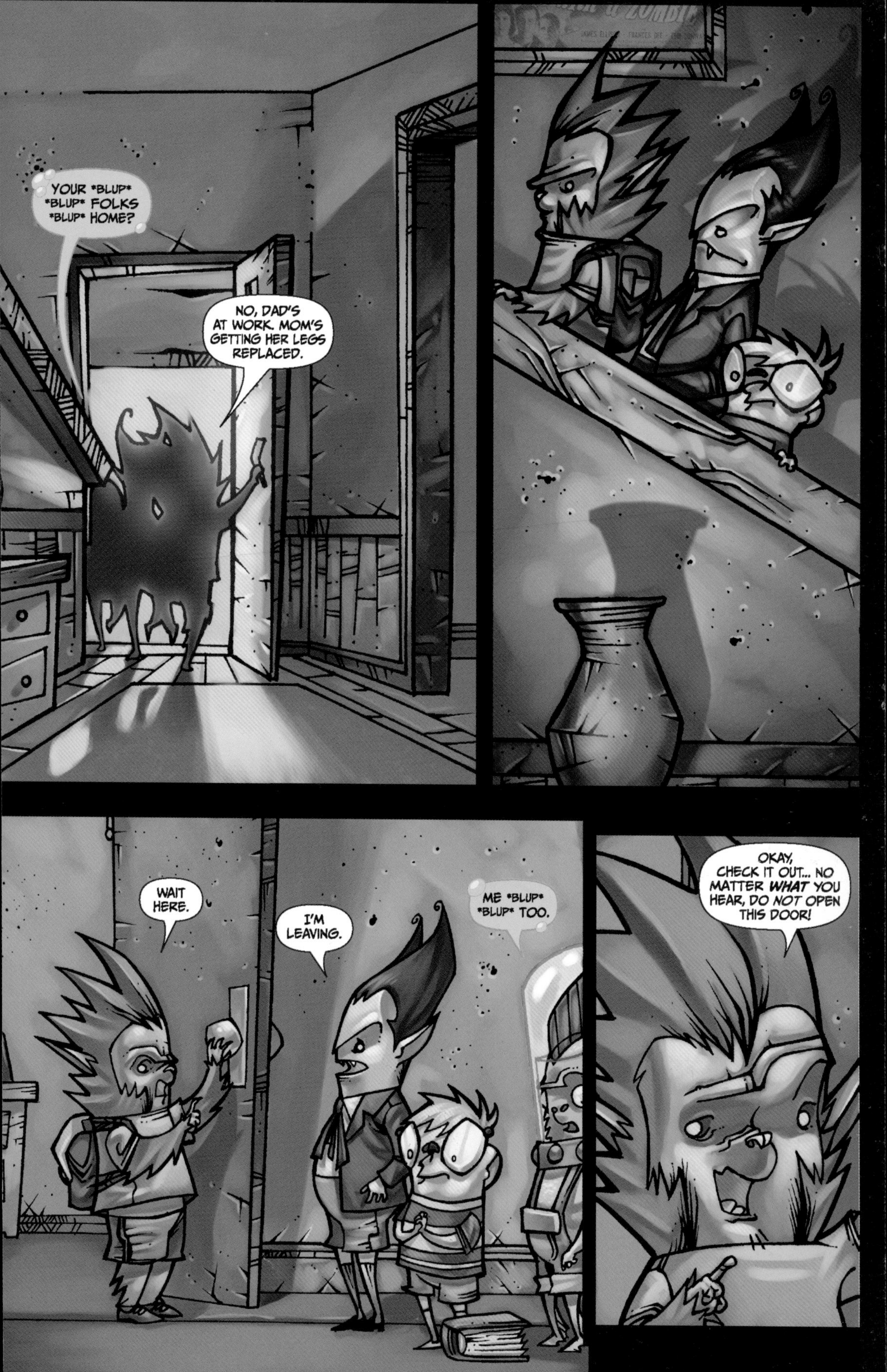
YOUR *BLUP* *BLUP* FOLKS *BLUP* HOME?
NO, DAD'S AT WORK. MOM'S GETTING HER LEGS REPLACED.
WAIT HERE.
I'M LEAVING.
ME *BLUP* *BLUP* TOO.
OKAY, CHECK IT OUT... NO MATTER WHAT YOU HEAR, DO NOT OPEN THIS DOOR!

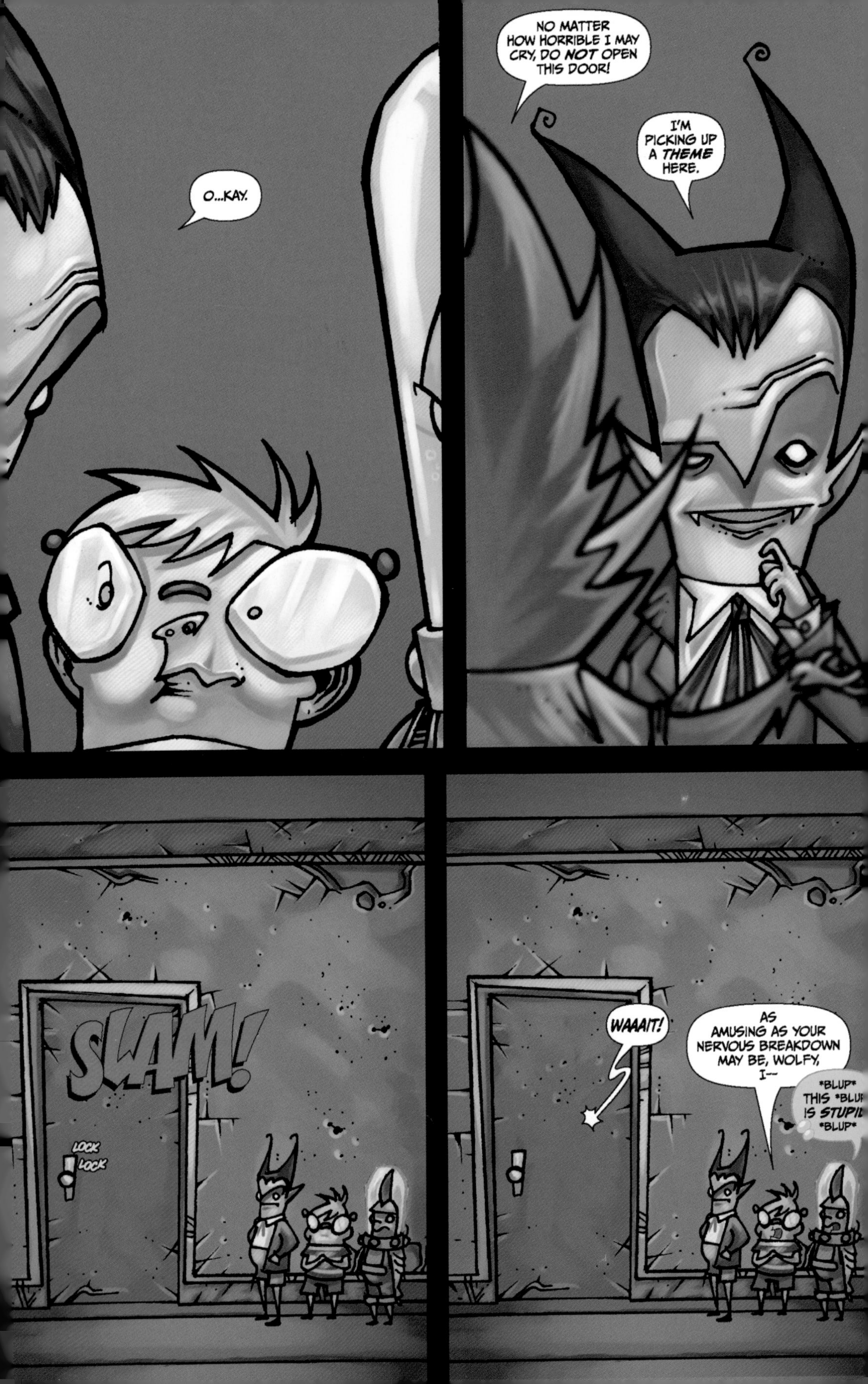
O...KAY.
NO MATTER HOW HORRIBLE I MAY CRY, DO NOT OPEN THIS DOOR!
I'M PICKING UP A THEME HERE.
SLAM!
LOCK
LOCK
WAAAIT!
AS AMUSING AS YOUR NERVOUS BREAKDOWN MAY BE, WOLFY, I--
BLUP

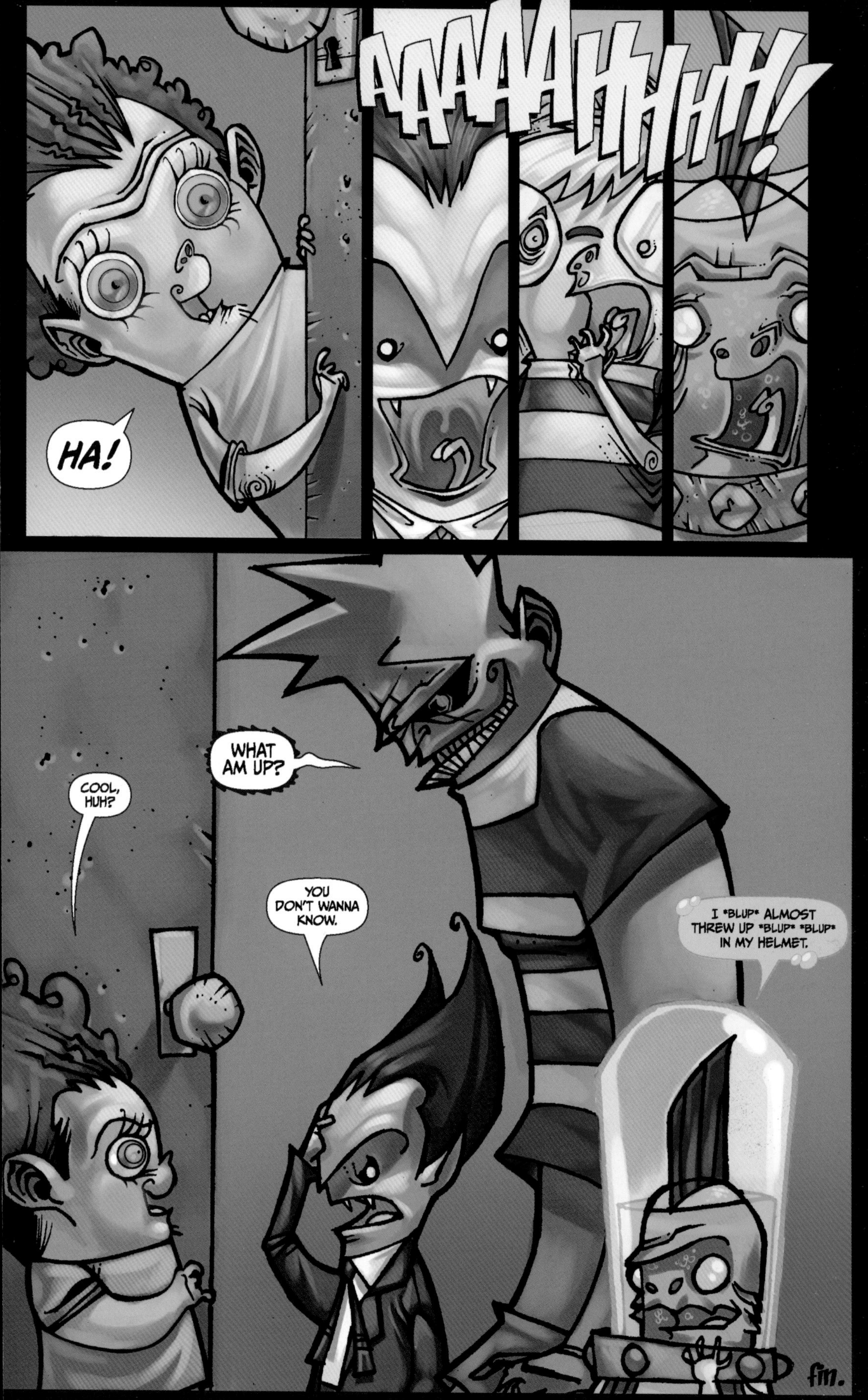
AAAAAHHHHH!
HA!
WHAT AM UP?
COOL, HUH?
YOU DON'T WANNA KNOW.
I *BLUP* ALMOST THREW UP *BLUP* *BLUP* IN MY HELMET.
fin.

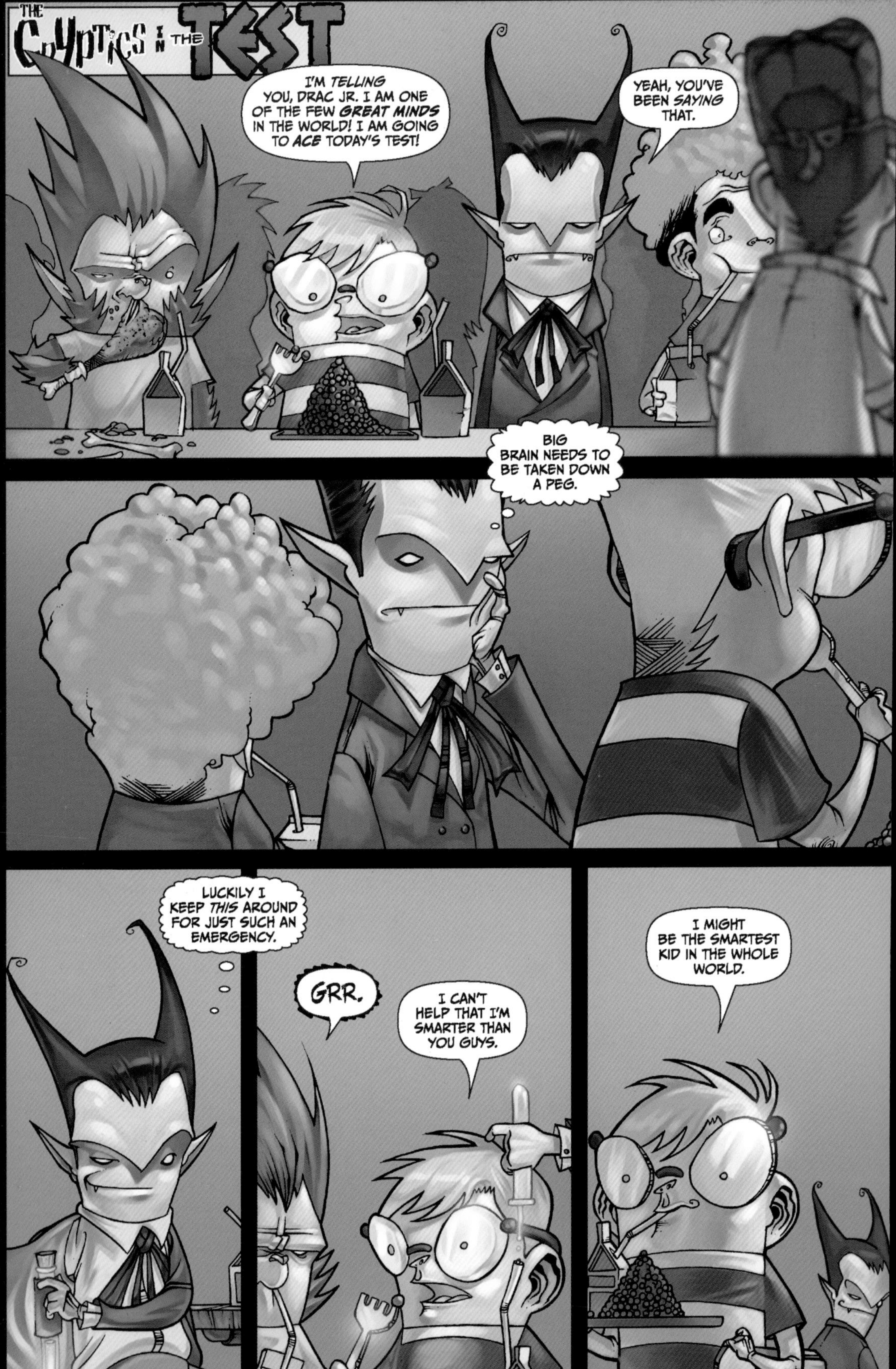
THE CRYPTICS IN THE TEST
I'M TELLING YOU, DRAC JR. I AM ONE OF THE FEW GREAT MINDS IN THE WORLD! I AM GOING TO ACE TODAY'S TEST!
YEAH, YOU'VE BEEN SAYING THAT.
BIG BRAIN NEEDS TO BE TAKEN DOWN A PEG.
LUCKILY I KEEP THIS AROUND FOR JUST SUCH AN EMERGENCY.
GRR.
I CAN'T HELP THAT I'M SMARTER THAN YOU GUYS.
I MIGHT BE THE SMARTEST KID IN THE WHOLE WORLD.

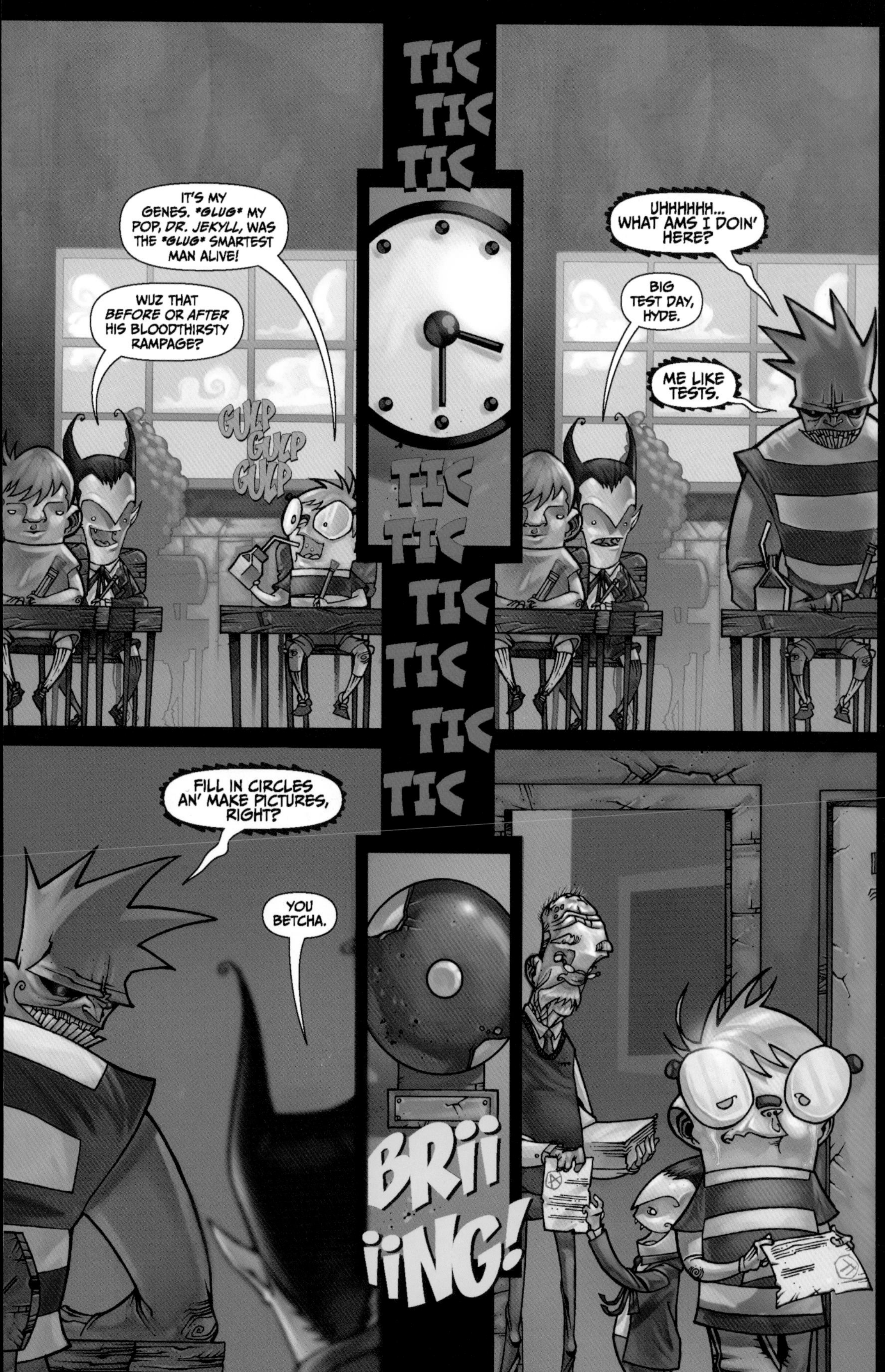
TIC TIC TIC
IT'S MY GENES. *GLUG* MY POP, DR. JEKYLL, WAS THE *GLUG* SMARTEST MAN ALIVE!
WUZ THAT BEFORE OR AFTER HIS BLOODTHIRSTY RAMPAGE?
GULP GULP GULP
UHHHHHH... WHAT AMS I DOIN' HERE?
BIG TEST DAY, HYDE.
ME LIKE TESTS.
TIC TIC TIC TIC TIC TIC
FILL IN CIRCLES AN' MAKE PICTURES, RIGHT?
YOU BETCHA.
BRii iiNG!
fin.

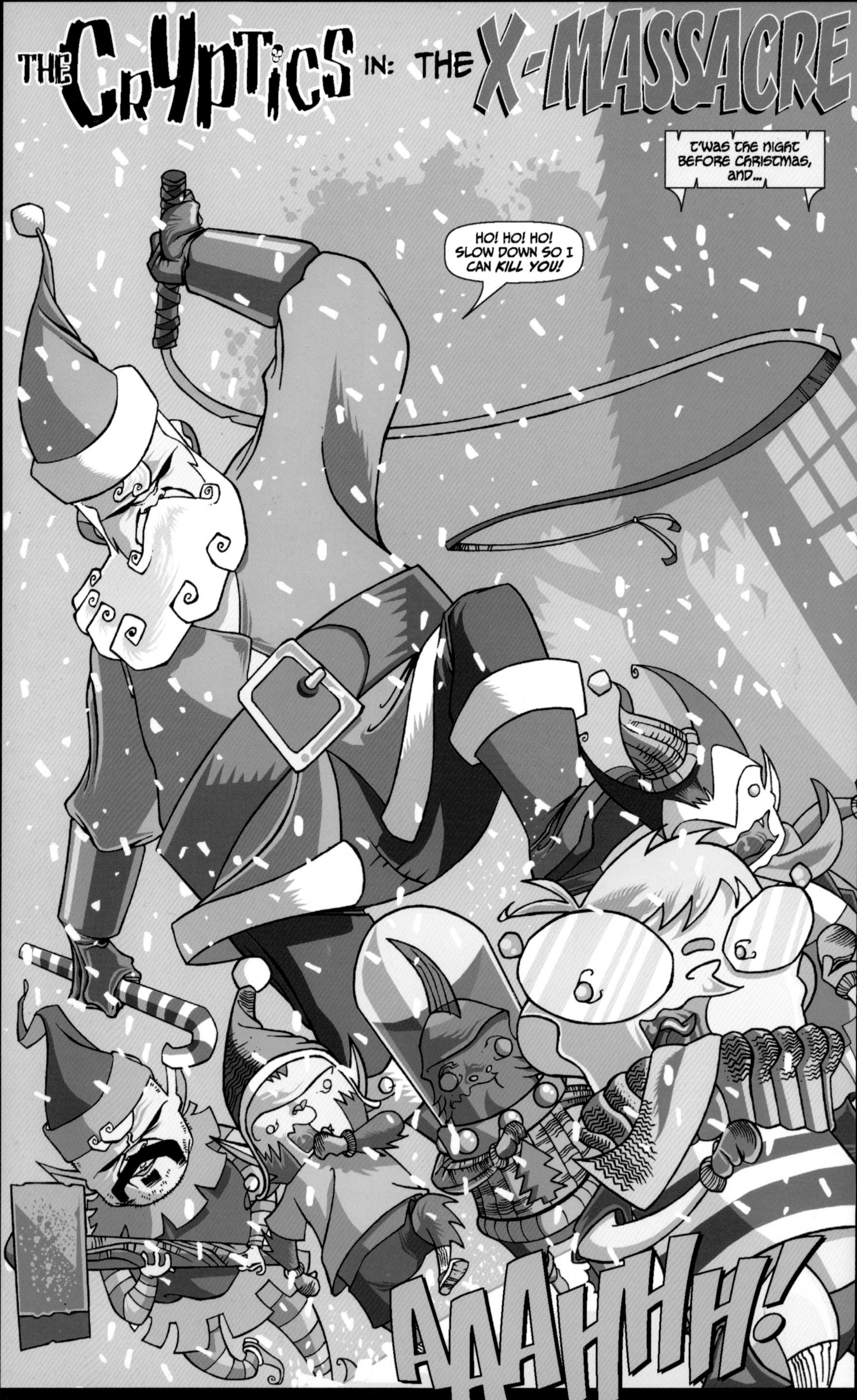

THE CRYPTICS IN: THE X-MASSACRE
T'WAS THE NIGHT BEFORE CHRISTMAS, AND...
HO! HO! HO! SLOW DOWN SO I CAN KILL YOU!
AAAHHH!

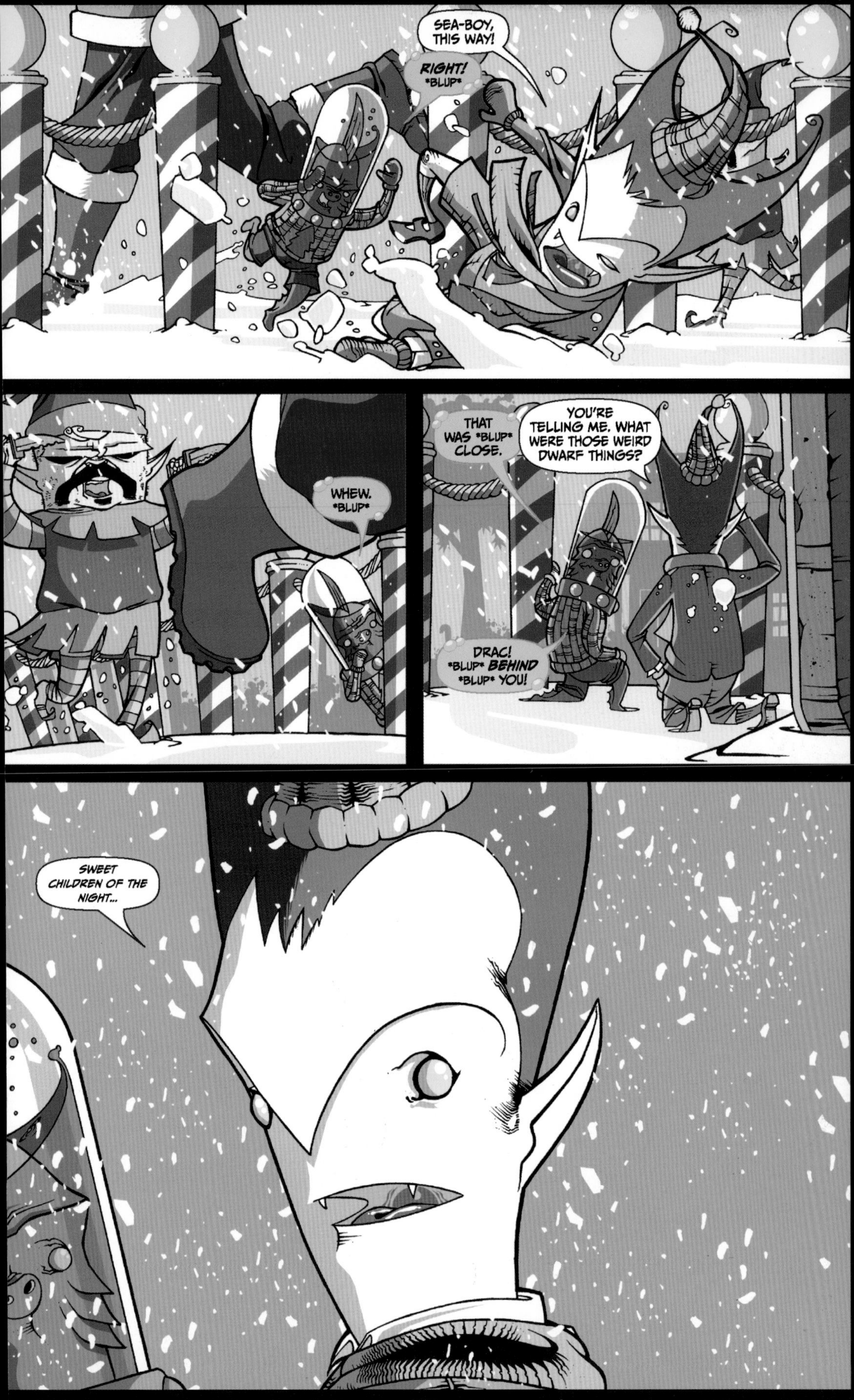
SEA-BOY, THIS WAY!
RIGHT! *BLUP*
WHEW. *BLUP*
THAT WAS *BLUP* CLOSE.
YOU'RE TELLING ME. WHAT WERE THOSE WEIRD DWARF THINGS?
DRAC! *BLUP* BEHIND *BLUP* YOU!
SWEET CHILDREN OF THE NIGHT...

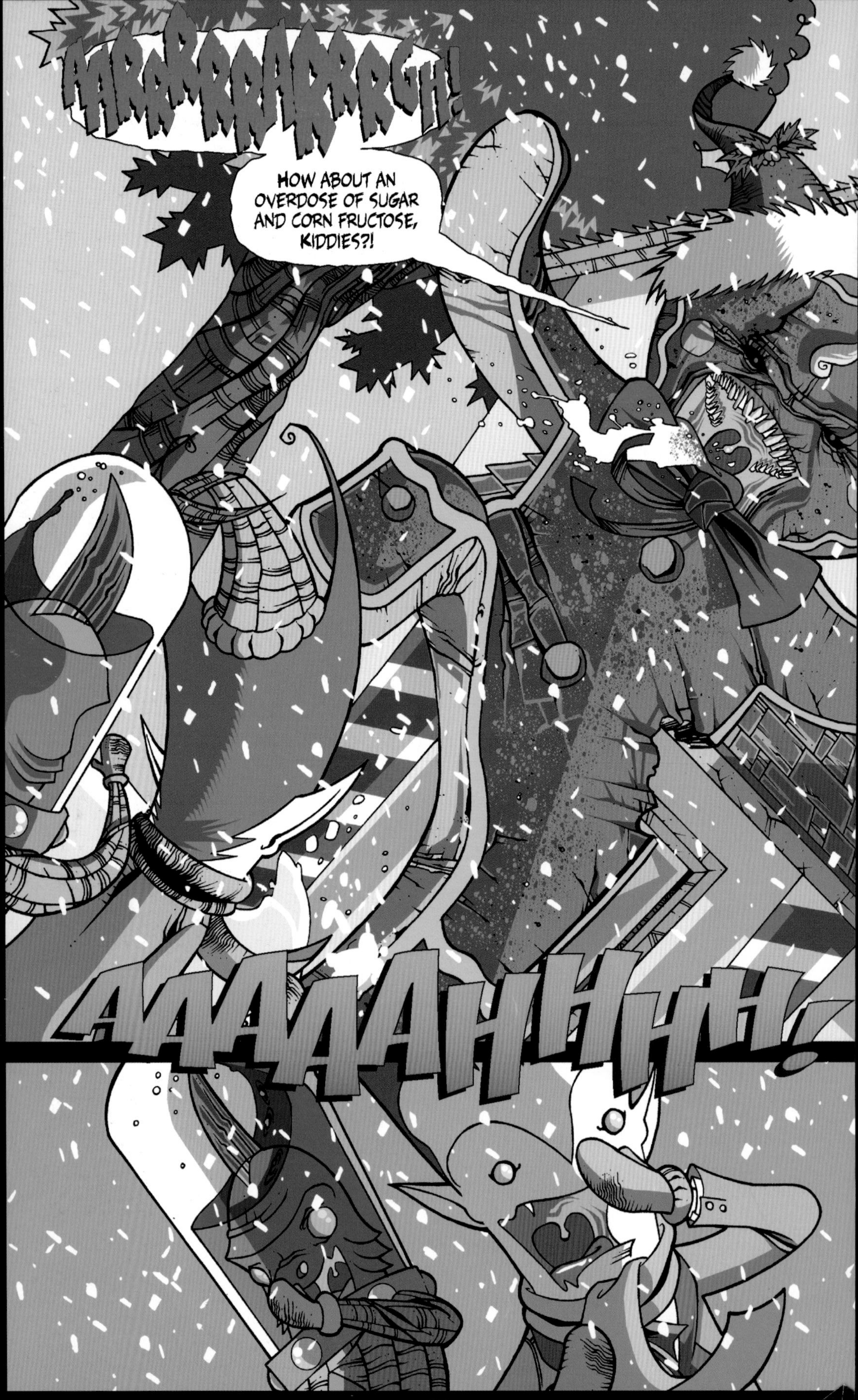
AARRRRRAARRRRGH!
HOW ABOUT AN OVERDOSE OF SUGAR AND CORN FRUCTOSE, KIDDIES?!
AAAAAHHHH!

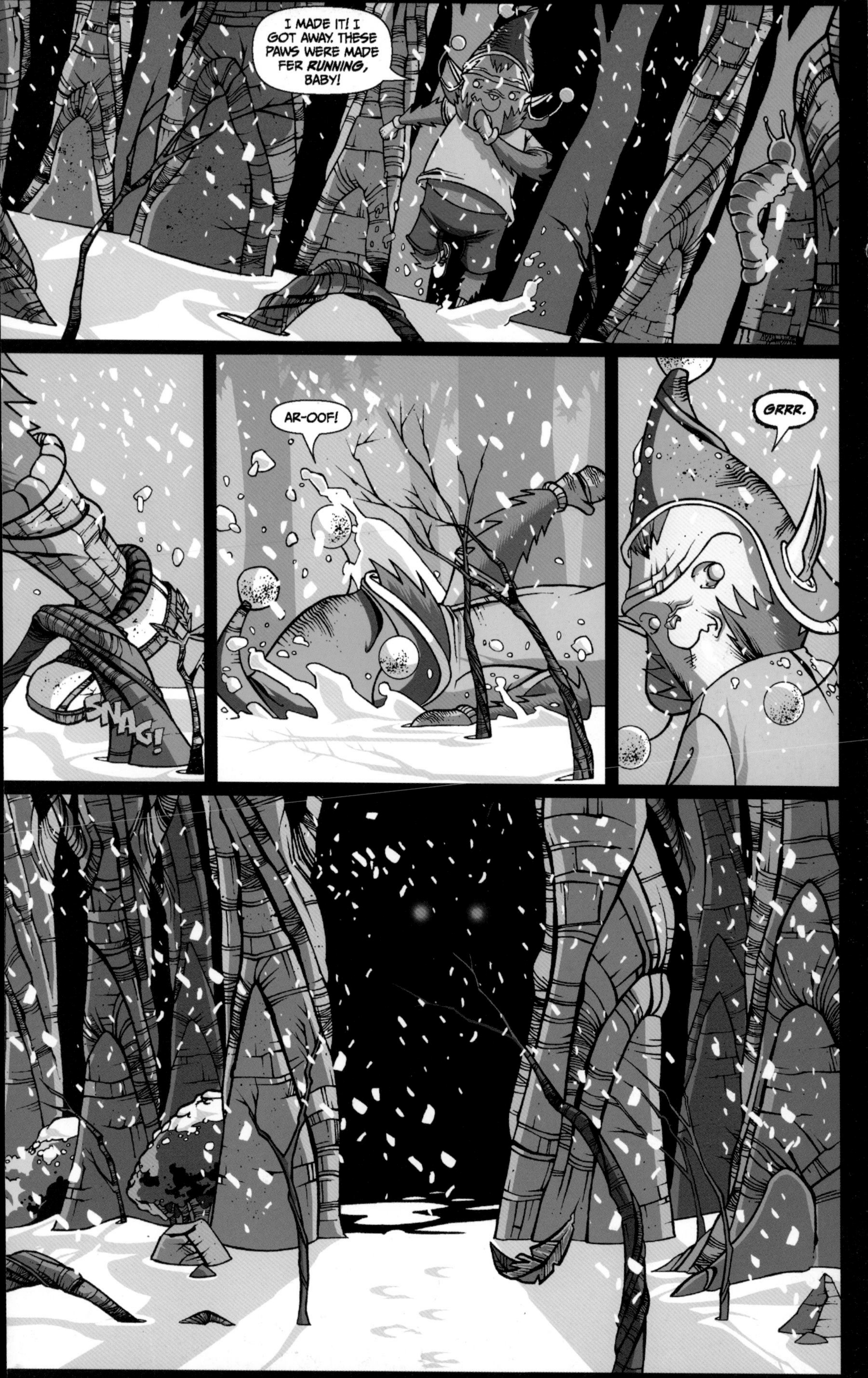
I MADE IT! I GOT AWAY. THESE PAWS WERE MADE FER *RUNNING*, BABY!
SNAG!
AR-OOF!
GRRR.

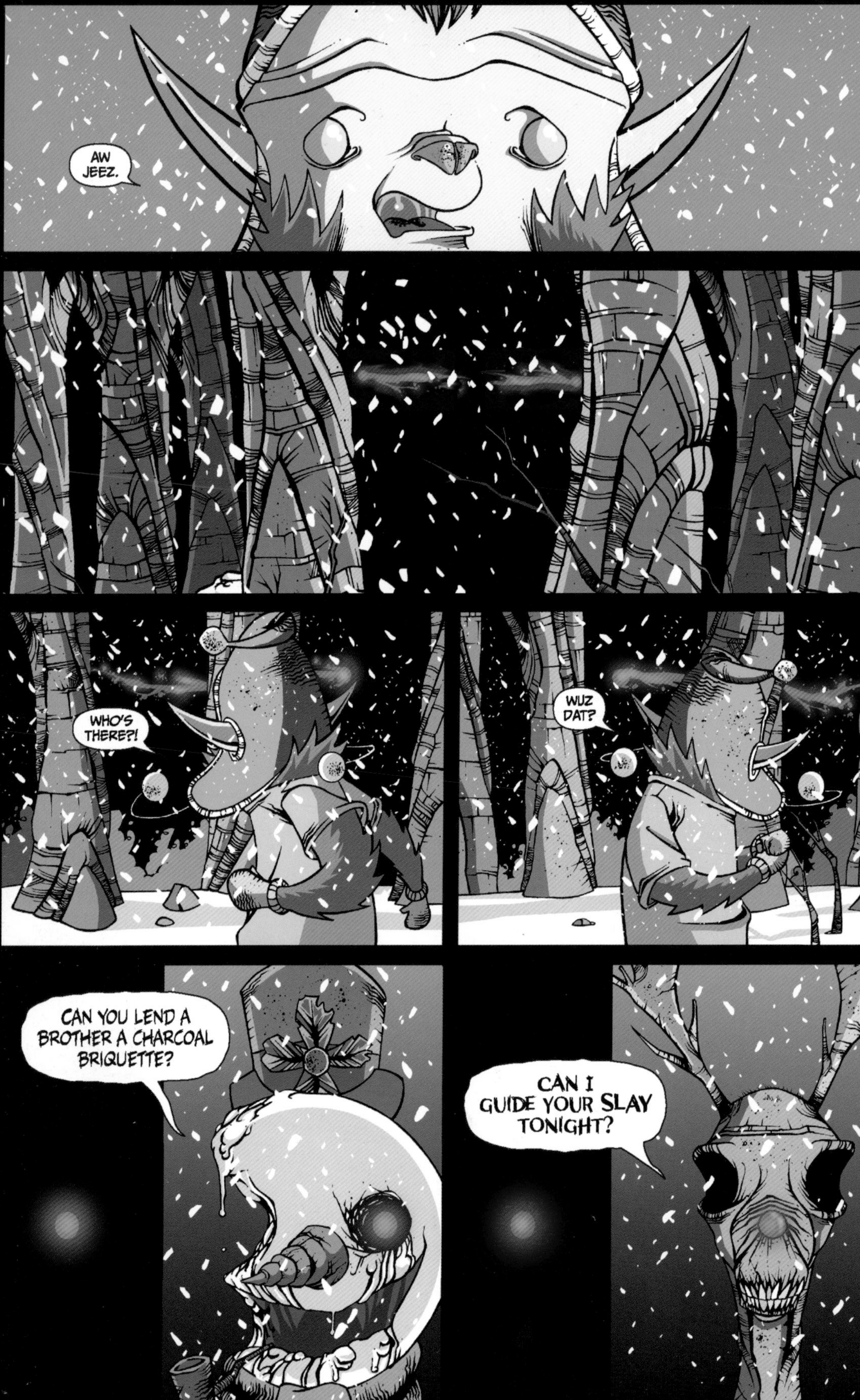
AW JEEZ.
WHO'S THERE?!
WUZ DAT?
CAN YOU LEND A BROTHER A CHARCOAL BRIQUETTE?
CAN I GUIDE YOUR SLAY TONIGHT?

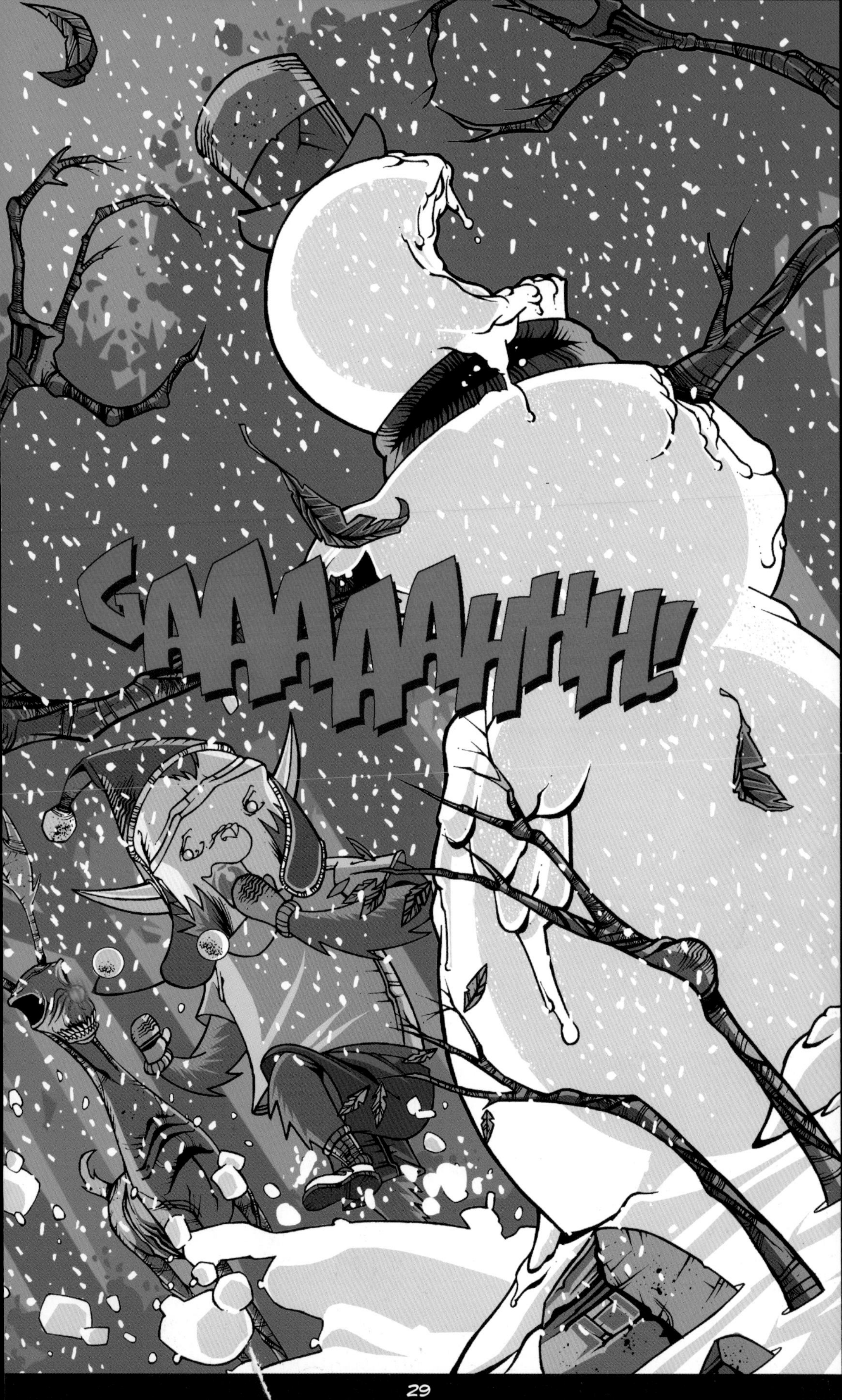
GAAAAAHHH!

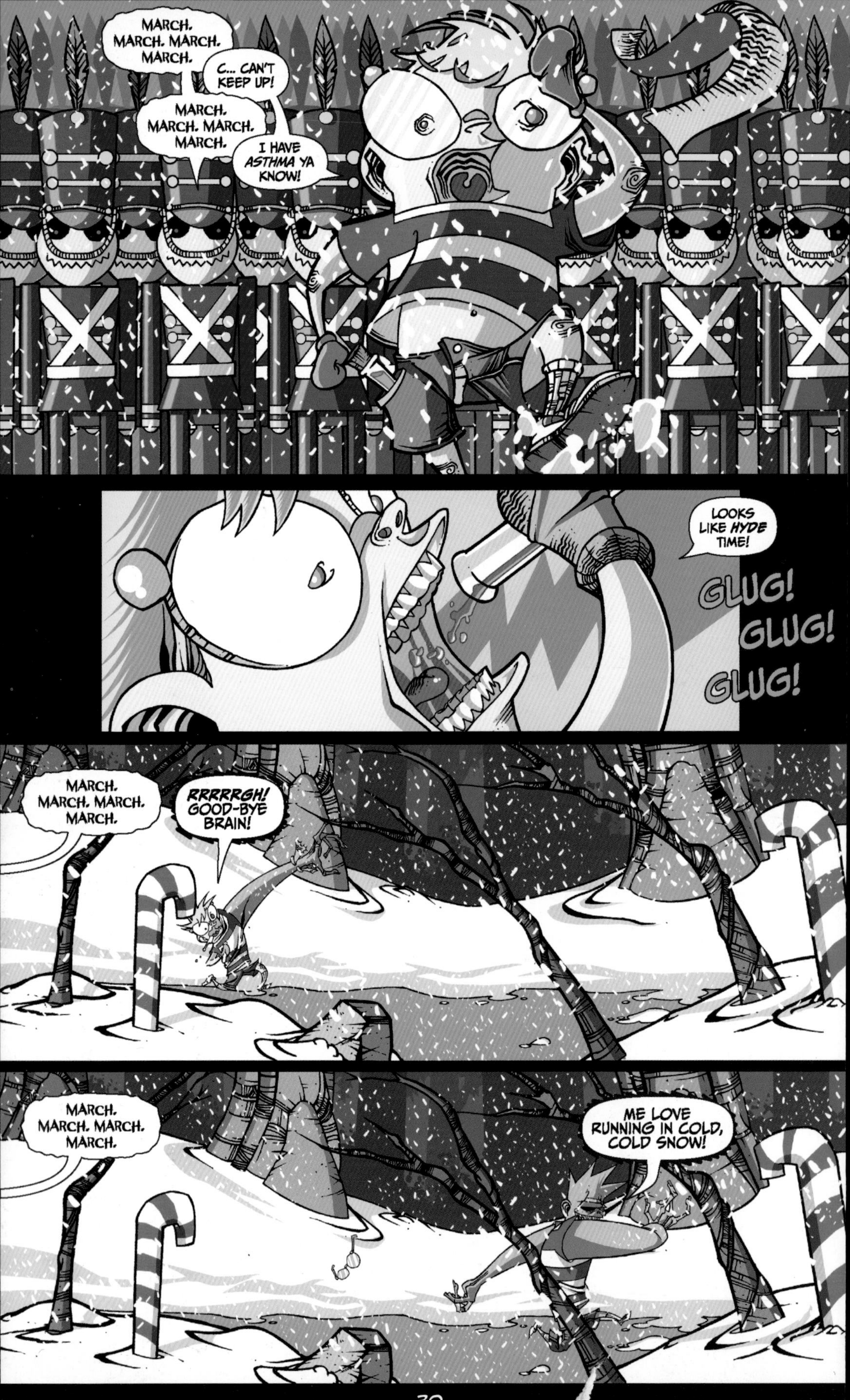
MARCH. MARCH. MARCH. MARCH.
C... CAN'T KEEP UP!
MARCH. MARCH. MARCH. MARCH.
I HAVE ASTHMA YA KNOW!
LOOKS LIKE HYDE TIME!
GLUG! GLUG! GLUG!
MARCH. MARCH. MARCH. MARCH.
RRRRRGH! GOOD-BYE BRAIN!
MARCH. MARCH. MARCH. MARCH.
ME LOVE RUNNING IN COLD, COLD SNOW!

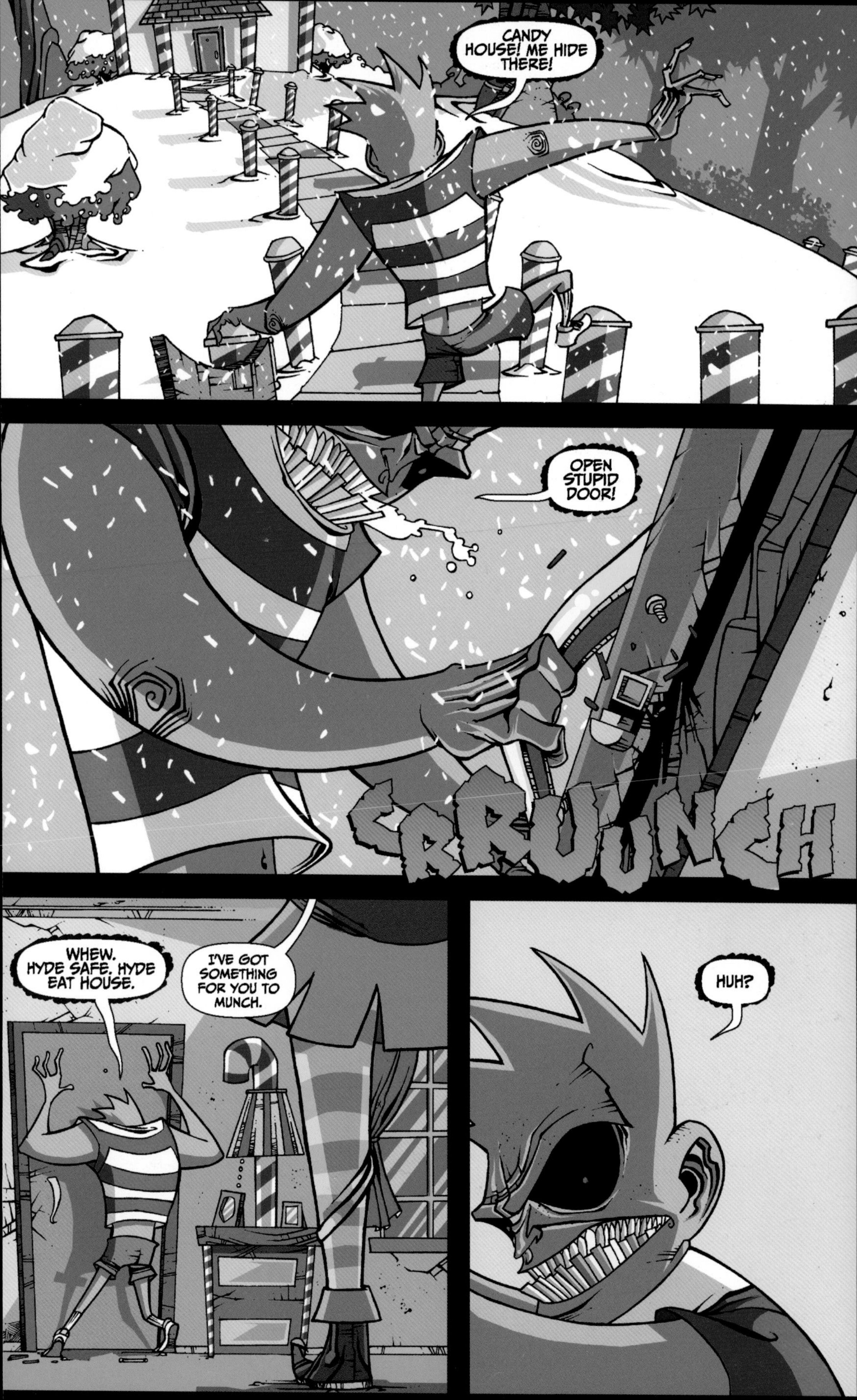
CANDY HOUSE! ME HIDE THERE!
OPEN STUPID DOOR!
CRRUUNCH
WHEW. HYDE SAFE. HYDE EAT HOUSE.
I'VE GOT SOMETHING FOR YOU TO MUNCH.
HUH?

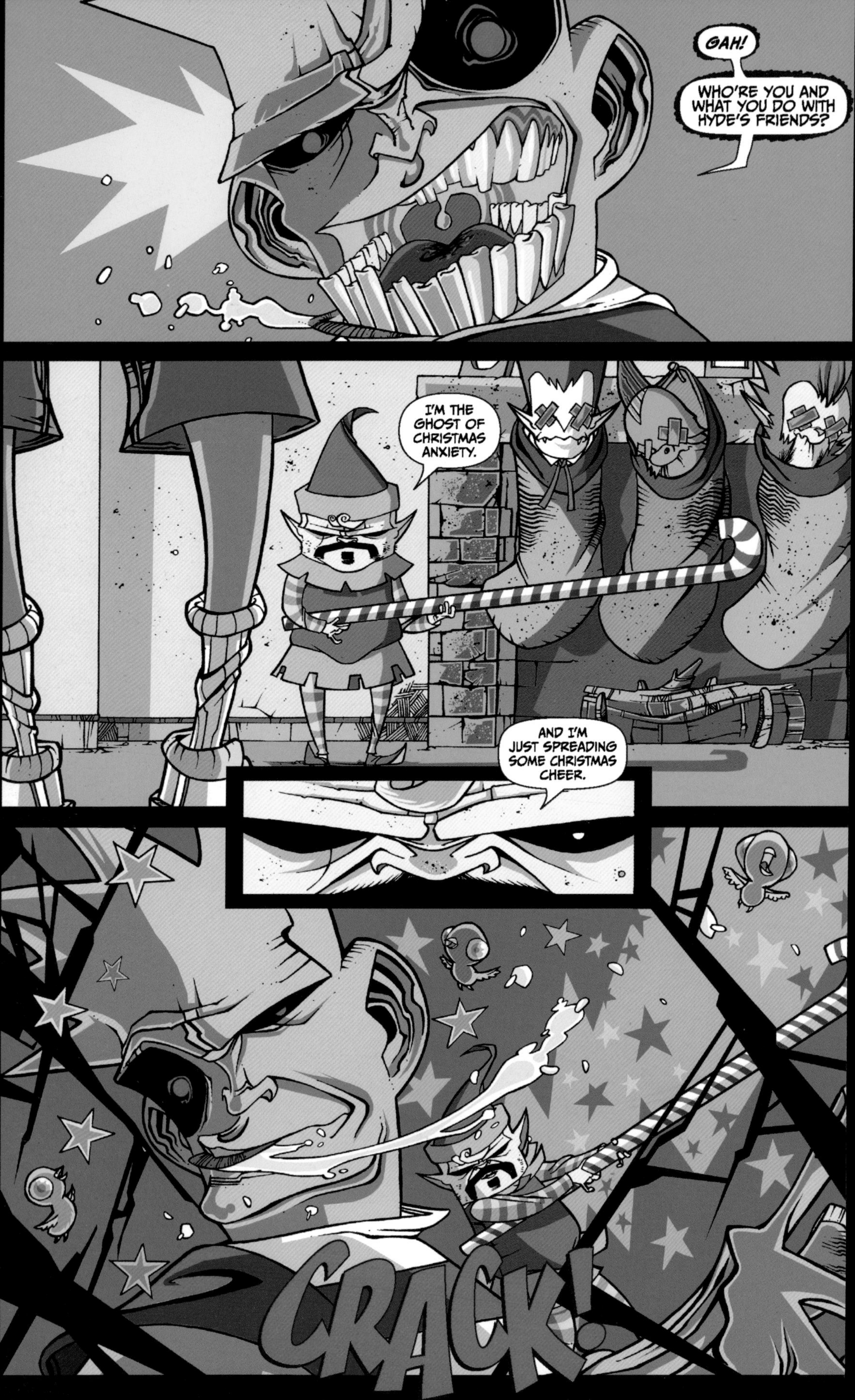
GAH!
WHO'RE YOU AND WHAT YOU DO WITH HYDE'S FRIENDS?
I'M THE GHOST OF CHRISTMAS ANXIETY.
AND I'M JUST SPREADING SOME CHRISTMAS CHEER.
CRACK!

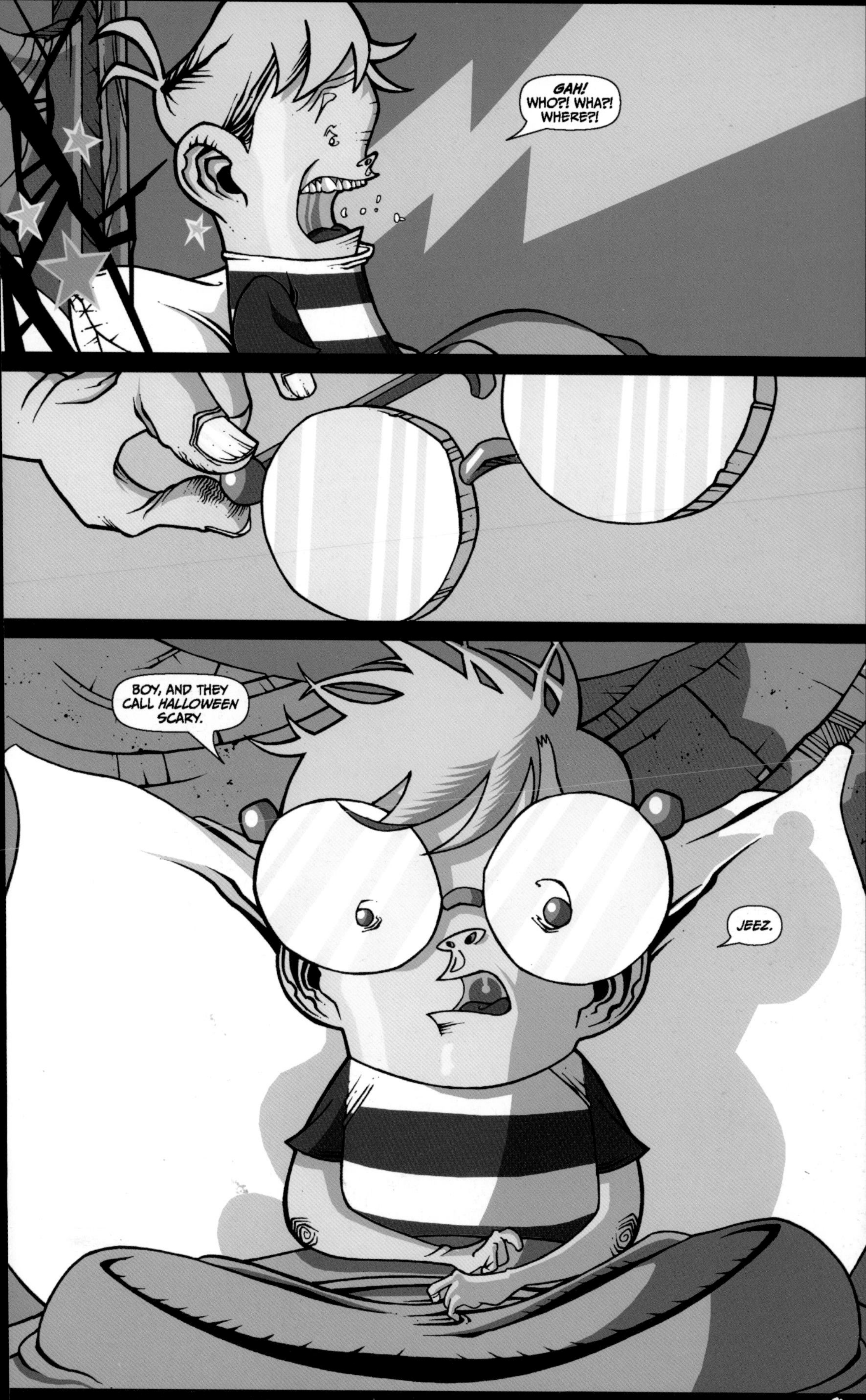
GAH! WHO?! WHA?! WHERE?!
BOY, AND THEY CALL HALLOWEEN SCARY.
JEEZ.

fin.

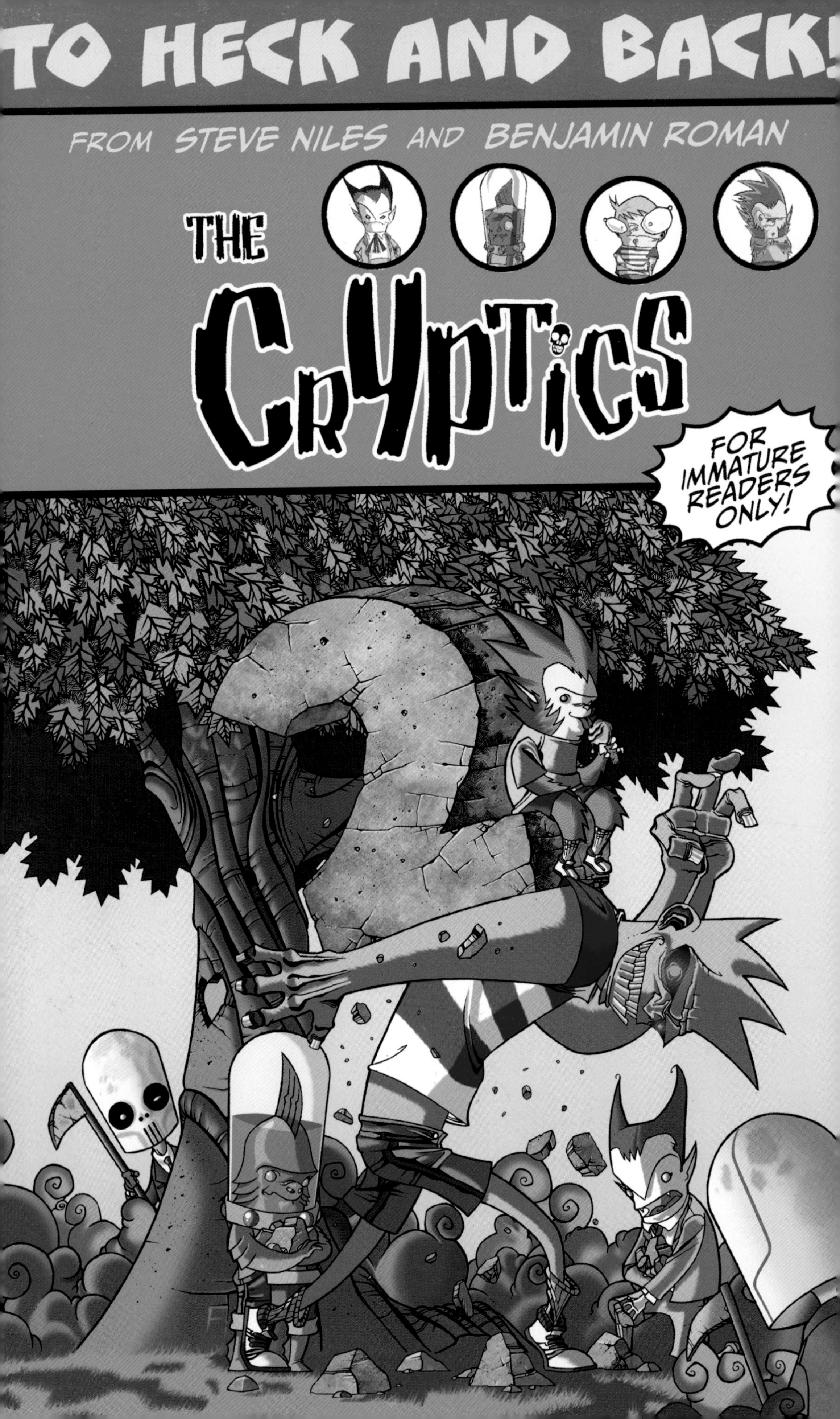
TO HECK AND BACK!
FROM STEVE NILES AND BENJAMIN ROMAN
THE CRYPTICS
FOR IMMATURE READERS ONLY!

THE CRYPTICS

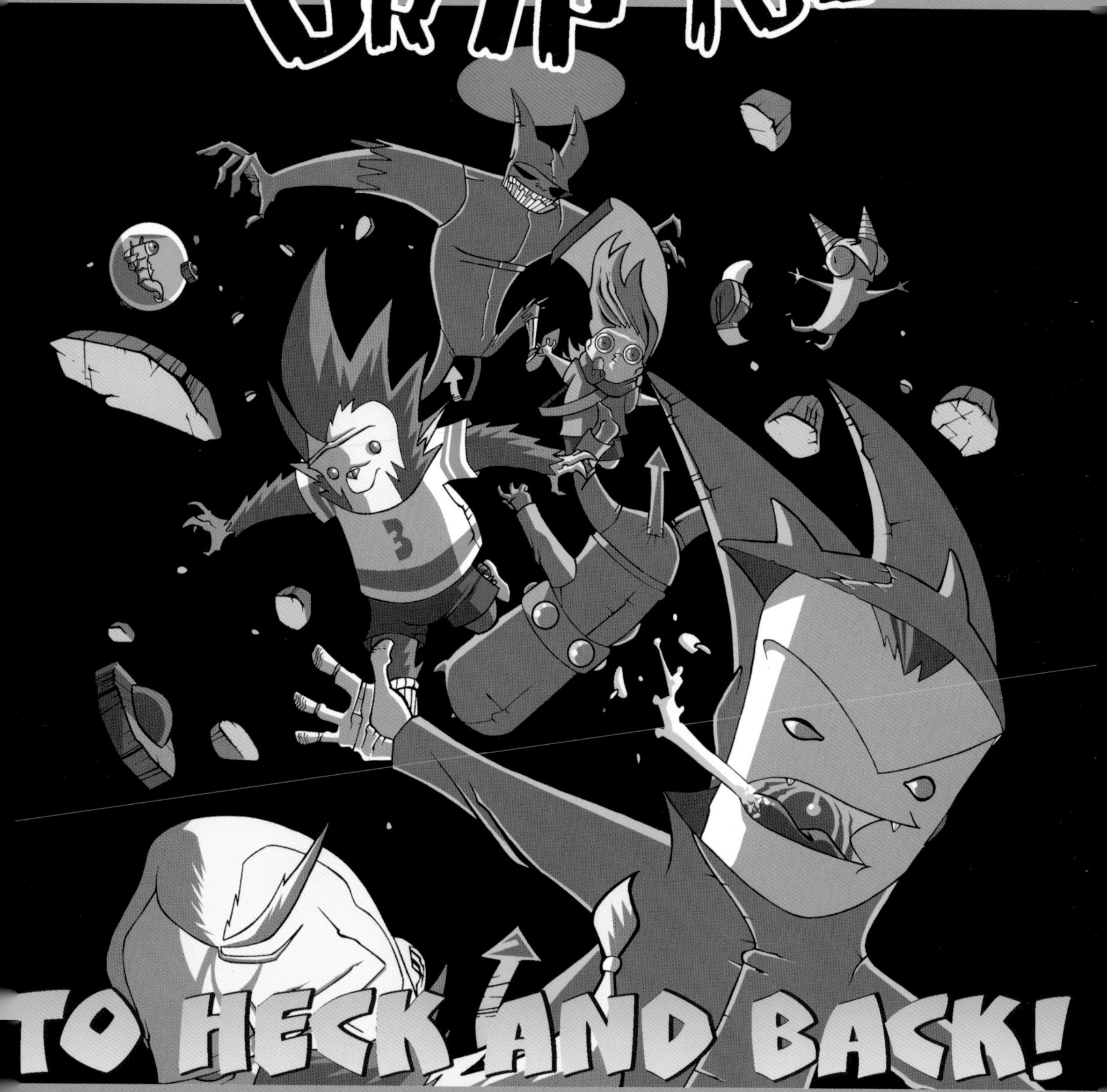

TO HECK AND BACK!

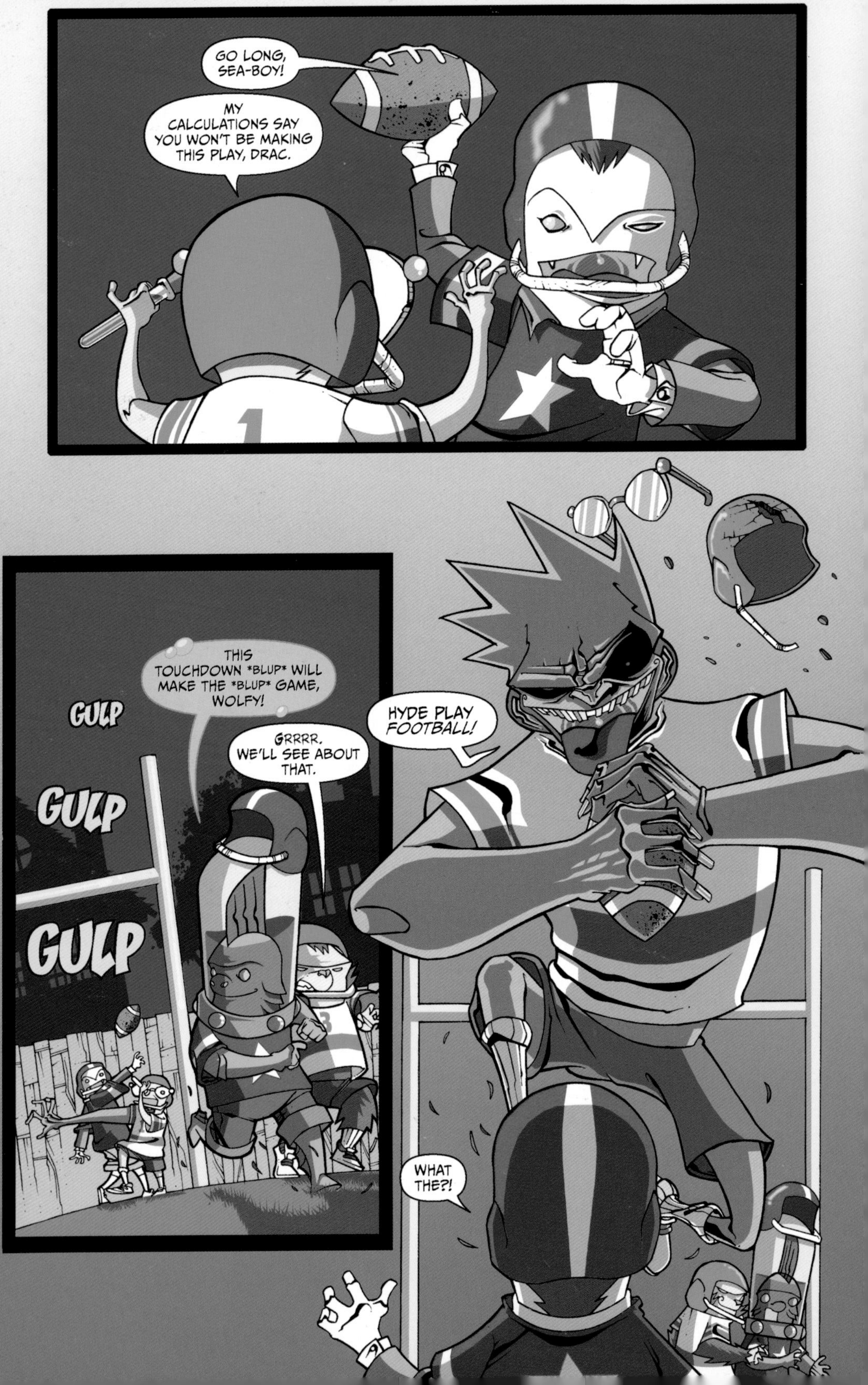

GO LONG, SEA-BOY!
MY CALCULATIONS SAY YOU WON'T BE MAKING THIS PLAY, DRAC.
GULP
GULP
GULP
THIS TOUCHDOWN *BLUP* WILL MAKE THE *BLUP* GAME, WOLFY!
GRRRR. WE'LL SEE ABOUT THAT.
HYDE PLAY FOOTBALL!
WHAT THE?!

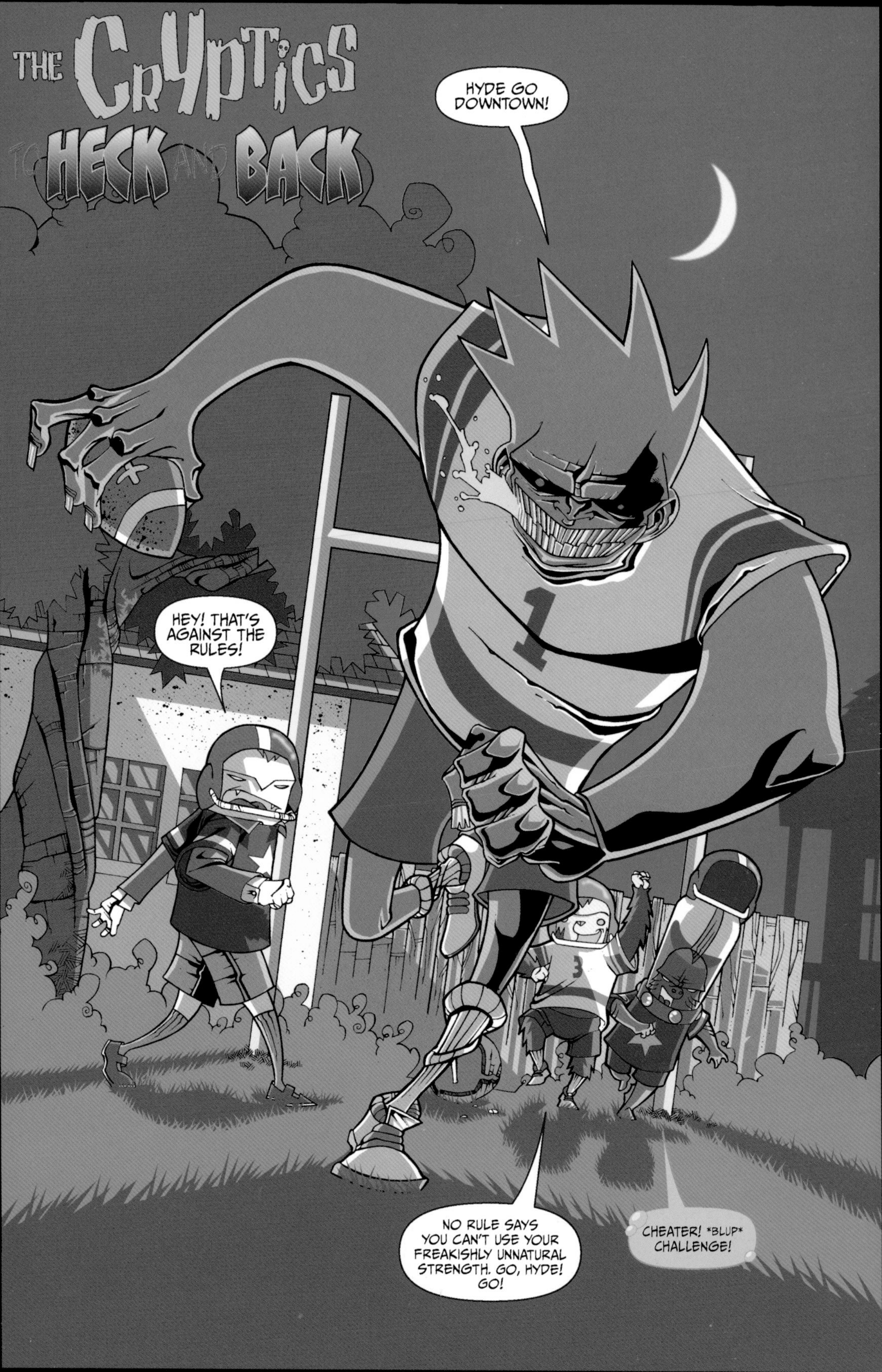
THE CRYPTICS
TO HECK AND BACK
HYDE GO DOWNTOWN!
HEY! THAT'S AGAINST THE RULES!
NO RULE SAYS YOU CAN'T USE YOUR FREAKISHLY UNNATURAL STRENGTH. GO, HYDE! GO!
CHEATER! *BLUP* CHALLENGE!

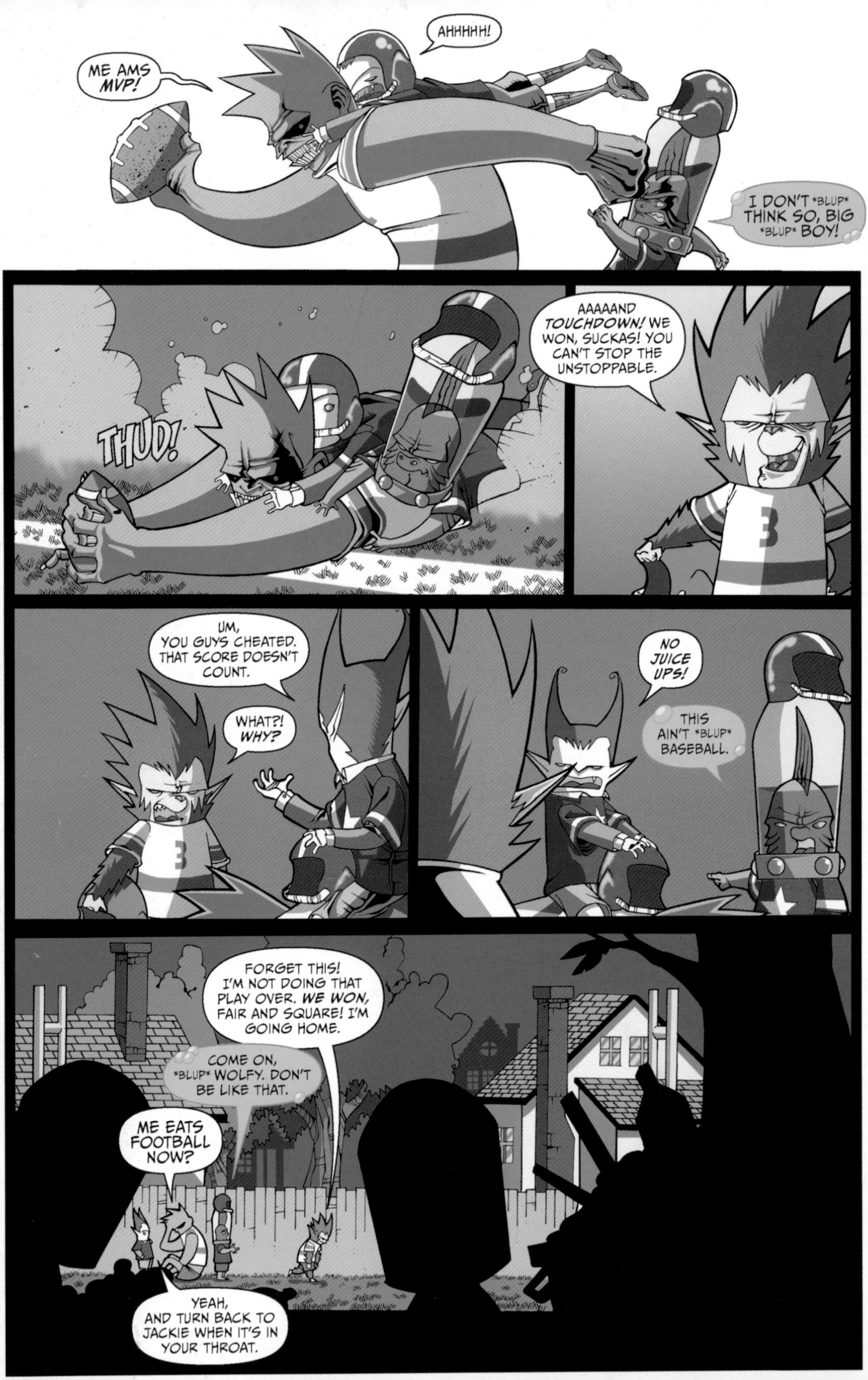
AHHHHH!
ME AMS MVP!
I DON'T *BLUP* THINK SO, BIG *BLUP* BOY!
THUD!
AAAAAND TOUCHDOWN! WE WON, SUCKAS! YOU CAN'T STOP THE UNSTOPPABLE.
UM, YOU GUYS CHEATED. THAT SCORE DOESN'T COUNT.
WHAT?! WHY?
NO JUICE UPS!
THIS AIN'T *BLUP* BASEBALL.
FORGET THIS! I'M NOT DOING THAT PLAY OVER. WE WON, FAIR AND SQUARE! I'M GOING HOME.
COME ON, *BLUP* WOLFY. DON'T BE LIKE THAT.
ME EATS FOOTBALL NOW?
YEAH, AND TURN BACK TO JACKIE WHEN IT'S IN YOUR THROAT.

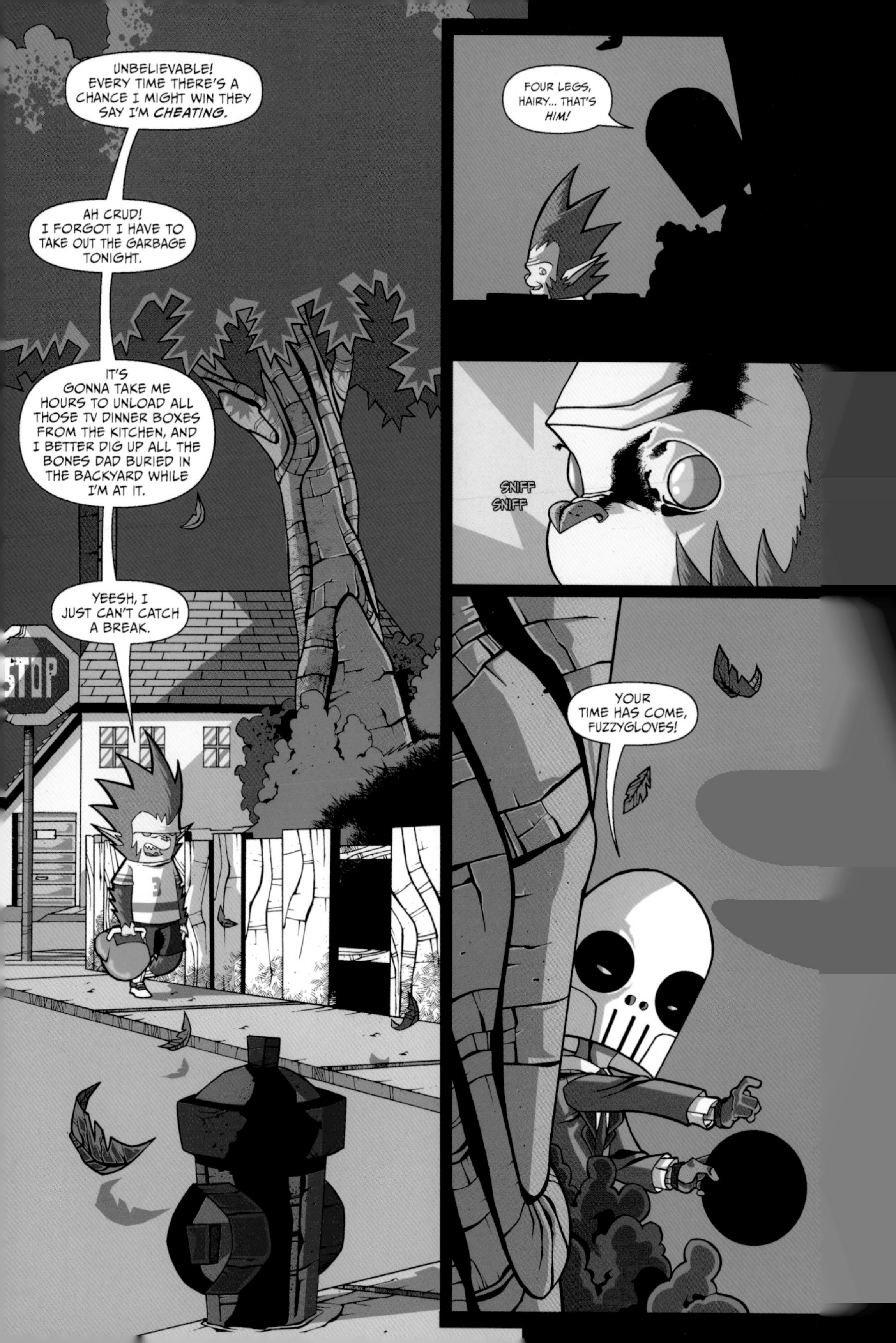
UNBELIEVABLE! EVERY TIME THERE'S A CHANCE I MIGHT WIN THEY SAY I'M *CHEATING.*
AH CRUD! I FORGOT I HAVE TO TAKE OUT THE GARBAGE TONIGHT.
IT'S GONNA TAKE ME HOURS TO UNLOAD ALL THOSE TV DINNER BOXES FROM THE KITCHEN, AND I BETTER DIG UP ALL THE BONES DAD BURIED IN THE BACKYARD WHILE I'M AT IT.
YEESH, I JUST CAN'T CATCH A BREAK.
STOP
FOUR LEGS, HAIRY... THAT'S *HIM!*
SNIFF
SNIFF
YOUR TIME HAS COME, FUZZYGLOVES!

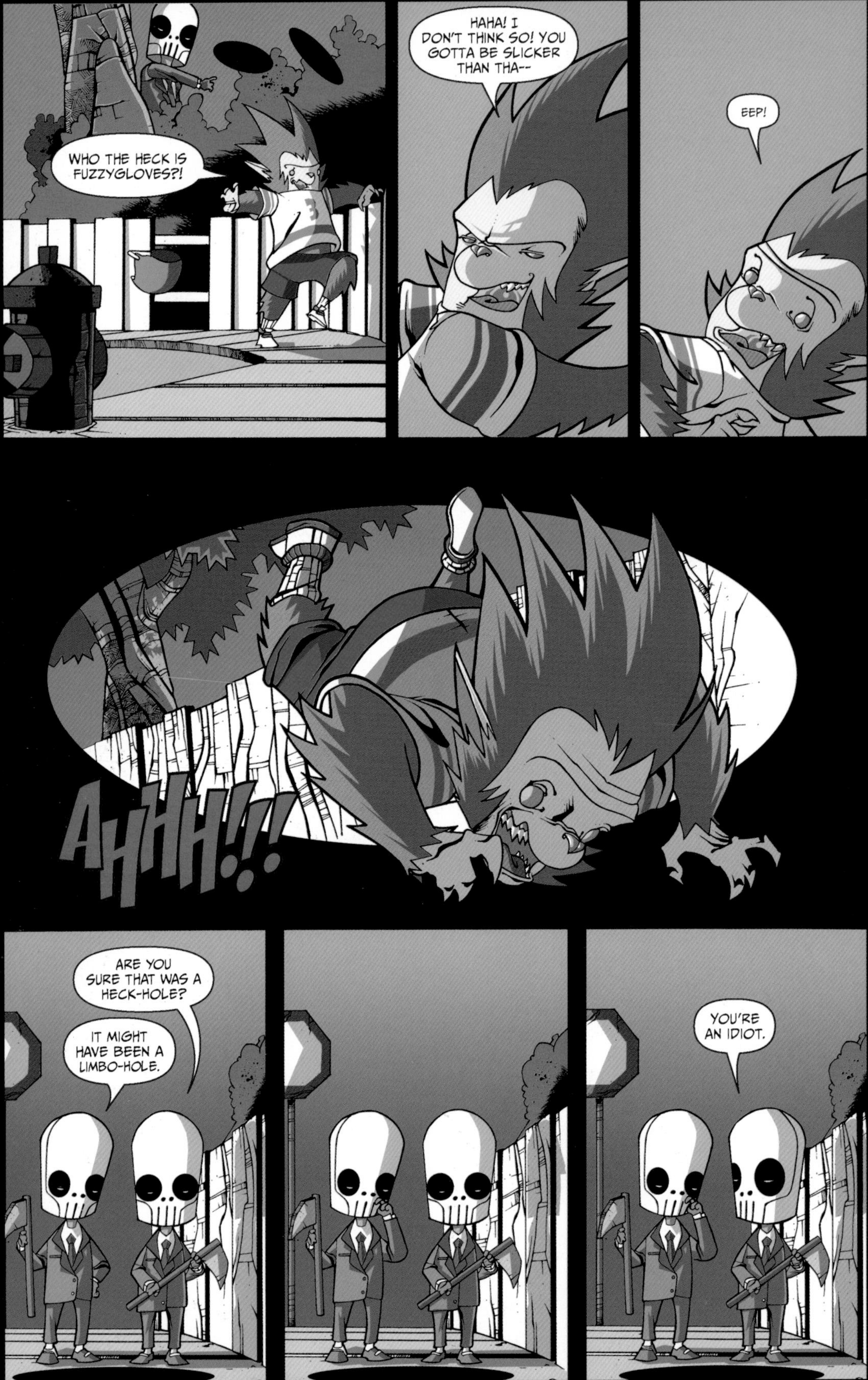
WHO THE HECK IS FUZZYGLOVES?!
HAHA! I DON'T THINK SO! YOU GOTTA BE SLICKER THAN THA--
EEP!
AHHH!!!
ARE YOU SURE THAT WAS A HECK-HOLE?
IT MIGHT HAVE BEEN A LIMBO-HOLE.
YOU'RE AN IDIOT.

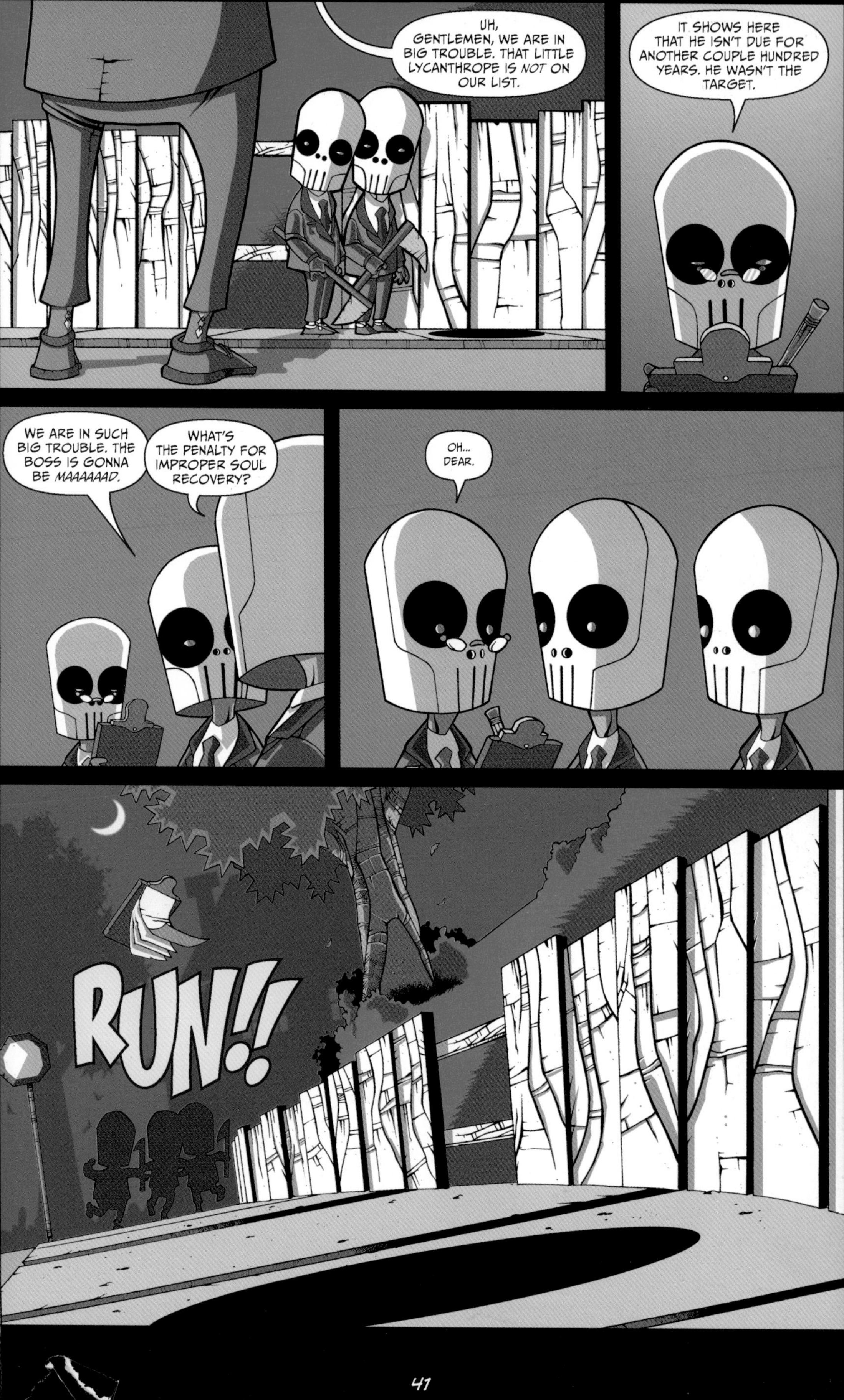
UH, GENTLEMEN, WE ARE IN BIG TROUBLE. THAT LITTLE LYCANTHROPE IS *NOT* ON OUR LIST.
IT SHOWS HERE THAT HE ISN'T DUE FOR ANOTHER COUPLE HUNDRED YEARS. HE WASN'T THE TARGET.
WE ARE IN SUCH BIG TROUBLE. THE BOSS IS GONNA BE *MAAAAAAD.*
WHAT'S THE PENALTY FOR IMPROPER SOUL RECOVERY?
OH... DEAR.
RUN!!

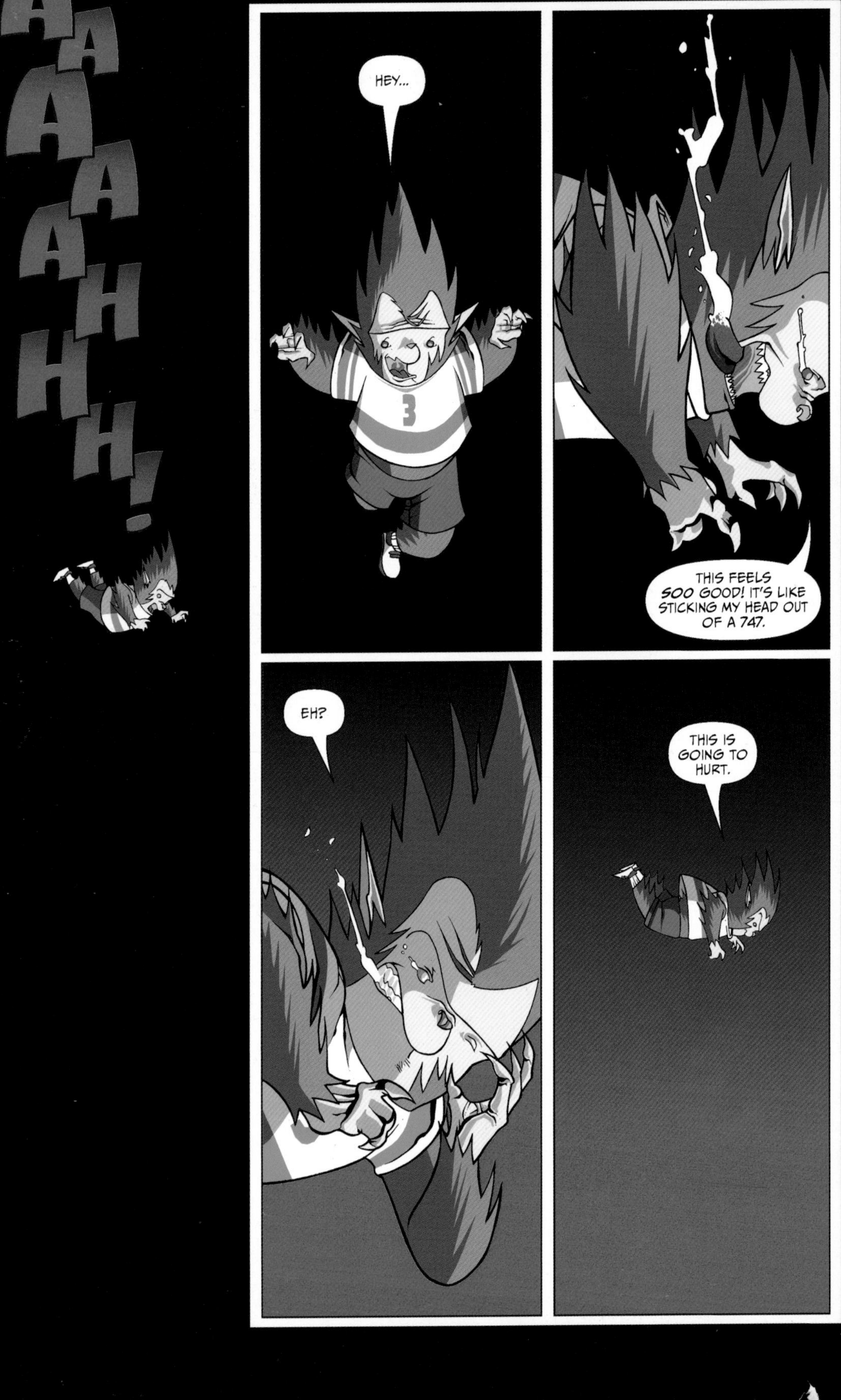
AAAAAAAHHH!
HEY...
THIS FEELS SOO GOOD! IT'S LIKE STICKING MY HEAD OUT OF A 747.
EH?
THIS IS GOING TO HURT.

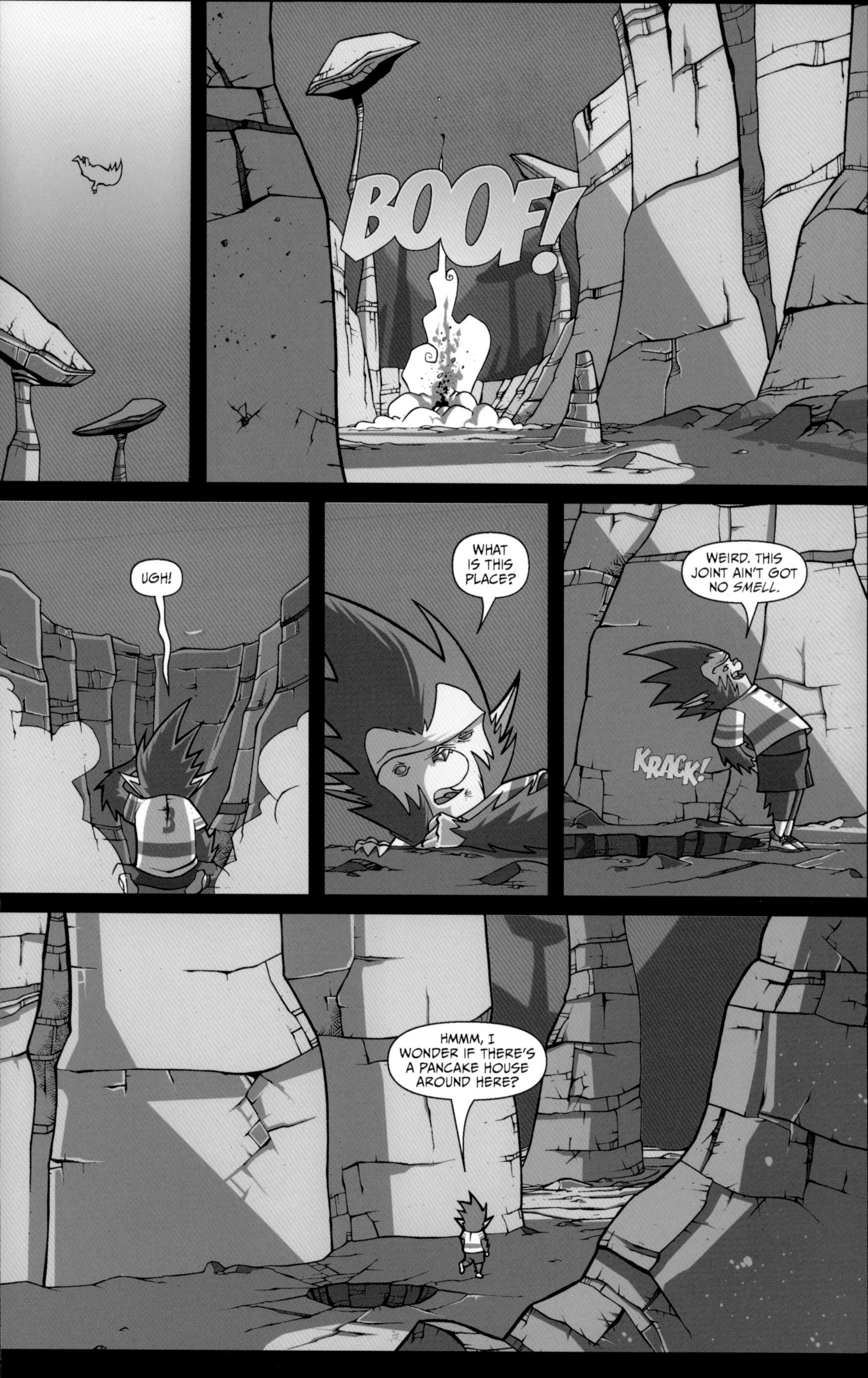
BOOF!
UGH!
WHAT IS THIS PLACE?
WEIRD. THIS JOINT AIN'T GOT NO *SMELL*.
KRACK!
HMMM, I WONDER IF THERE'S A PANCAKE HOUSE AROUND HERE?

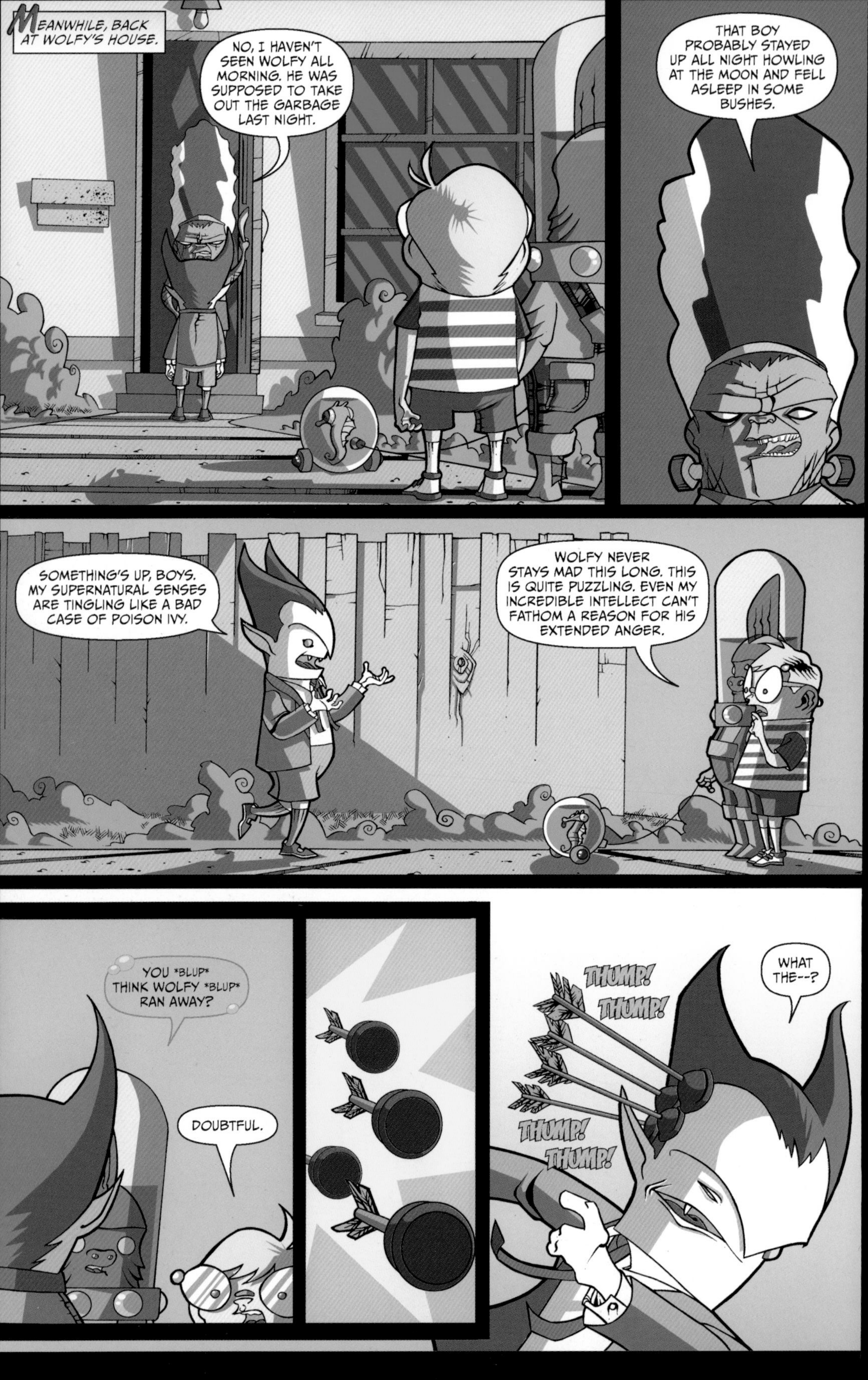
MEANWHILE, BACK AT WOLFY'S HOUSE.
NO, I HAVEN'T SEEN WOLFY ALL MORNING. HE WAS SUPPOSED TO TAKE OUT THE GARBAGE LAST NIGHT.
THAT BOY PROBABLY STAYED UP ALL NIGHT HOWLING AT THE MOON AND FELL ASLEEP IN SOME BUSHES.
SOMETHING'S UP, BOYS. MY SUPERNATURAL SENSES ARE TINGLING LIKE A BAD CASE OF POISON IVY.
WOLFY NEVER STAYS MAD THIS LONG. THIS IS QUITE PUZZLING. EVEN MY INCREDIBLE INTELLECT CAN'T FATHOM A REASON FOR HIS EXTENDED ANGER.
YOU *BLUP* THINK WOLFY *BLUP* RAN AWAY?
DOUBTFUL.
THUMP!
THUMP!
THUMP!
THUMP!
WHAT THE--?

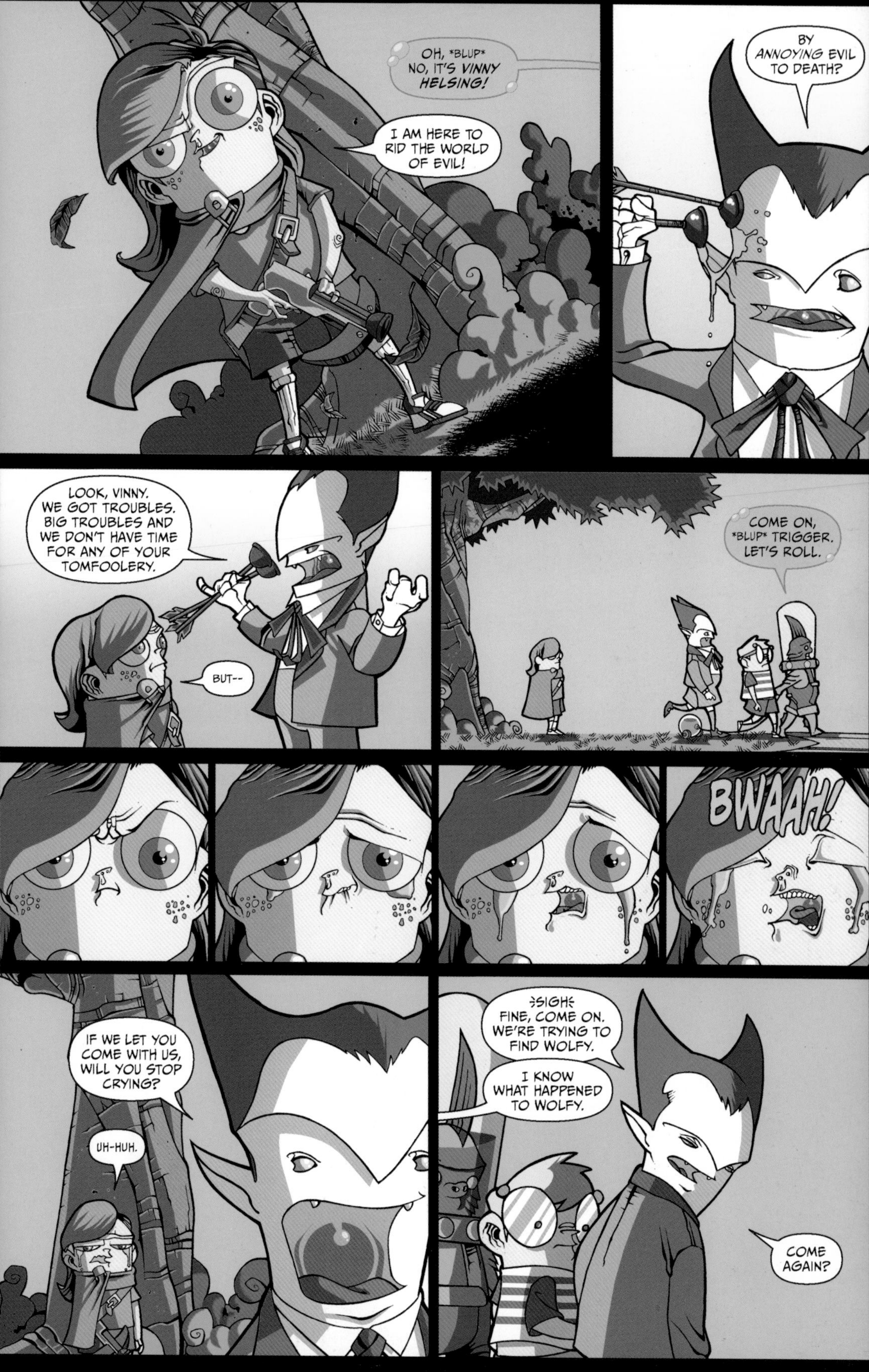
OH, *BLUP* NO, IT'S VINNY HELSING!
I AM HERE TO RID THE WORLD OF EVIL!
BY ANNOYING EVIL TO DEATH?
LOOK, VINNY. WE GOT TROUBLES. BIG TROUBLES AND WE DON'T HAVE TIME FOR ANY OF YOUR TOMFOOLERY.
BUT--
COME ON, *BLUP* TRIGGER. LET'S ROLL.
BWAAH!
IF WE LET YOU COME WITH US, WILL YOU STOP CRYING?
UH-HUH.
SIGH
FINE, COME ON. WE'RE TRYING TO FIND WOLFY.
I KNOW WHAT HAPPENED TO WOLFY.
COME AGAIN?

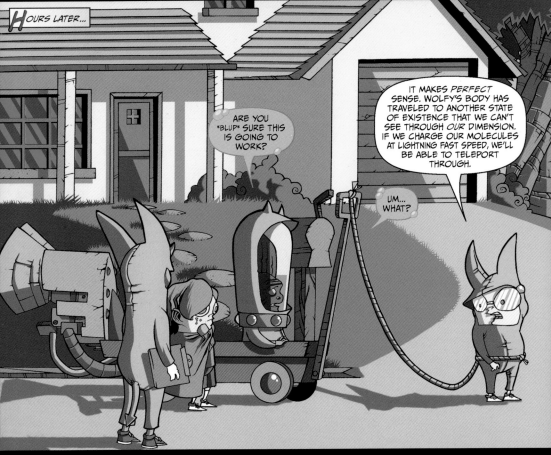

ARE YOU *BLUP* SURE THIS IS GOING TO WORK?

IT MAKES *PERFECT* SENSE. WOLFY'S BODY HAS TRAVELED TO ANOTHER STATE OF EXISTENCE THAT WE CAN'T SEE THROUGH *OUR* DIMENSION. IF WE CHARGE OUR MOLECULES AT LIGHTNING FAST SPEED, WE'LL BE ABLE TO TELEPORT THROUGH.

UM... WHAT?

WE'RE GOING TO JUMP IN THE WAGON AND JACKIE'S GOING TO JUICE IT UP AND RUN REALLY FAST SO WE CAN TELEPORT! GOT IT?

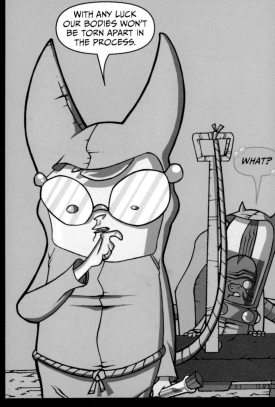

WITH ANY LUCK OUR BODIES WON'T BE TORN APART IN THE PROCESS.

WHAT?

46

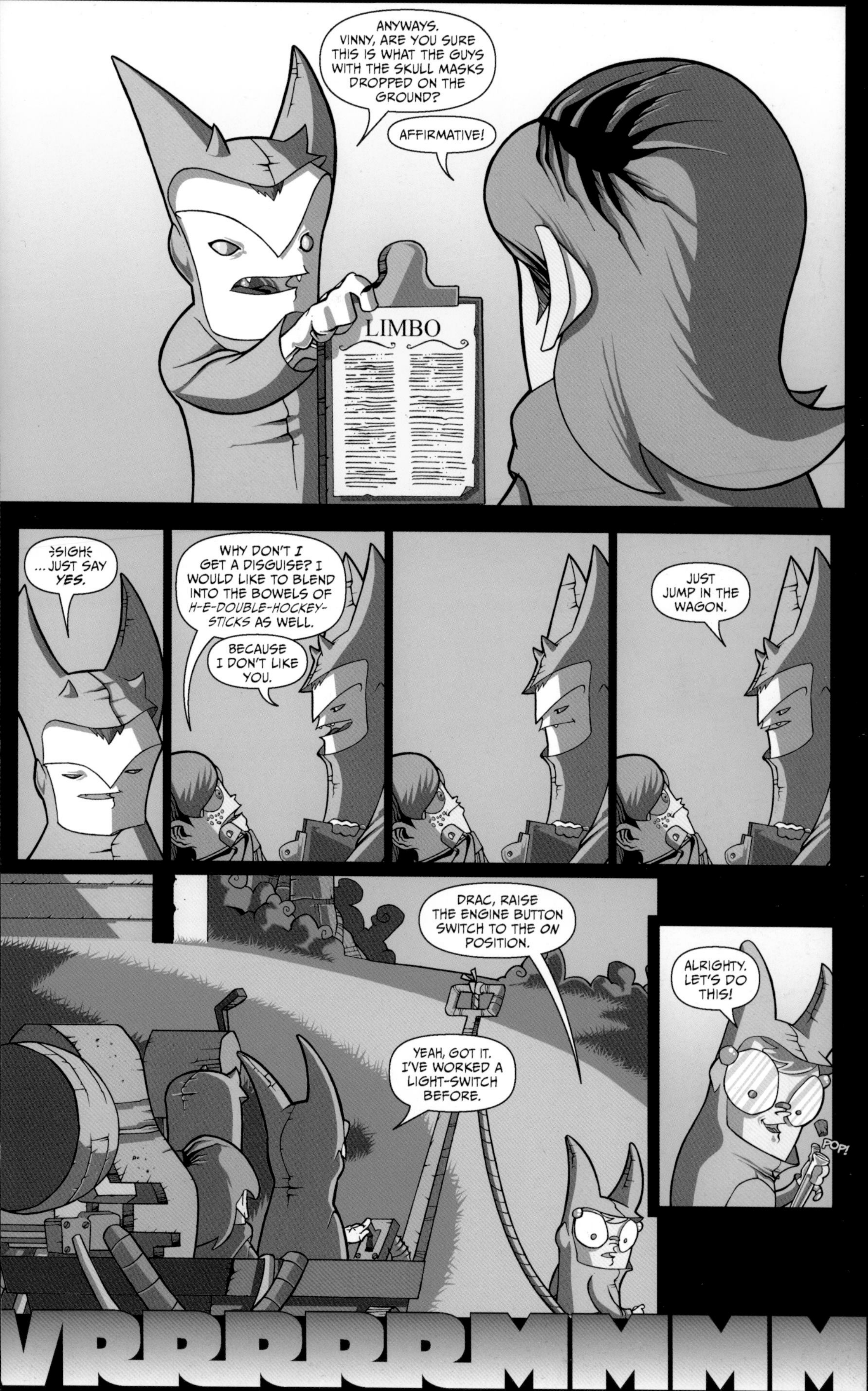
ANYWAYS. VINNY, ARE YOU SURE THIS IS WHAT THE GUYS WITH THE SKULL MASKS DROPPED ON THE GROUND?
AFFIRMATIVE!
LIMBO
SIGH ...JUST SAY *YES.*
WHY DON'T *I* GET A DISGUISE? I WOULD LIKE TO BLEND INTO THE BOWELS OF *H-E-DOUBLE-HOCKEY-STICKS* AS WELL.
BECAUSE I DON'T LIKE YOU.
JUST JUMP IN THE WAGON.
DRAC, RAISE THE ENGINE BUTTON SWITCH TO THE *ON* POSITION.
YEAH, GOT IT. I'VE WORKED A LIGHT-SWITCH BEFORE.
ALRIGHTY. LET'S DO THIS!
POP!
VRRRRRMMMMM

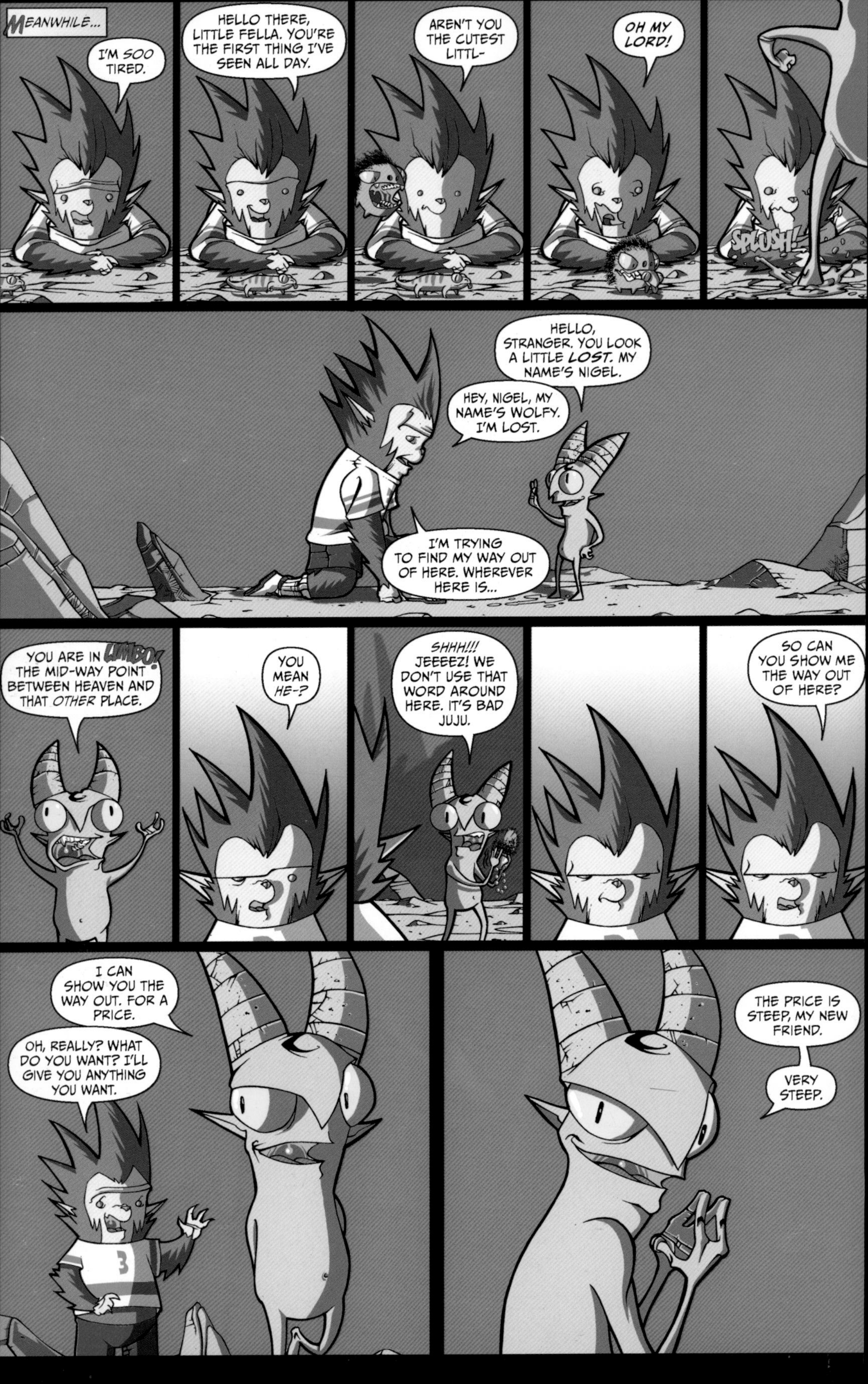

MEANWHILE...
I'M SOO TIRED.
HELLO THERE, LITTLE FELLA. YOU'RE THE FIRST THING I'VE SEEN ALL DAY.
AREN'T YOU THE CUTEST LITTL-
OH MY LORD!
SPLUSH!
HELLO, STRANGER. YOU LOOK A LITTLE LOST. MY NAME'S NIGEL.
HEY, NIGEL, MY NAME'S WOLFY. I'M LOST.
I'M TRYING TO FIND MY WAY OUT OF HERE. WHEREVER HERE IS...
YOU ARE IN LIMBO! THE MID-WAY POINT BETWEEN HEAVEN AND THAT OTHER PLACE.
YOU MEAN HE-?
SHHH!!! JEEEEZ! WE DON'T USE THAT WORD AROUND HERE. IT'S BAD JUJU.
SO CAN YOU SHOW ME THE WAY OUT OF HERE?
I CAN SHOW YOU THE WAY OUT. FOR A PRICE.
OH, REALLY? WHAT DO YOU WANT? I'LL GIVE YOU ANYTHING YOU WANT.
THE PRICE IS STEEP, MY NEW FRIEND.
VERY STEEP.

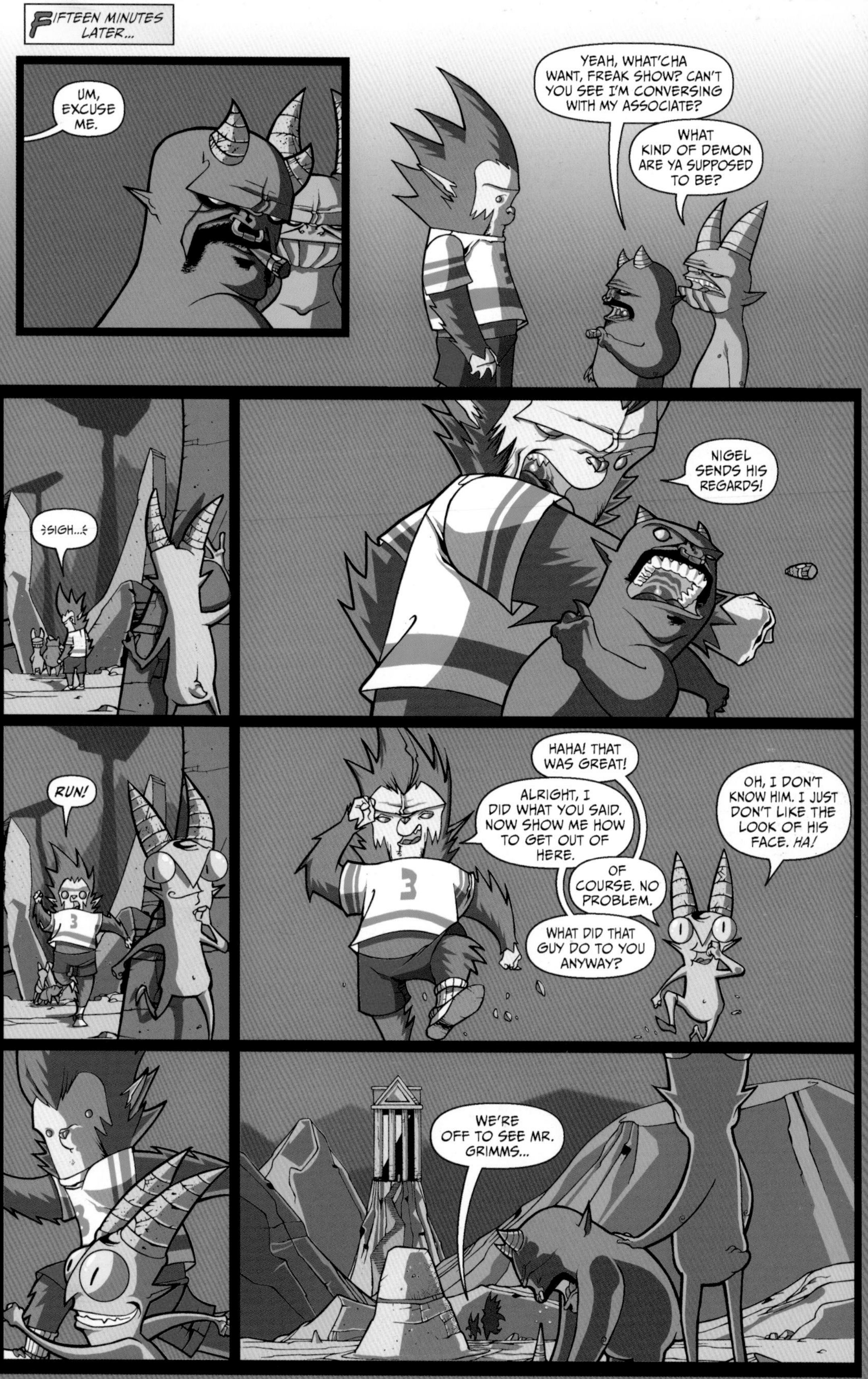
FIFTEEN MINUTES LATER...
UM, EXCUSE ME.
YEAH, WHAT'CHA WANT, FREAK SHOW? CAN'T YOU SEE I'M CONVERSING WITH MY ASSOCIATE?
WHAT KIND OF DEMON ARE YA SUPPOSED TO BE?
SIGH...
NIGEL SENDS HIS REGARDS!
RUN!
HAHA! THAT WAS GREAT!
ALRIGHT, I DID WHAT YOU SAID. NOW SHOW ME HOW TO GET OUT OF HERE.
OF COURSE. NO PROBLEM.
WHAT DID THAT GUY DO TO YOU ANYWAY?
OH, I DON'T KNOW HIM. I JUST DON'T LIKE THE LOOK OF HIS FACE. HA!
WE'RE OFF TO SEE MR. GRIMMS...

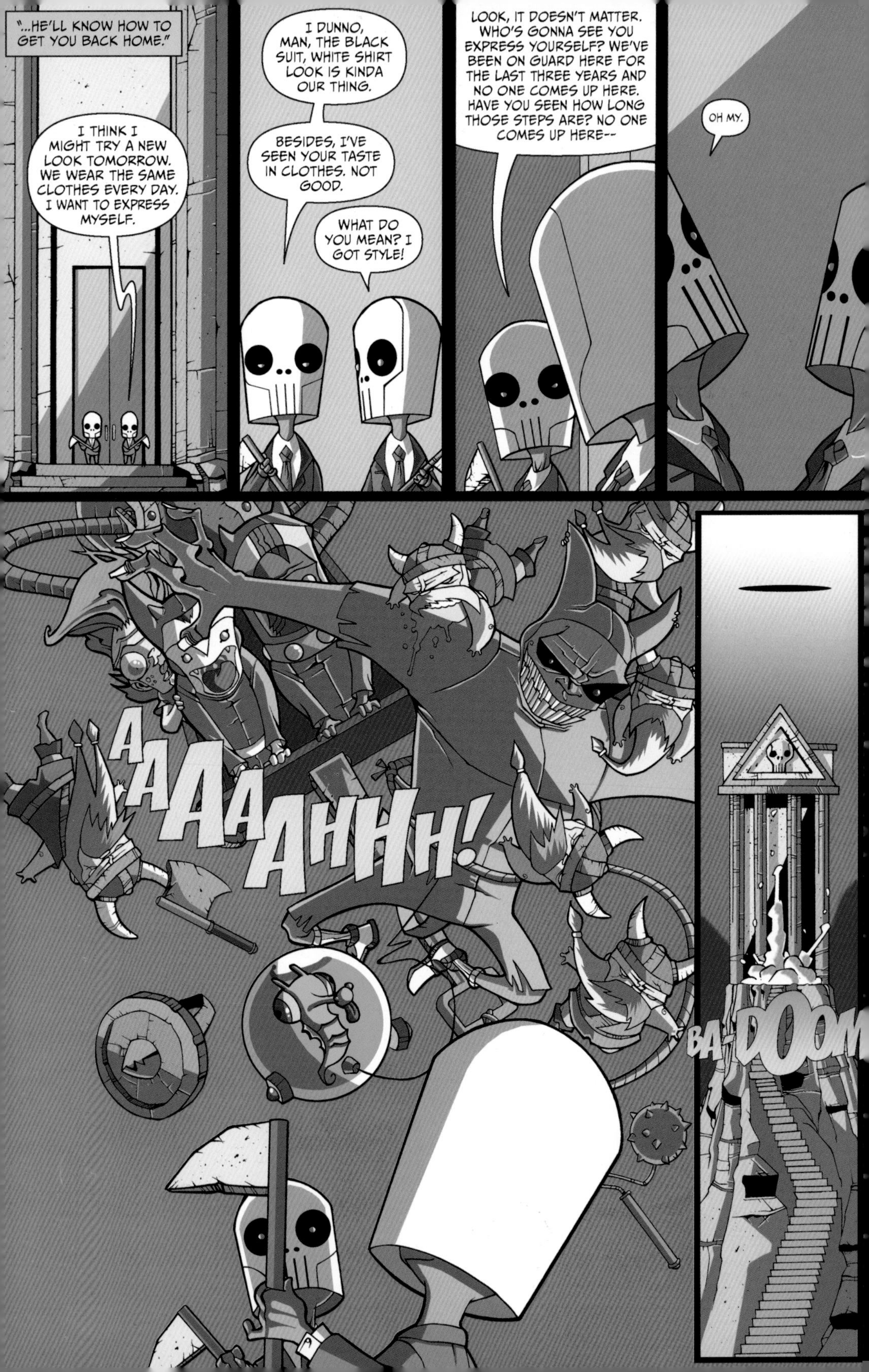
"...HE'LL KNOW HOW TO GET YOU BACK HOME."
I THINK I MIGHT TRY A NEW LOOK TOMORROW. WE WEAR THE SAME CLOTHES EVERY DAY. I WANT TO EXPRESS MYSELF.
I DUNNO, MAN, THE BLACK SUIT, WHITE SHIRT LOOK IS KINDA OUR THING.
BESIDES, I'VE SEEN YOUR TASTE IN CLOTHES. NOT GOOD.
WHAT DO YOU MEAN? I GOT STYLE!
LOOK, IT DOESN'T MATTER. WHO'S GONNA SEE YOU EXPRESS YOURSELF? WE'VE BEEN ON GUARD HERE FOR THE LAST THREE YEARS AND NO ONE COMES UP HERE. HAVE YOU SEEN HOW LONG THOSE STEPS ARE? NO ONE COMES UP HERE--
OH MY.
AAAAAHHHH!
BA-DOOM

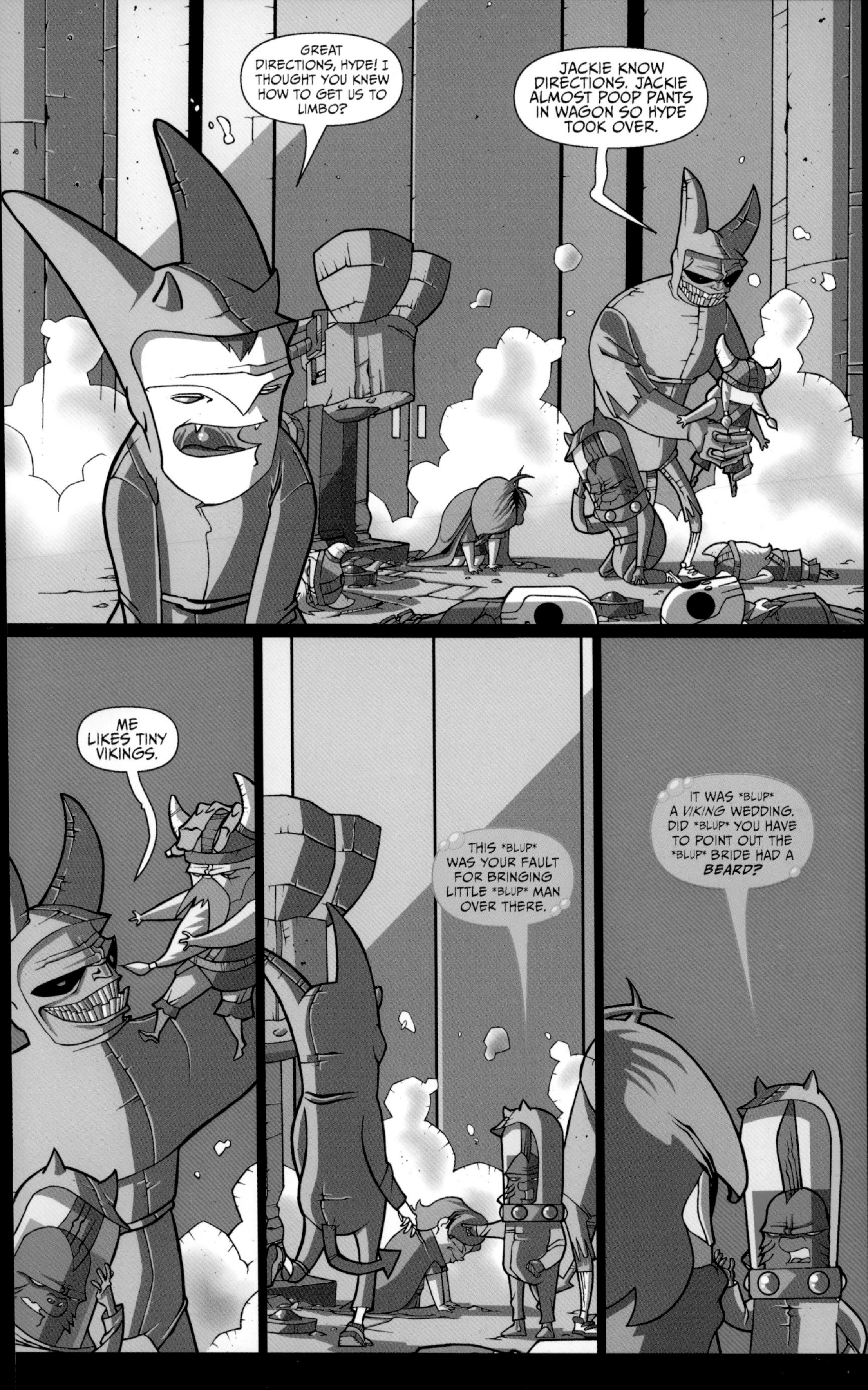
GREAT DIRECTIONS, HYDE! I THOUGHT YOU KNEW HOW TO GET US TO LIMBO?
JACKIE KNOW DIRECTIONS. JACKIE ALMOST POOP PANTS IN WAGON SO HYDE TOOK OVER.
ME LIKES TINY VIKINGS.
THIS *BLUP* WAS YOUR FAULT FOR BRINGING LITTLE *BLUP* MAN OVER THERE.
IT WAS *BLUP* A VIKING WEDDING. DID *BLUP* YOU HAVE TO POINT OUT THE *BLUP* BRIDE HAD A BEARD?

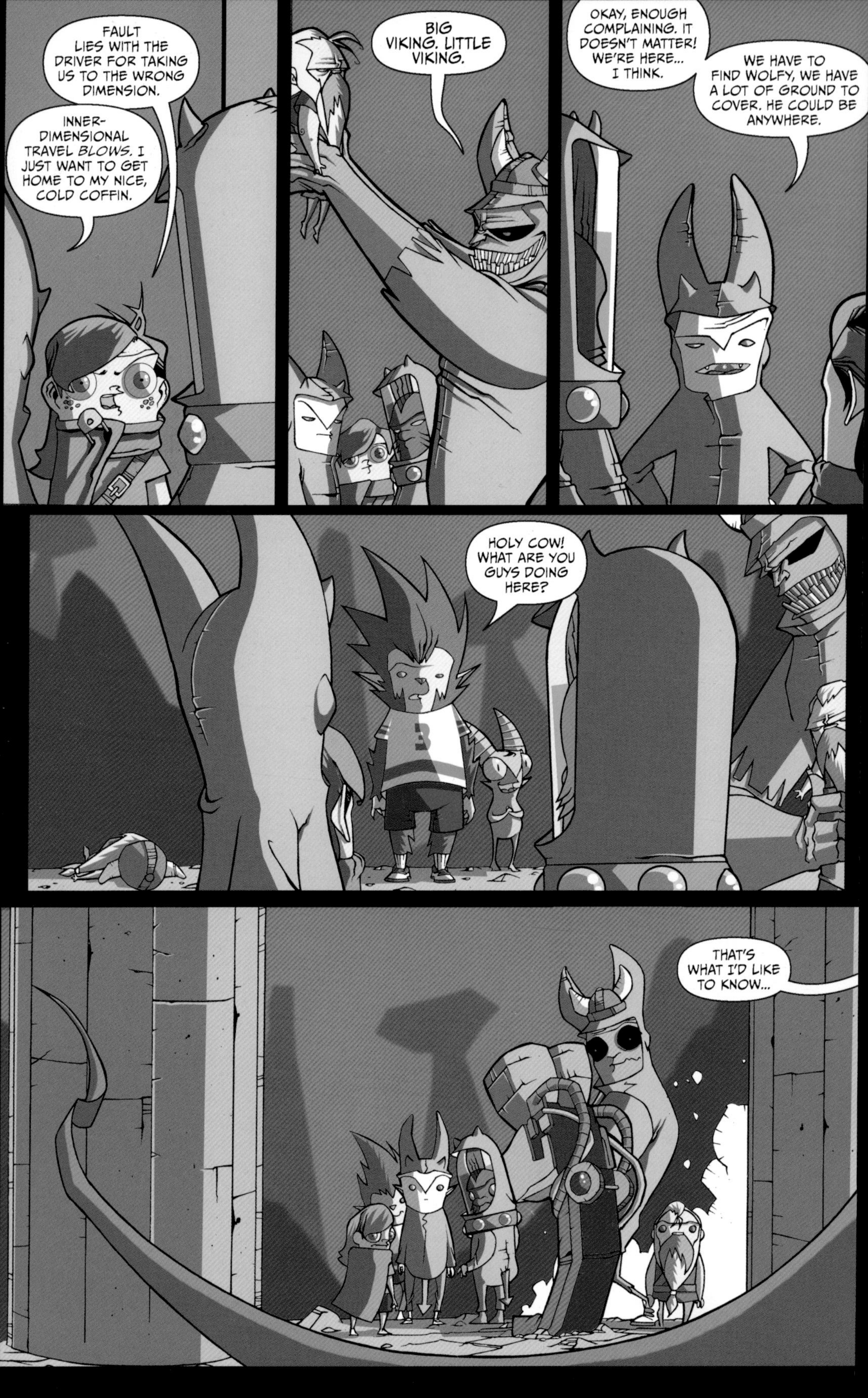
FAULT LIES WITH THE DRIVER FOR TAKING US TO THE WRONG DIMENSION.
INNER-DIMENSIONAL TRAVEL BLOWS. I JUST WANT TO GET HOME TO MY NICE, COLD COFFIN.
BIG VIKING. LITTLE VIKING.
OKAY, ENOUGH COMPLAINING. IT DOESN'T MATTER! WE'RE HERE... I THINK.
WE HAVE TO FIND WOLFY, WE HAVE A LOT OF GROUND TO COVER. HE COULD BE ANYWHERE.
HOLY COW! WHAT ARE YOU GUYS DOING HERE?
THAT'S WHAT I'D LIKE TO KNOW...

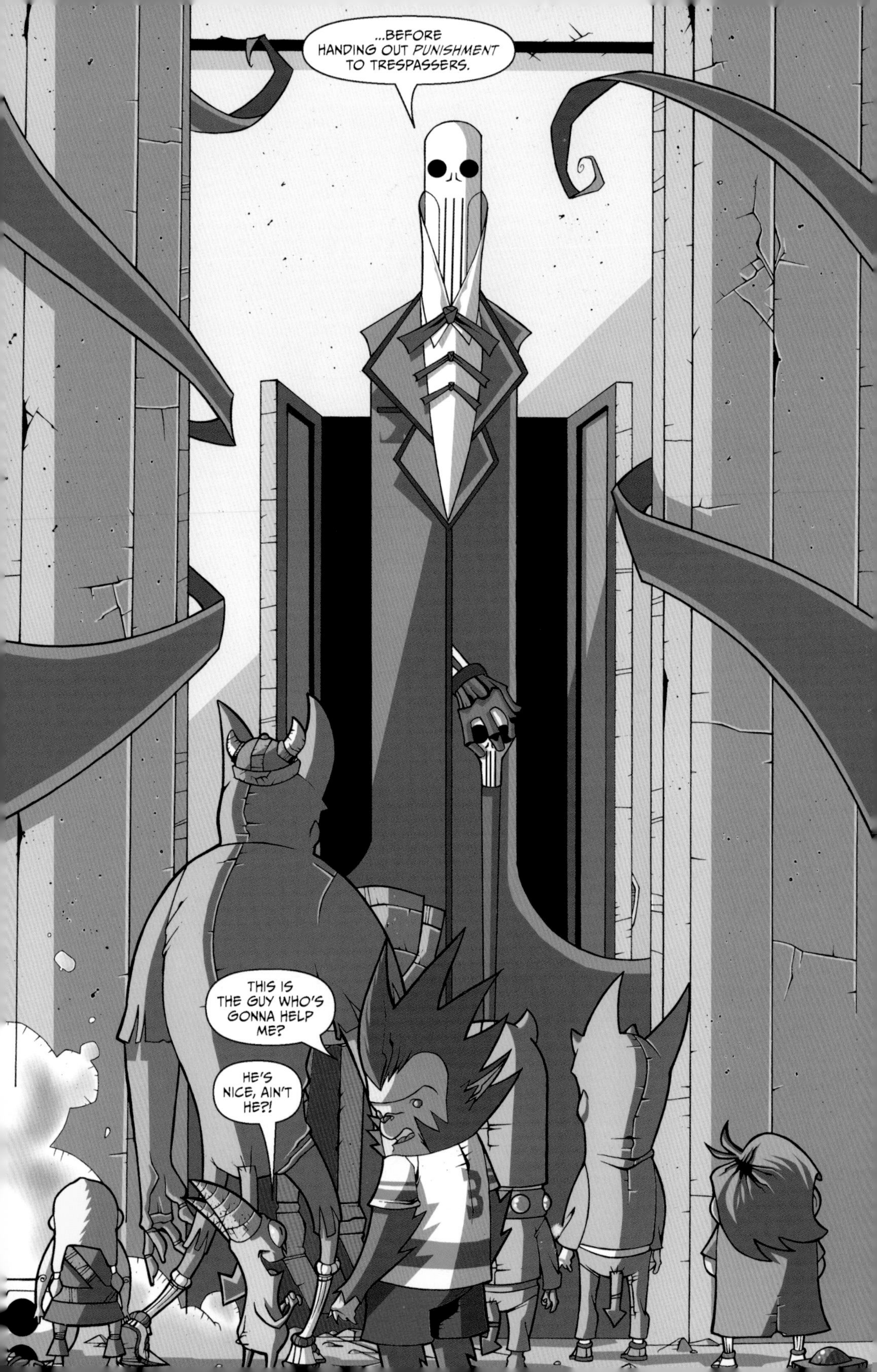
...BEFORE HANDING OUT *PUNISHMENT* TO TRESPASSERS.
THIS IS THE GUY WHO'S GONNA HELP ME?
HE'S NICE, AIN'T HE?!

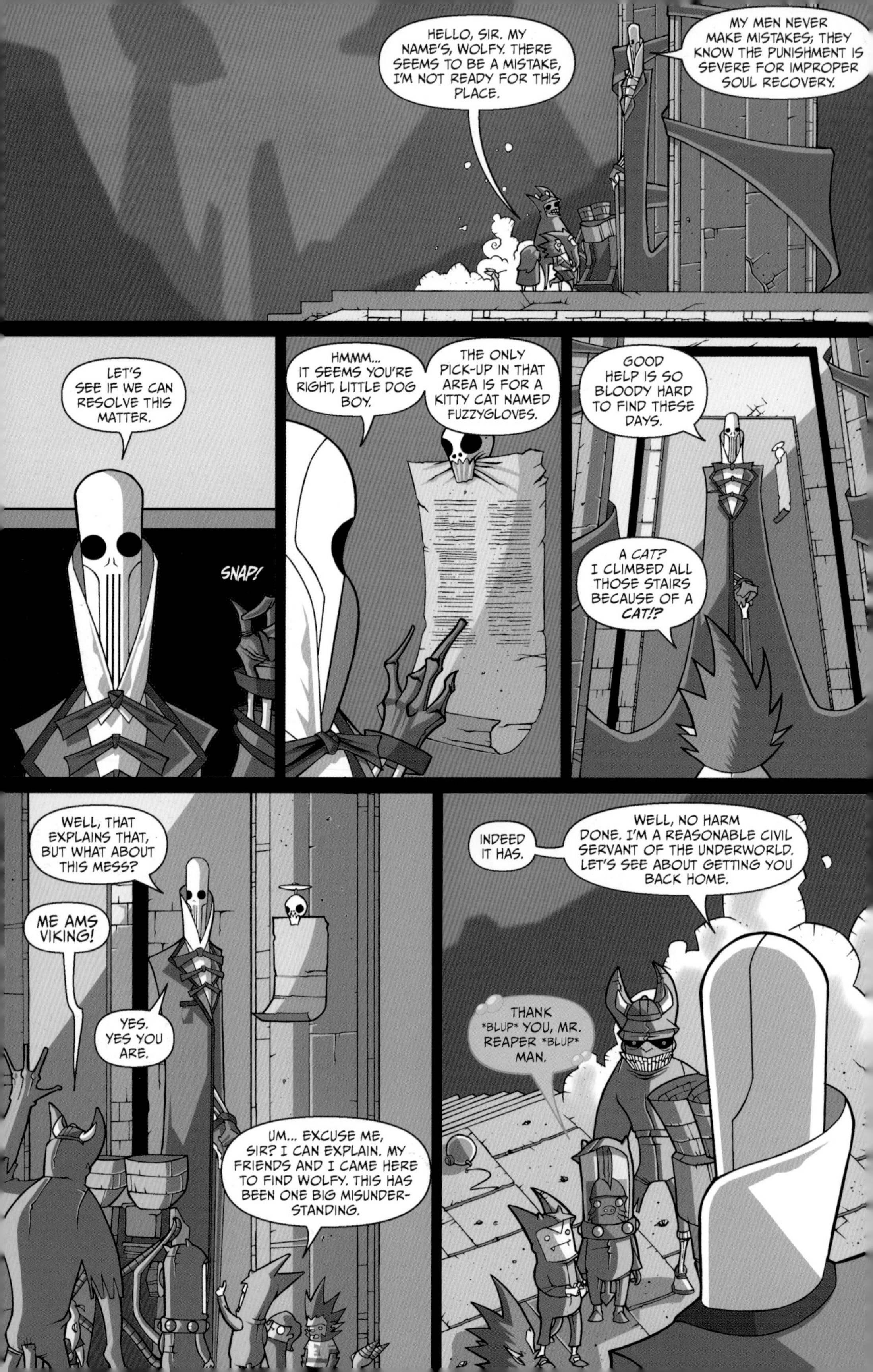
HELLO, SIR. MY NAME'S, WOLFY. THERE SEEMS TO BE A MISTAKE, I'M NOT READY FOR THIS PLACE.
MY MEN NEVER MAKE MISTAKES; THEY KNOW THE PUNISHMENT IS SEVERE FOR IMPROPER SOUL RECOVERY.
LET'S SEE IF WE CAN RESOLVE THIS MATTER.
SNAP!
HMMM... IT SEEMS YOU'RE RIGHT, LITTLE DOG BOY.
THE ONLY PICK-UP IN THAT AREA IS FOR A KITTY CAT NAMED FUZZYGLOVES.
GOOD HELP IS SO BLOODY HARD TO FIND THESE DAYS.
A CAT? I CLIMBED ALL THOSE STAIRS BECAUSE OF A CAT!?
WELL, THAT EXPLAINS THAT, BUT WHAT ABOUT THIS MESS?
ME AMS VIKING!
YES. YES YOU ARE.
UM... EXCUSE ME, SIR? I CAN EXPLAIN. MY FRIENDS AND I CAME HERE TO FIND WOLFY. THIS HAS BEEN ONE BIG MISUNDER-STANDING.
INDEED IT HAS.
WELL, NO HARM DONE. I'M A REASONABLE CIVIL SERVANT OF THE UNDERWORLD. LET'S SEE ABOUT GETTING YOU BACK HOME.
THANK *BLUP* YOU, MR. REAPER *BLUP* MAN.

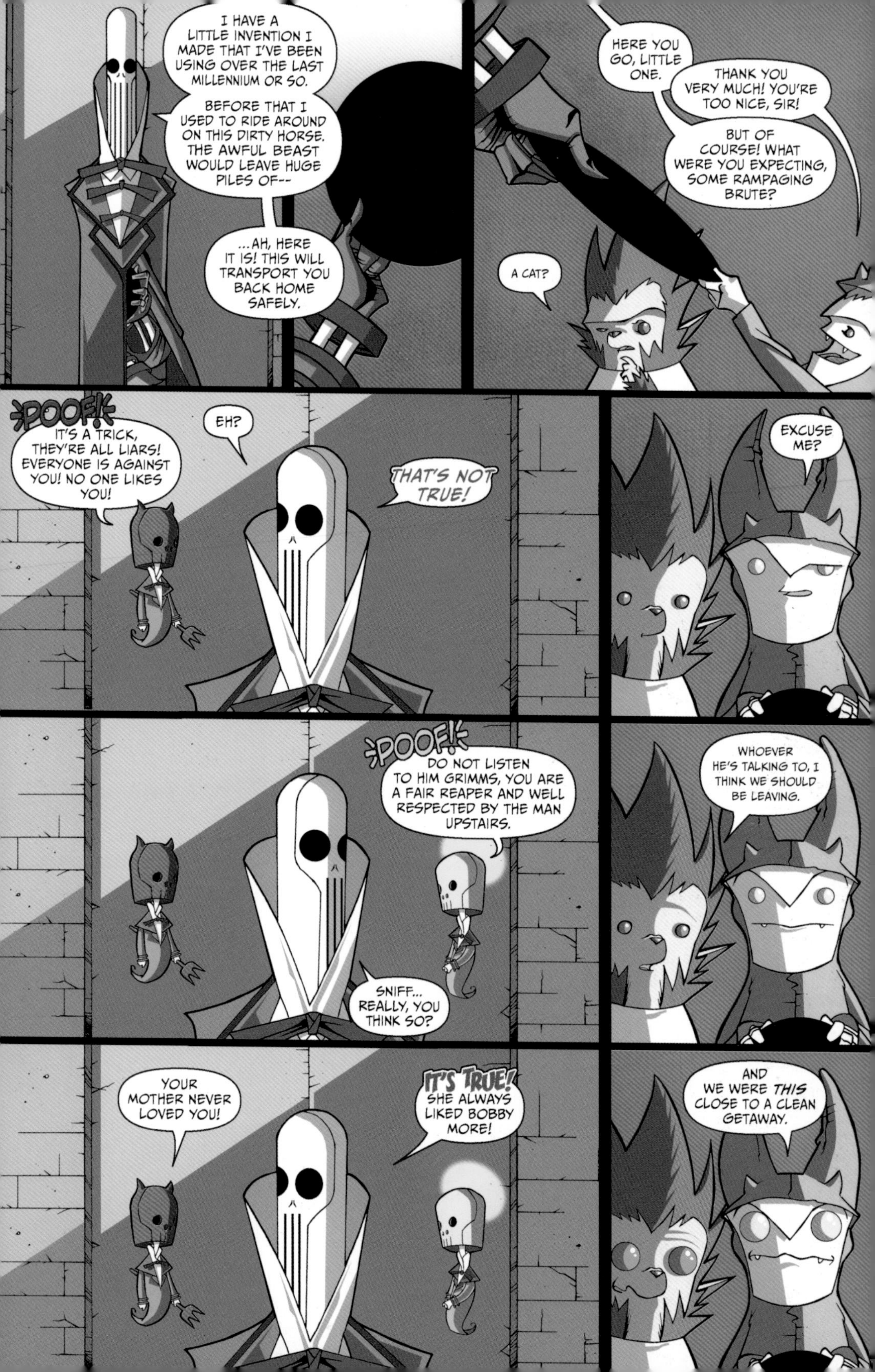

I HAVE A LITTLE INVENTION I MADE THAT I'VE BEEN USING OVER THE LAST MILLENNIUM OR SO.
BEFORE THAT I USED TO RIDE AROUND ON THIS DIRTY HORSE. THE AWFUL BEAST WOULD LEAVE HUGE PILES OF--
...AH, HERE IT IS! THIS WILL TRANSPORT YOU BACK HOME SAFELY.
HERE YOU GO, LITTLE ONE.
THANK YOU VERY MUCH! YOU'RE TOO NICE, SIR!
BUT OF COURSE! WHAT WERE YOU EXPECTING, SOME RAMPAGING BRUTE?
A CAT?
POOF!
IT'S A TRICK, THEY'RE ALL LIARS! EVERYONE IS AGAINST YOU! NO ONE LIKES YOU!
EH?
THAT'S NOT TRUE!
EXCUSE ME?
POOF!
DO NOT LISTEN TO HIM GRIMMS, YOU ARE A FAIR REAPER AND WELL RESPECTED BY THE MAN UPSTAIRS.
SNIFF... REALLY, YOU THINK SO?
WHOEVER HE'S TALKING TO, I THINK WE SHOULD BE LEAVING.
YOUR MOTHER NEVER LOVED YOU!
IT'S TRUE! SHE ALWAYS LIKED BOBBY MORE!
AND WE WERE THIS CLOSE TO A CLEAN GETAWAY.

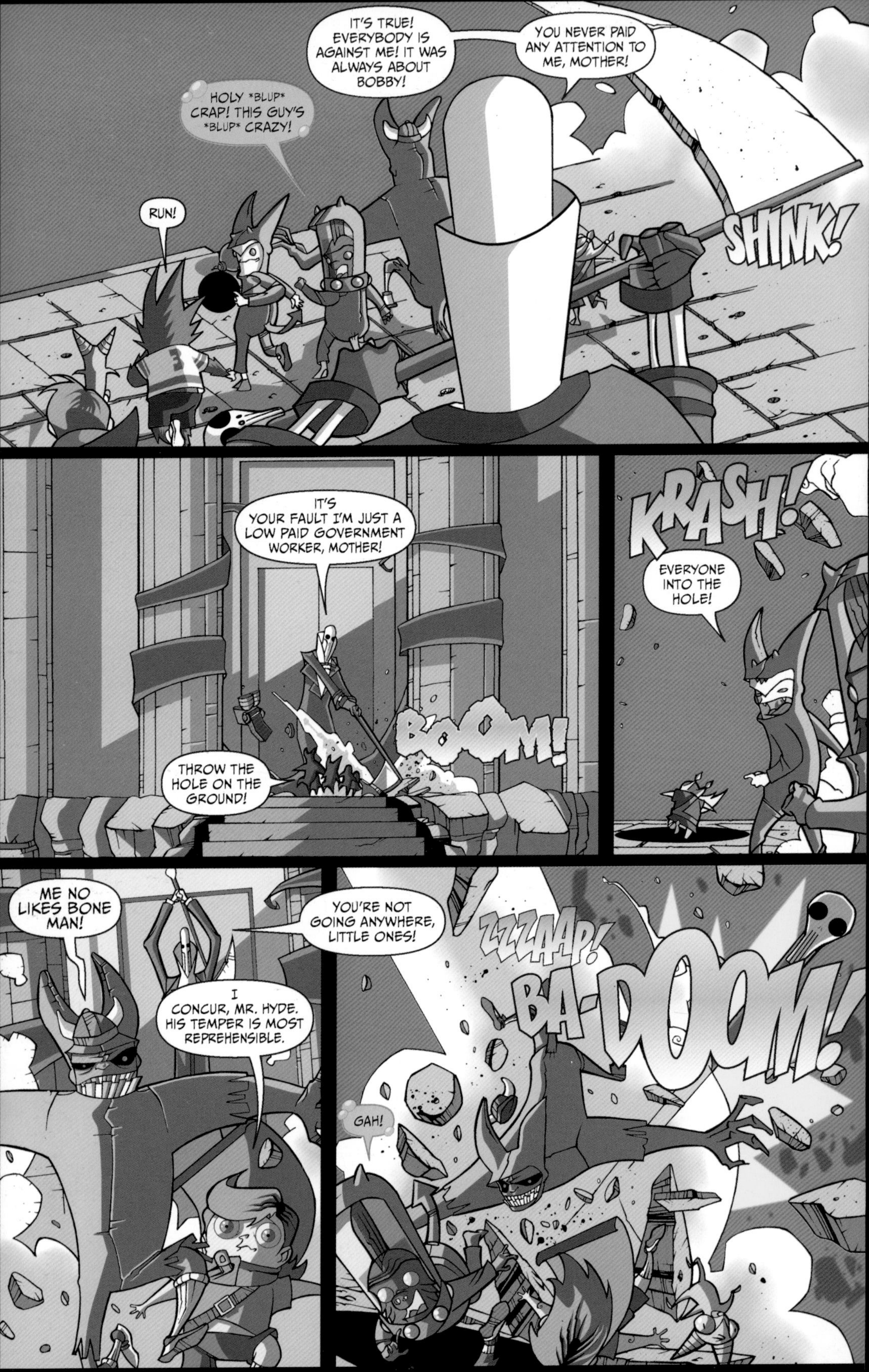
IT'S TRUE! EVERYBODY IS AGAINST ME! IT WAS ALWAYS ABOUT BOBBY!
YOU NEVER PAID ANY ATTENTION TO ME, MOTHER!
HOLY *BLUP* CRAP! THIS GUY'S *BLUP* CRAZY!
RUN!
SHINK!
IT'S YOUR FAULT I'M JUST A LOW PAID GOVERNMENT WORKER, MOTHER!
BOOM!
THROW THE HOLE ON THE GROUND!
KRASH!
EVERYONE INTO THE HOLE!
ME NO LIKES BONE MAN!
YOU'RE NOT GOING ANYWHERE, LITTLE ONES!
I CONCUR, MR. HYDE. HIS TEMPER IS MOST REPREHENSIBLE.
ZZZAAP!
BA-DOOM!
GAH!

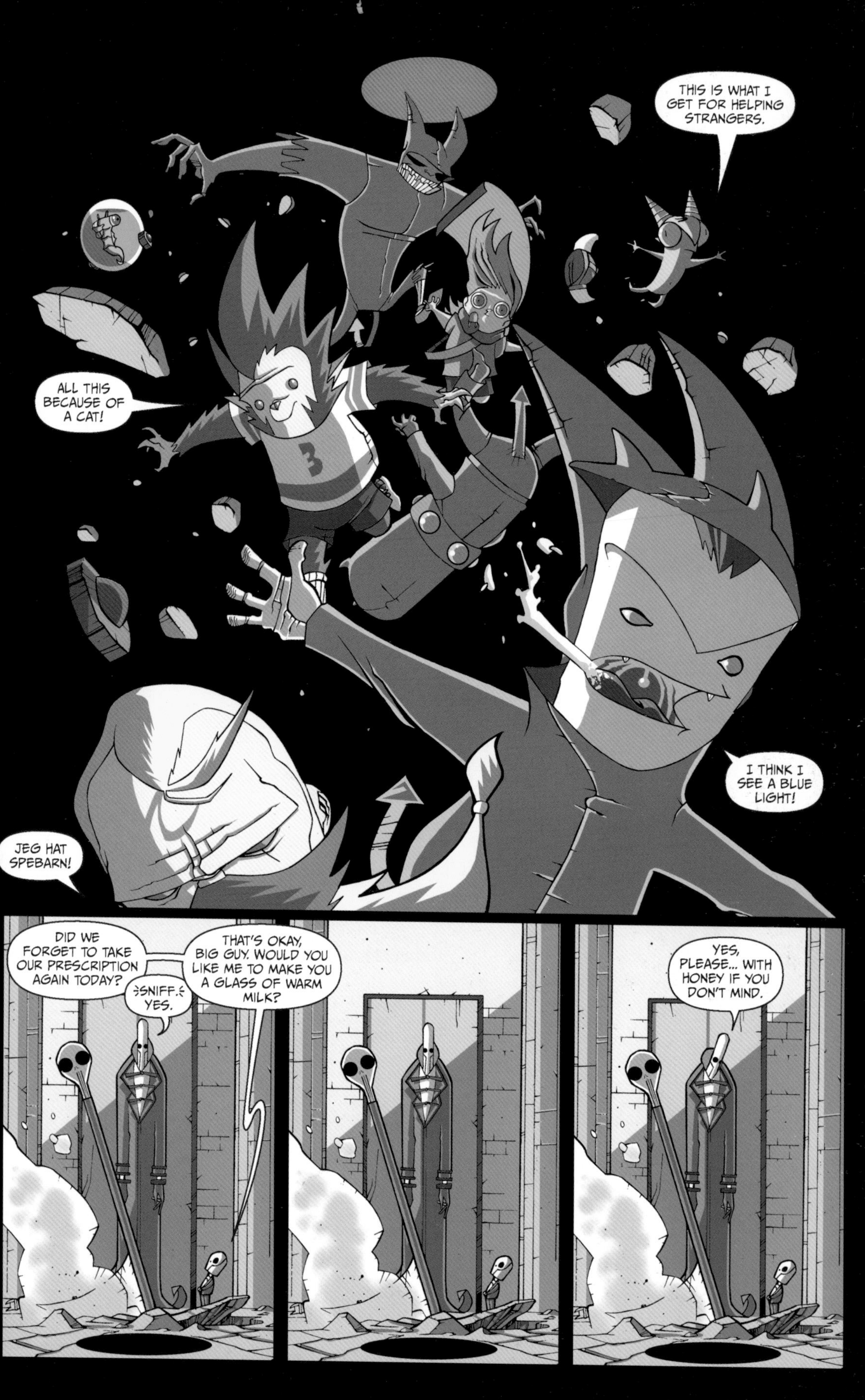

THIS IS WHAT I GET FOR HELPING STRANGERS.
ALL THIS BECAUSE OF A CAT!
I THINK I SEE A BLUE LIGHT!
JEG HAT SPEBARN!
DID WE FORGET TO TAKE OUR PRESCRIPTION AGAIN TODAY?
SNIFF. YES.
THAT'S OKAY, BIG GUY. WOULD YOU LIKE ME TO MAKE YOU A GLASS OF WARM MILK?
YES, PLEASE... WITH HONEY IF YOU DON'T MIND.

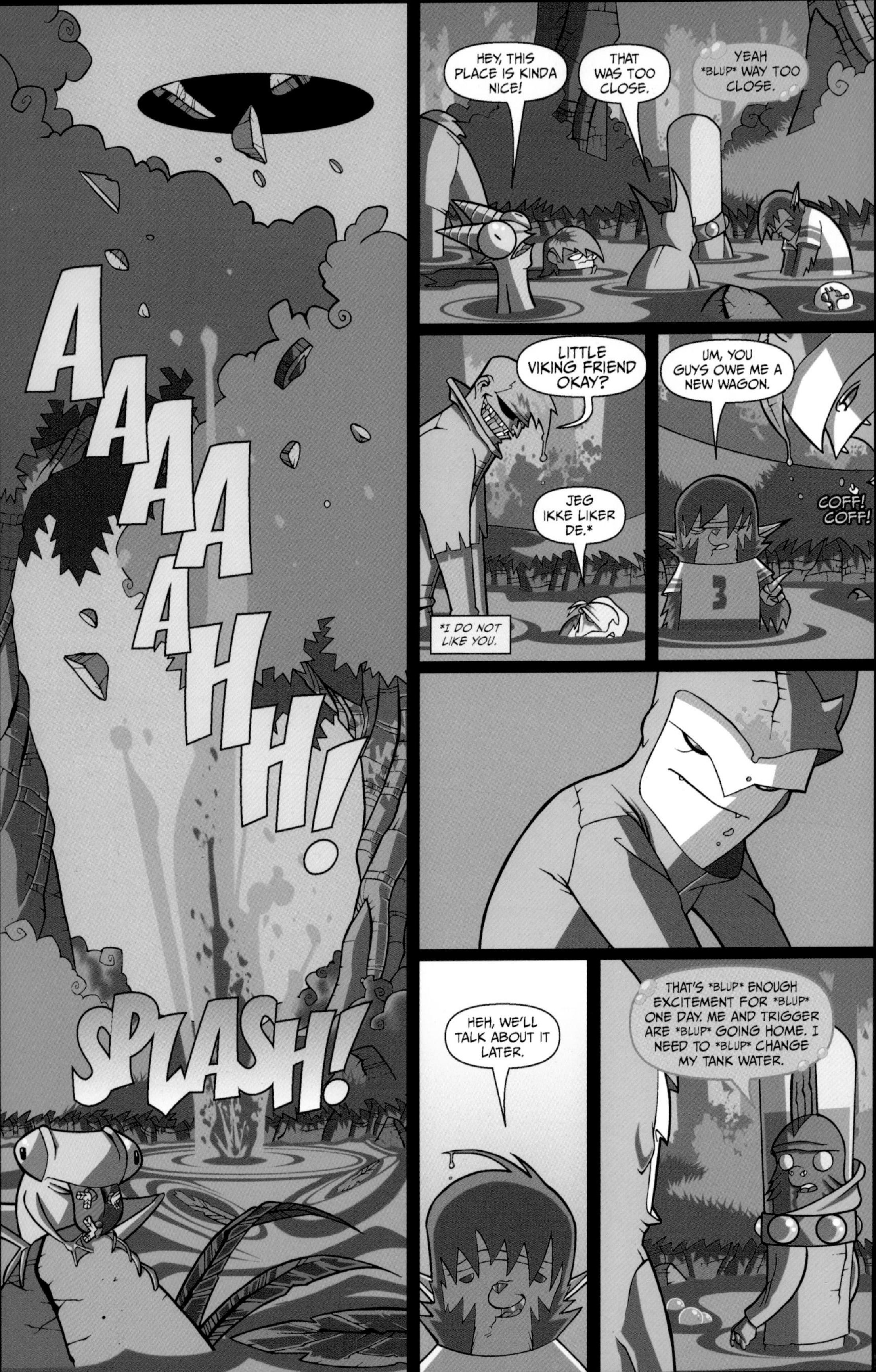
AAAAAAAHHH!
SPLASH!
HEY, THIS PLACE IS KINDA NICE!
THAT WAS TOO CLOSE.
YEAH *BLUP* WAY TOO CLOSE.
LITTLE VIKING FRIEND OKAY?
JEG IKKE LIKER DE.*
*I DO NOT LIKE YOU.
UM, YOU GUYS OWE ME A NEW WAGON.
COFF! COFF!
HEH, WE'LL TALK ABOUT IT LATER.
THAT'S *BLUP* ENOUGH EXCITEMENT FOR *BLUP* ONE DAY. ME AND TRIGGER ARE *BLUP* GOING HOME. I NEED TO *BLUP* CHANGE MY TANK WATER.

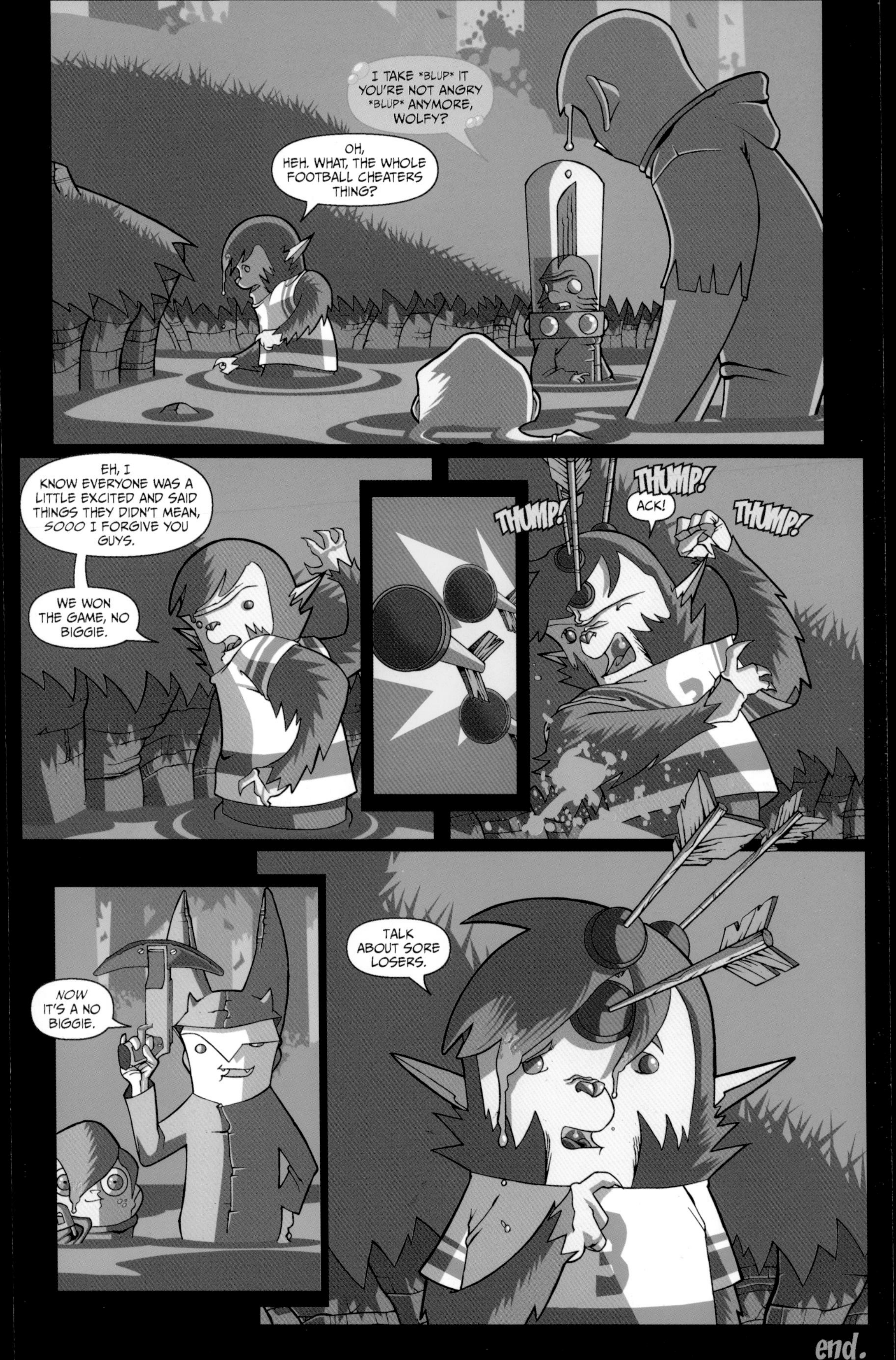
I TAKE *BLUP* IT YOU'RE NOT ANGRY *BLUP* ANYMORE, WOLFY?
OH, HEH. WHAT, THE WHOLE FOOTBALL CHEATERS THING?
EH, I KNOW EVERYONE WAS A LITTLE EXCITED AND SAID THINGS THEY DIDN'T MEAN, SOOO I FORGIVE YOU GUYS.
WE WON THE GAME, NO BIGGIE.
THUMP!
THUMP!
ACK!
THUMP!
NOW IT'S A NO BIGGIE.
TALK ABOUT SORE LOSERS.
end.

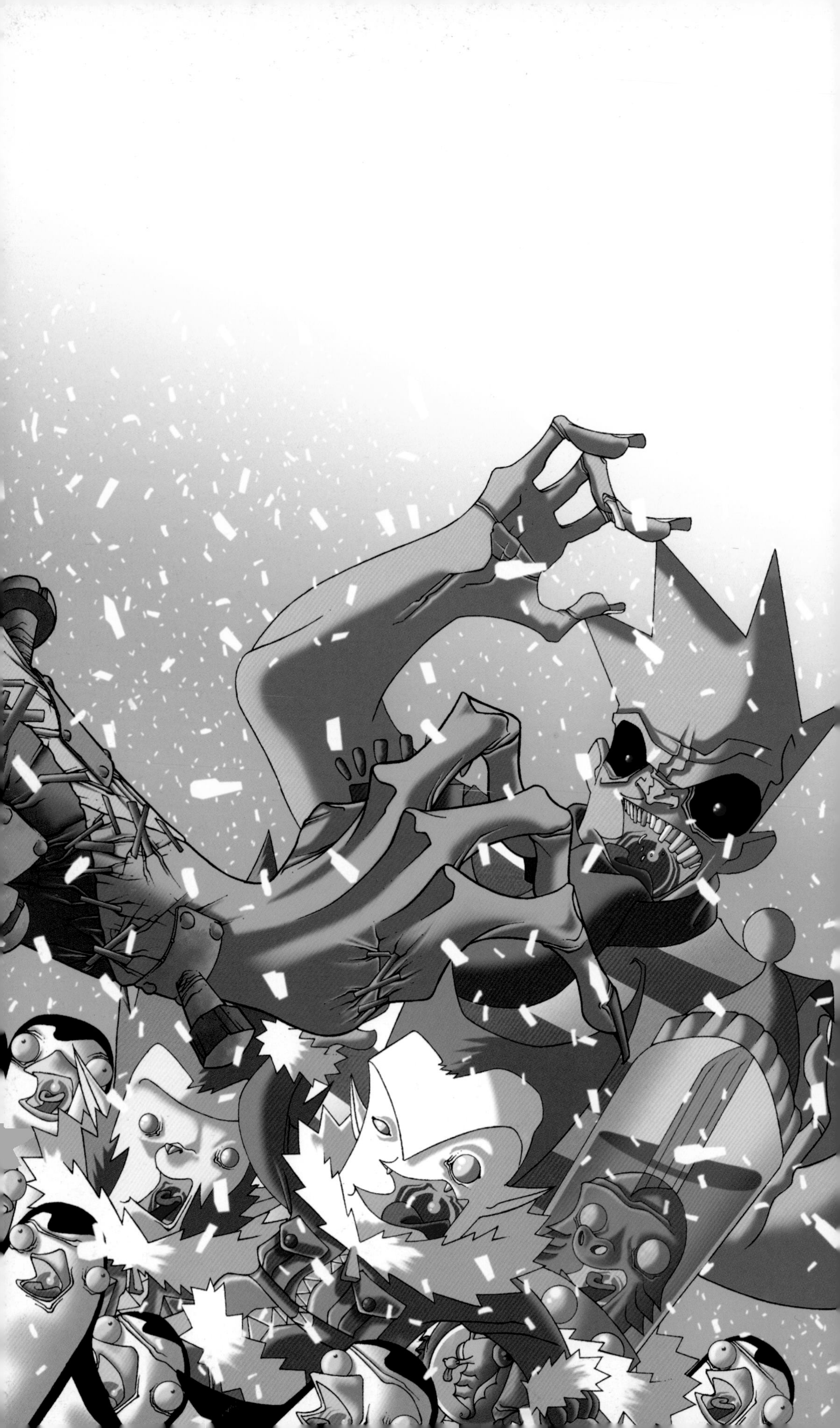

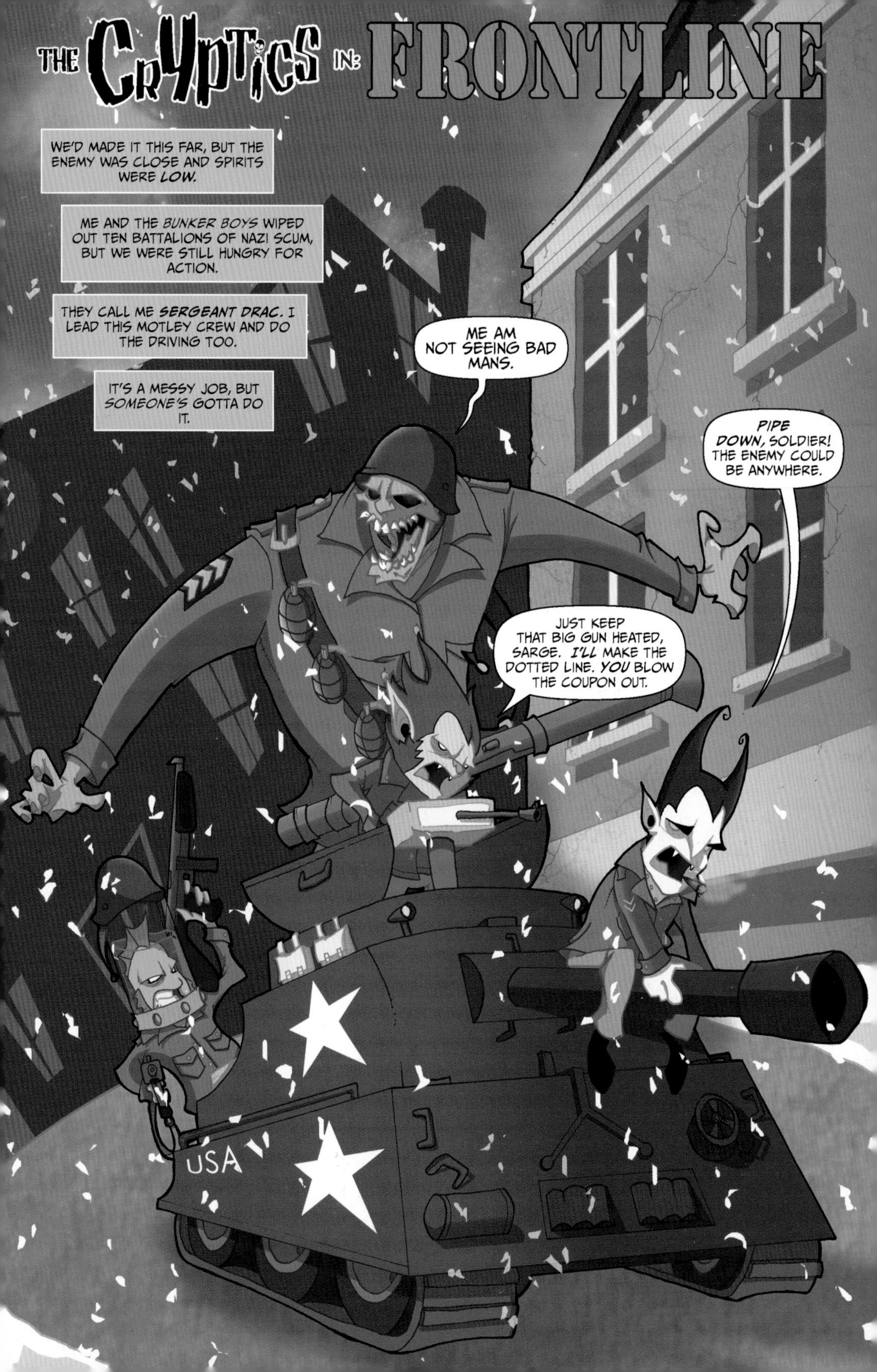
THE CRYPTICS IN: FRONTLINE
WE'D MADE IT THIS FAR, BUT THE ENEMY WAS CLOSE AND SPIRITS WERE *LOW.*
ME AND THE *BUNKER BOYS* WIPED OUT TEN BATTALIONS OF NAZI SCUM, BUT WE WERE STILL HUNGRY FOR ACTION.
THEY CALL ME ***SERGEANT DRAC.*** I LEAD THIS MOTLEY CREW AND DO THE DRIVING TOO.
IT'S A MESSY JOB, BUT *SOMEONE'S* GOTTA DO IT.
ME AM NOT SEEING BAD MANS.
PIPE DOWN, SOLDIER! THE ENEMY COULD BE ANYWHERE.
JUST KEEP THAT BIG GUN HEATED, SARGE. ***I'LL*** MAKE THE DOTTED LINE. ***YOU*** BLOW THE COUPON OUT.
USA

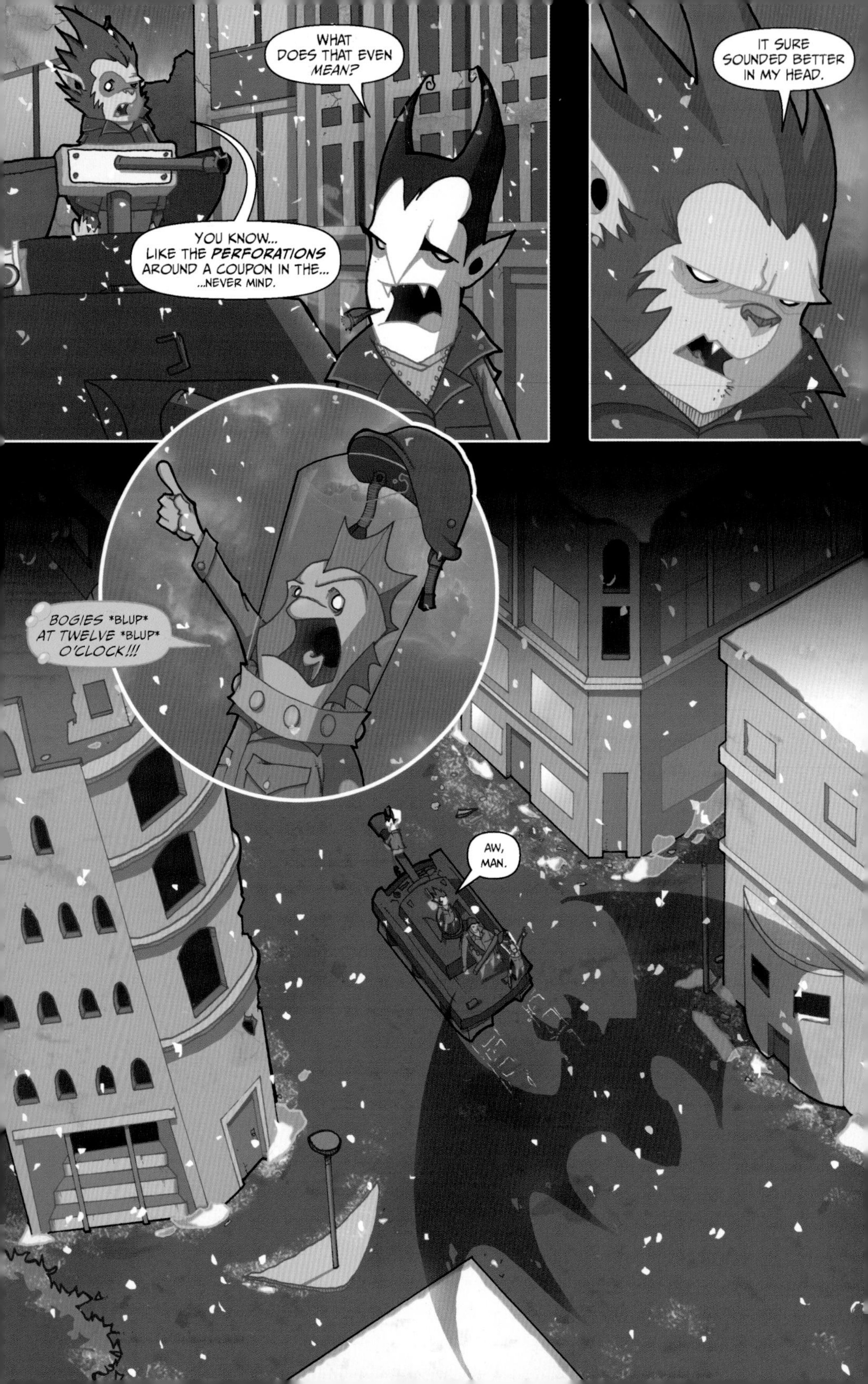
WHAT DOES THAT EVEN *MEAN?*
YOU KNOW... LIKE THE *PERFORATIONS* AROUND A COUPON IN THE... ...NEVER MIND.
IT SURE SOUNDED BETTER IN MY HEAD.
BOGIES *BLUP* AT TWELVE *BLUP* O'CLOCK!!!
AW, MAN.

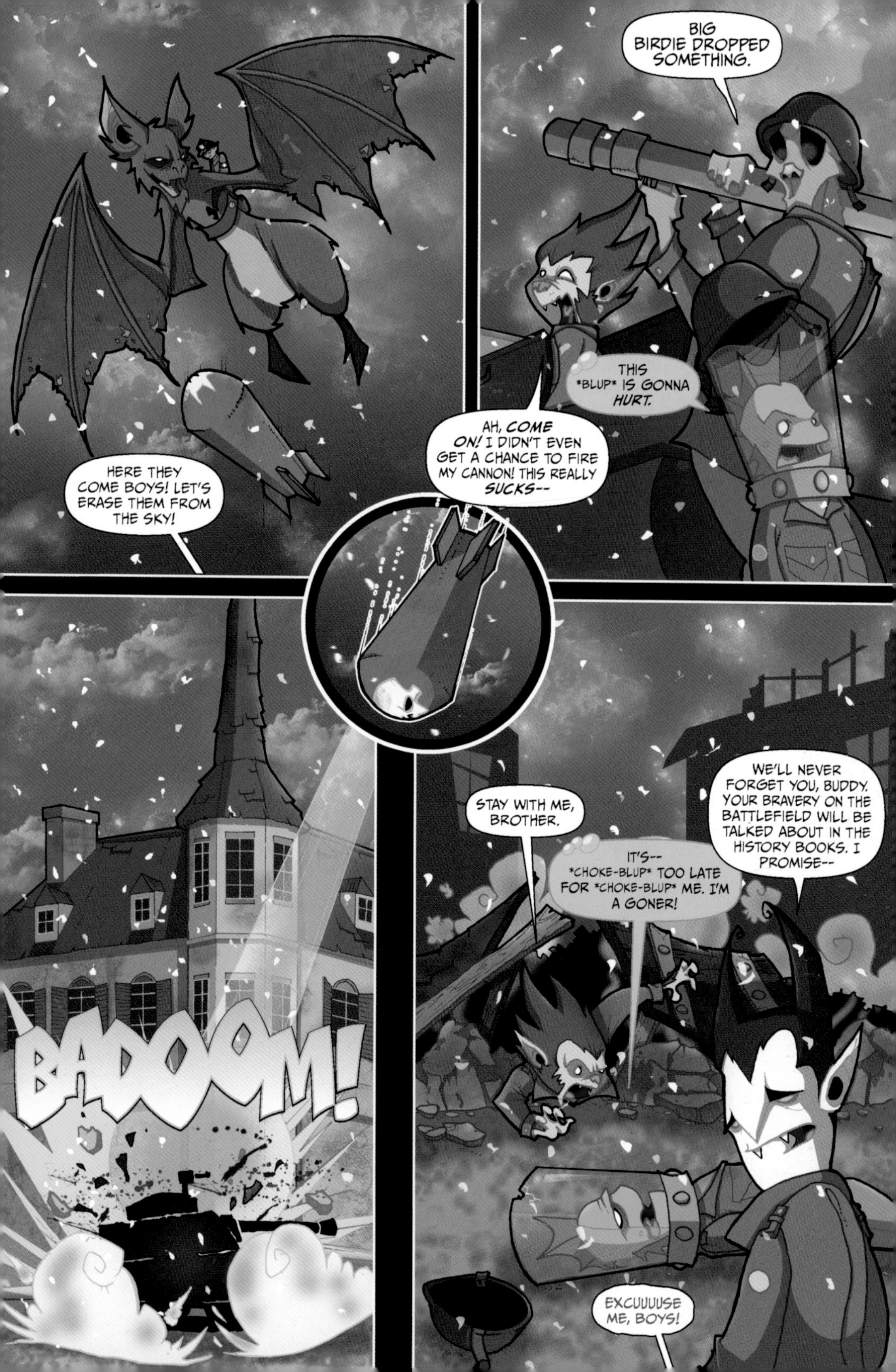
HERE THEY COME BOYS! LET'S ERASE THEM FROM THE SKY!
BIG BIRDIE DROPPED SOMETHING.
THIS *BLUP* IS GONNA HURT.
AH, COME ON! I DIDN'T EVEN GET A CHANCE TO FIRE MY CANNON! THIS REALLY SUCKS--
BADOOM!
STAY WITH ME, BROTHER.
IT'S-- *CHOKE-BLUP* TOO LATE FOR *CHOKE-BLUP* ME. I'M A GONER!
WE'LL NEVER FORGET YOU, BUDDY. YOUR BRAVERY ON THE BATTLEFIELD WILL BE TALKED ABOUT IN THE HISTORY BOOKS. I PROMISE--
EXCUUUUSE ME, BOYS!

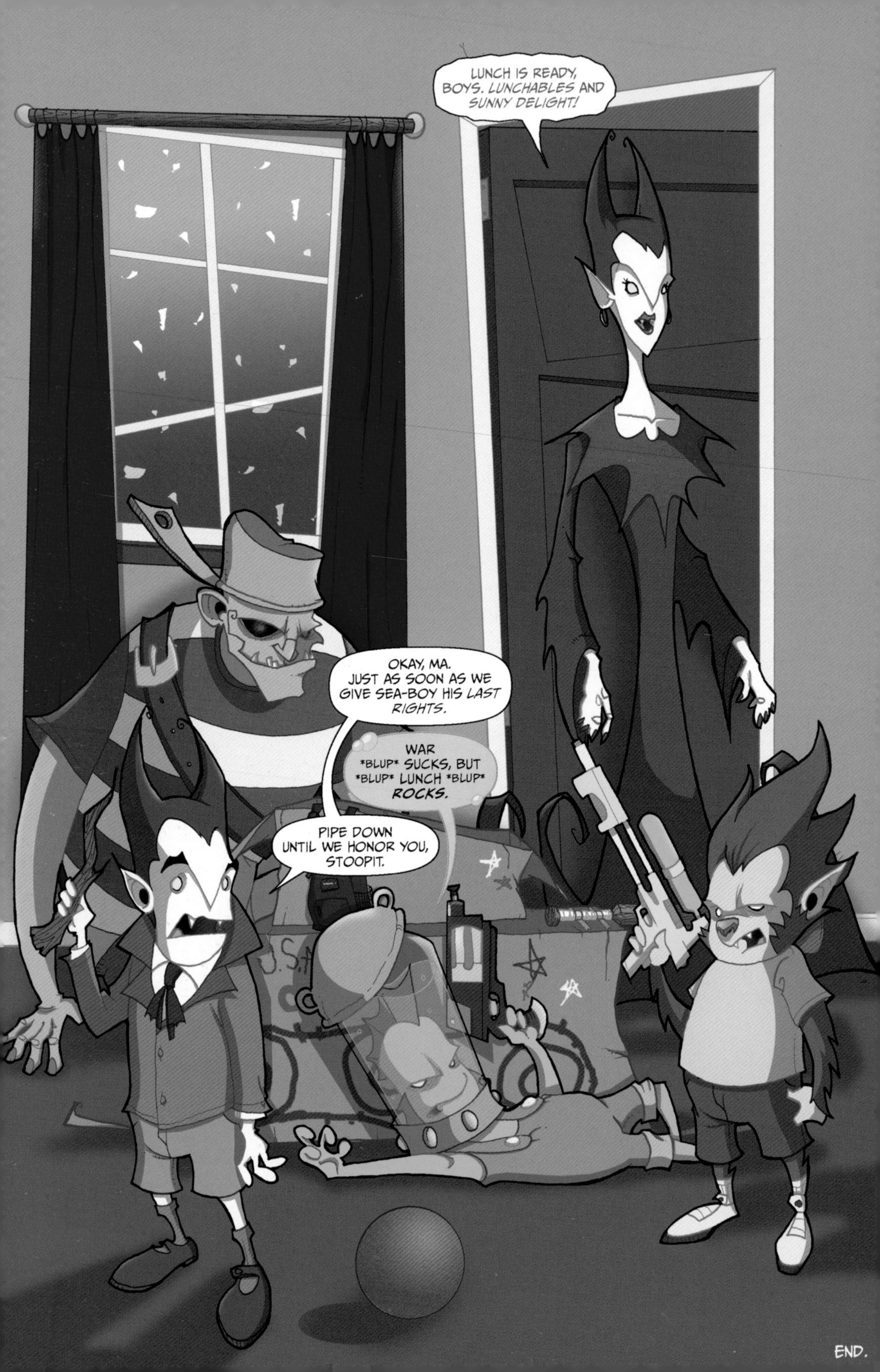
LUNCH IS READY, BOYS. LUNCHABLES AND SUNNY DELIGHT!
OKAY, MA. JUST AS SOON AS WE GIVE SEA-BOY HIS LAST RIGHTS.
WAR *BLUP* SUCKS, BUT *BLUP* LUNCH *BLUP* ROCKS.
PIPE DOWN UNTIL WE HONOR YOU, STOOPIT.
END.

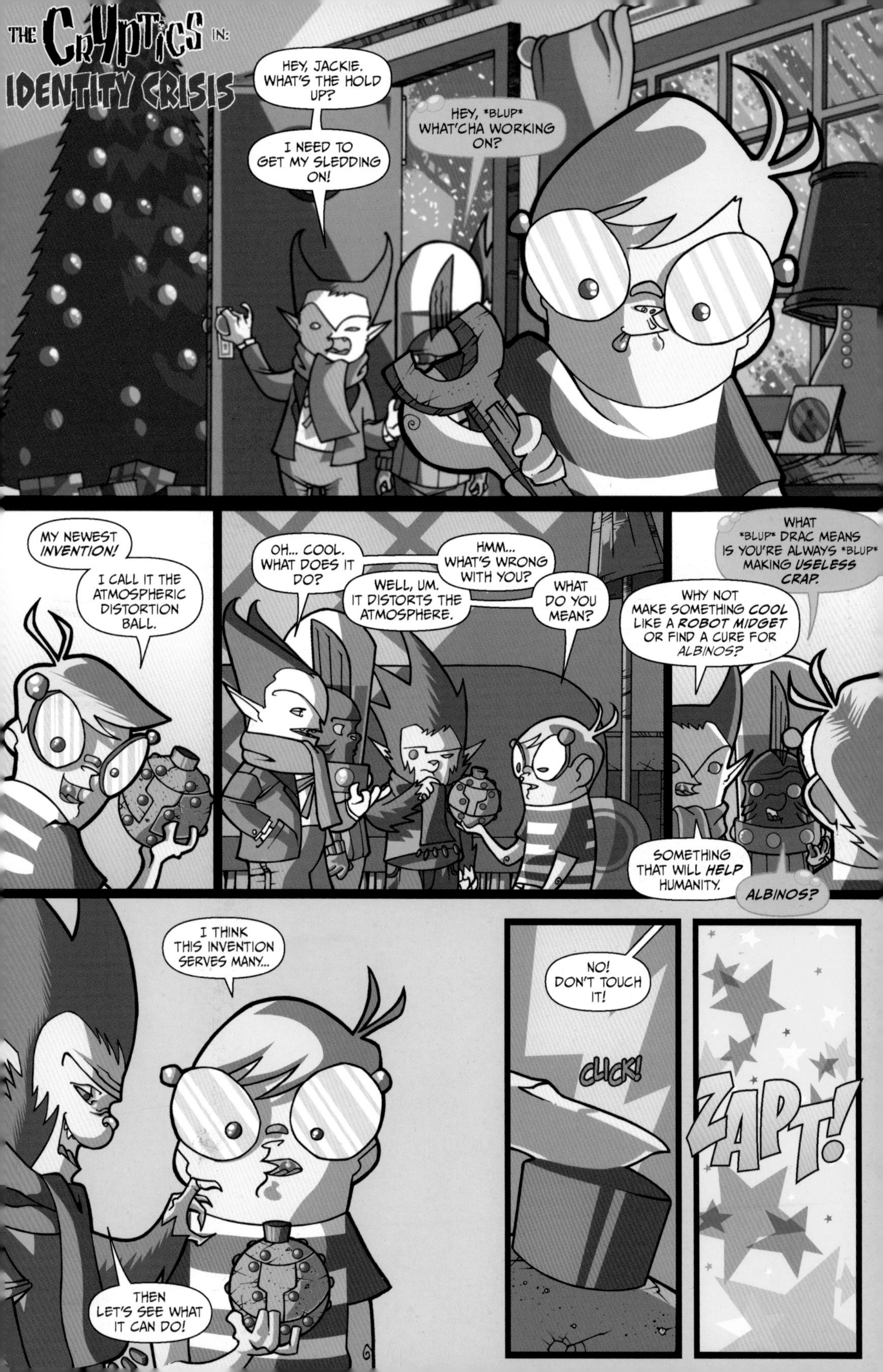
THE CRYPTICS IN:
IDENTITY CRISIS
HEY, JACKIE. WHAT'S THE HOLD UP?
I NEED TO GET MY SLEDDING ON!
HEY, *BLUP* WHAT'CHA WORKING ON?
MY NEWEST INVENTION!
I CALL IT THE ATMOSPHERIC DISTORTION BALL.
OH... COOL. WHAT DOES IT DO?
WELL, UM. IT DISTORTS THE ATMOSPHERE.
HMM... WHAT'S WRONG WITH YOU?
WHAT DO YOU MEAN?
WHAT *BLUP* DRAC MEANS IS YOU'RE ALWAYS *BLUP* MAKING USELESS CRAP.
WHY NOT MAKE SOMETHING COOL LIKE A ROBOT MIDGET OR FIND A CURE FOR ALBINOS?
SOMETHING THAT WILL HELP HUMANITY.
ALBINOS?
I THINK THIS INVENTION SERVES MANY...
THEN LET'S SEE WHAT IT CAN DO!
NO! DON'T TOUCH IT!
CLICK!
ZAPT!

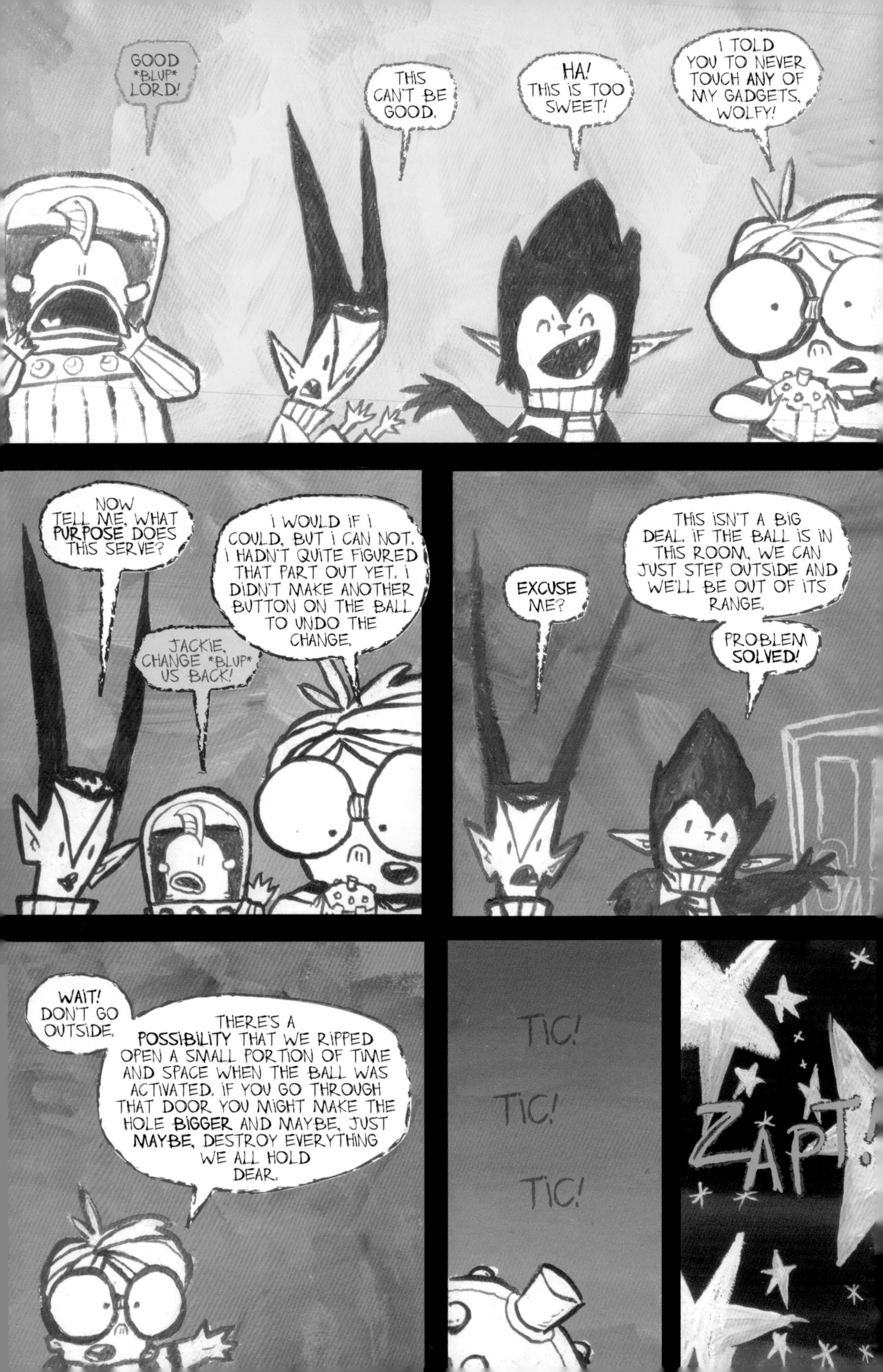
GOOD *BLUP* LORD!
THIS CAN'T BE GOOD.
HA! THIS IS TOO SWEET!
I TOLD YOU TO NEVER TOUCH ANY OF MY GADGETS, WOLFY!
NOW TELL ME, WHAT PURPOSE DOES THIS SERVE?
I WOULD IF I COULD, BUT I CAN NOT. I HADN'T QUITE FIGURED THAT PART OUT YET. I DIDN'T MAKE ANOTHER BUTTON ON THE BALL TO UNDO THE CHANGE.
JACKIE, CHANGE *BLUP* US BACK!
EXCUSE ME?
THIS ISN'T A BIG DEAL. IF THE BALL IS IN THIS ROOM, WE CAN JUST STEP OUTSIDE AND WE'LL BE OUT OF ITS RANGE.
PROBLEM SOLVED!
WAIT! DON'T GO OUTSIDE.
THERE'S A POSSIBILITY THAT WE RIPPED OPEN A SMALL PORTION OF TIME AND SPACE WHEN THE BALL WAS ACTIVATED. IF YOU GO THROUGH THAT DOOR YOU MIGHT MAKE THE HOLE BIGGER AND MAYBE, JUST MAYBE, DESTROY EVERYTHING WE ALL HOLD DEAR.
TIC!
TIC!
TIC!
ZAPT!

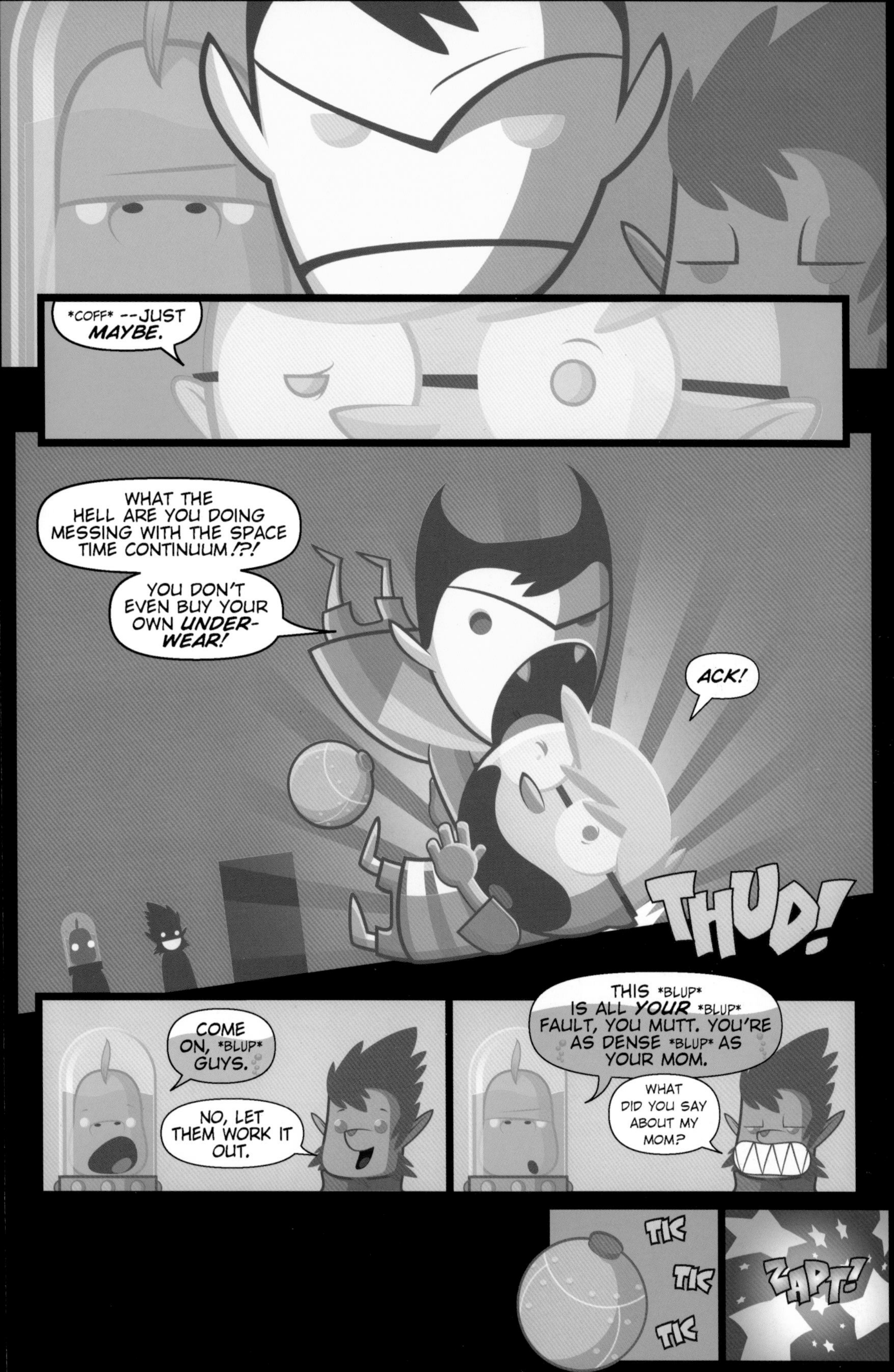
COFF --JUST MAYBE.
WHAT THE HELL ARE YOU DOING MESSING WITH THE SPACE TIME CONTINUUM!?!
YOU DON'T EVEN BUY YOUR OWN UNDER-WEAR!
ACK!
THUD!
COME ON, *BLUP* GUYS.
NO, LET THEM WORK IT OUT.
THIS *BLUP* IS ALL YOUR *BLUP* FAULT, YOU MUTT. YOU'RE AS DENSE *BLUP* AS YOUR MOM.
WHAT DID YOU SAY ABOUT MY MOM?
TIC
TIC
TIC
ZAPT!

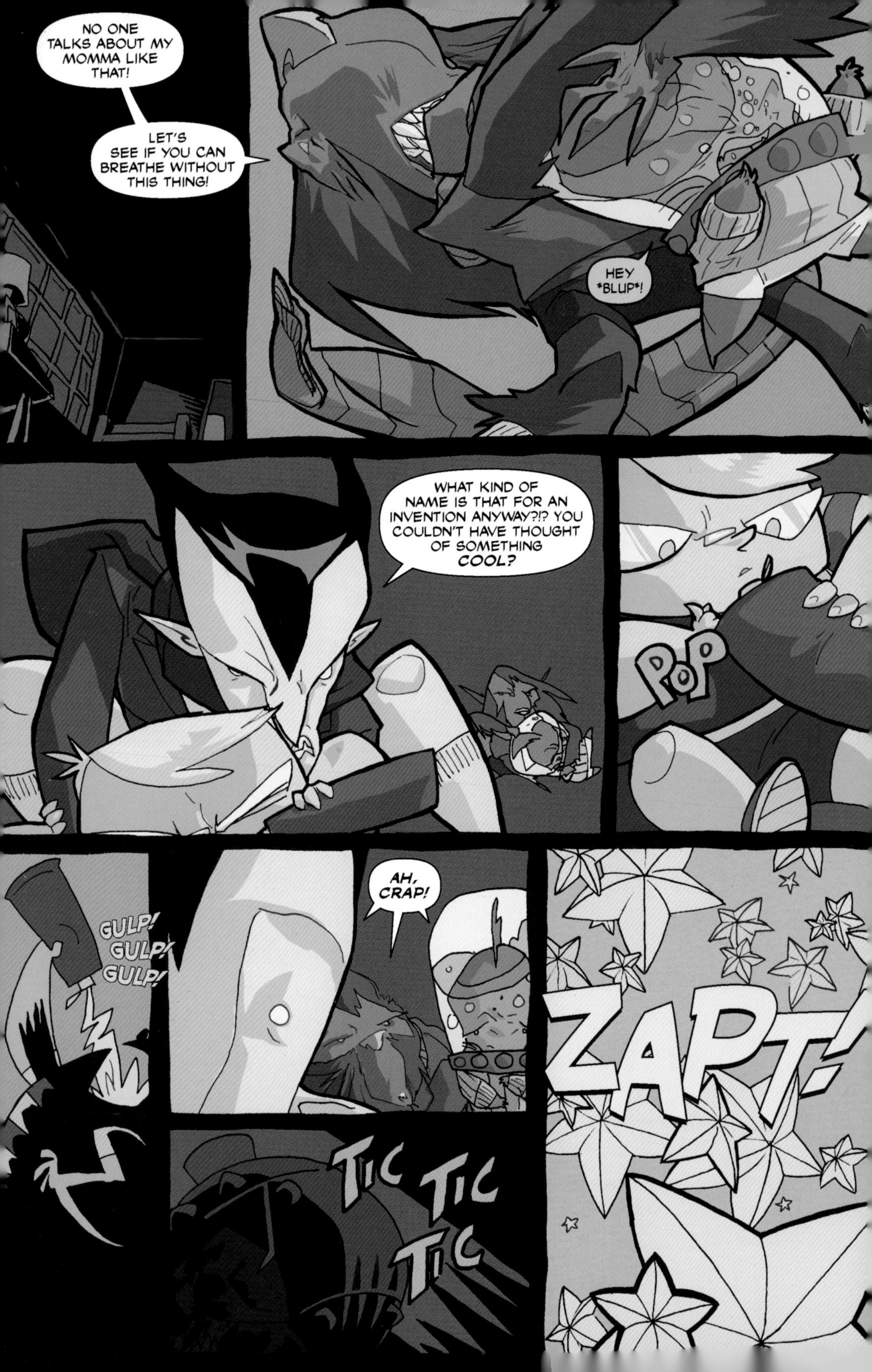
NO ONE TALKS ABOUT MY MOMMA LIKE THAT!
LET'S SEE IF YOU CAN BREATHE WITHOUT THIS THING!
HEY *BLUP*!
WHAT KIND OF NAME IS THAT FOR AN INVENTION ANYWAY?!? YOU COULDN'T HAVE THOUGHT OF SOMETHING COOL?
POP
GULP! GULP! GULP!
AH, CRAP!
ZAPT!
TIC TIC TIC

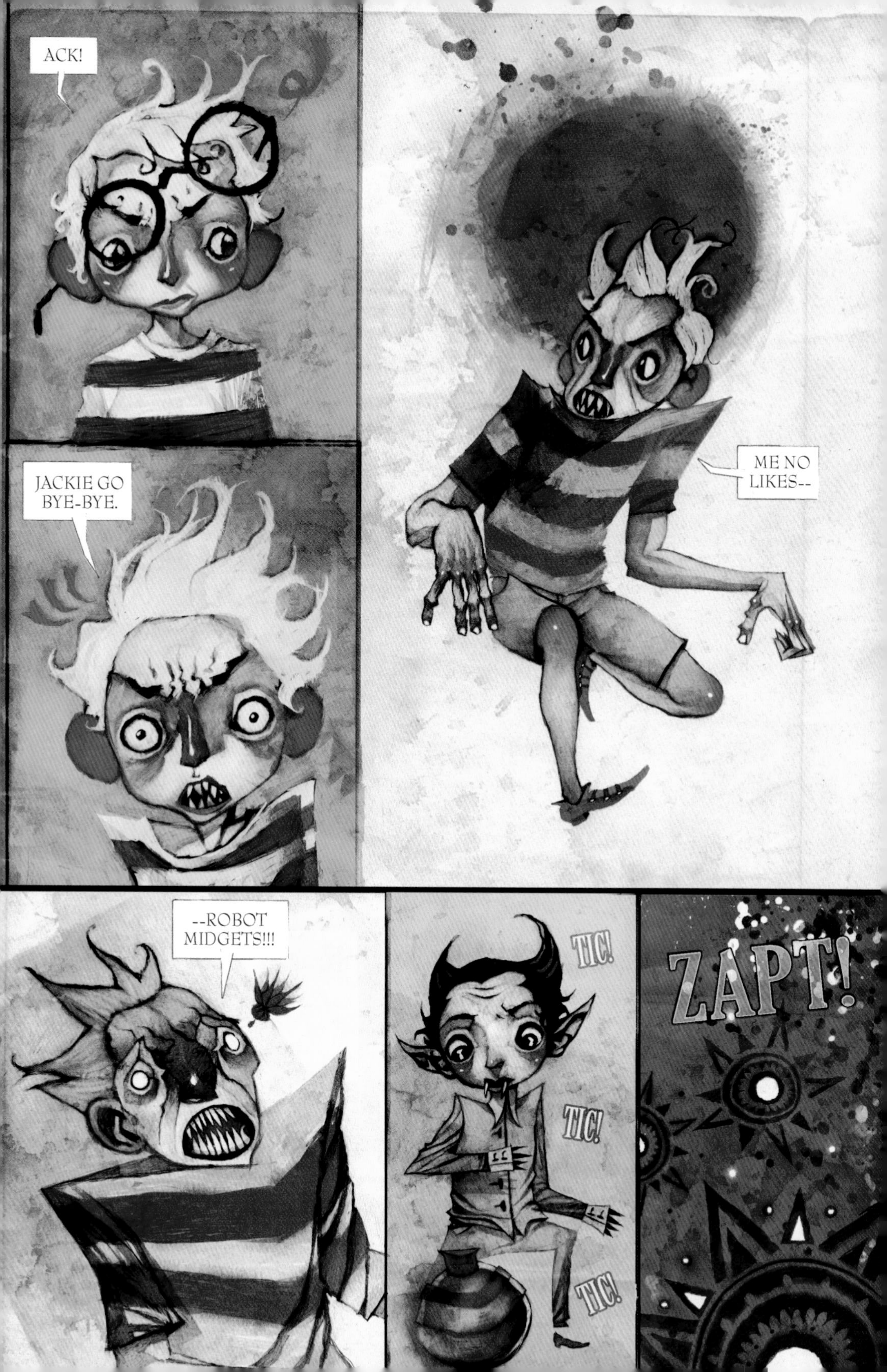
ACK!
JACKIE GO BYE-BYE.
ME NO LIKES--
--ROBOT MIDGETS!!!
TIC!
TIC!
TIC!
ZAPT!

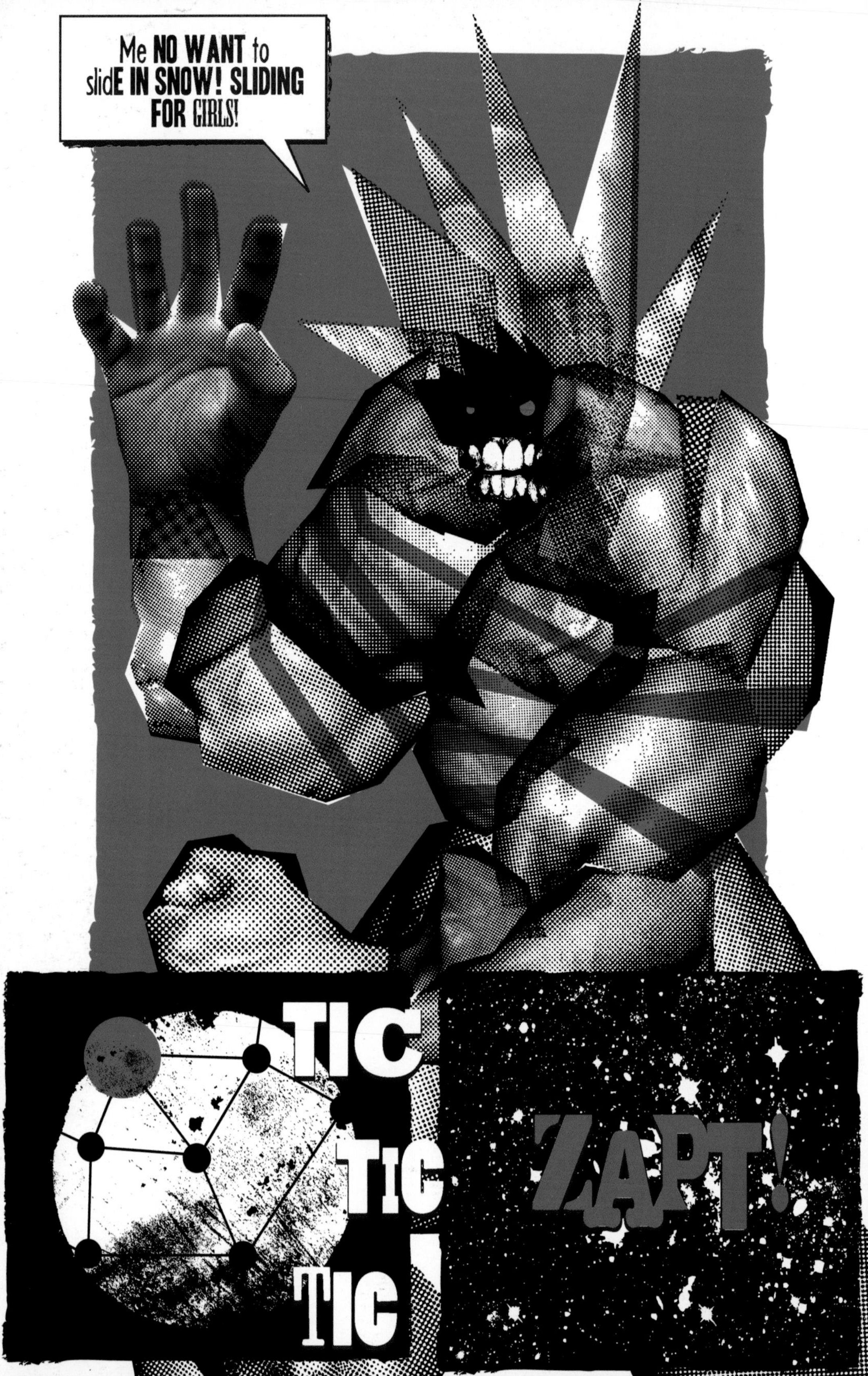
Me NO WANT to slidE IN SNOW! SLIDING FOR GIRLS!
TIC
TIC
TIC
ZAPT!

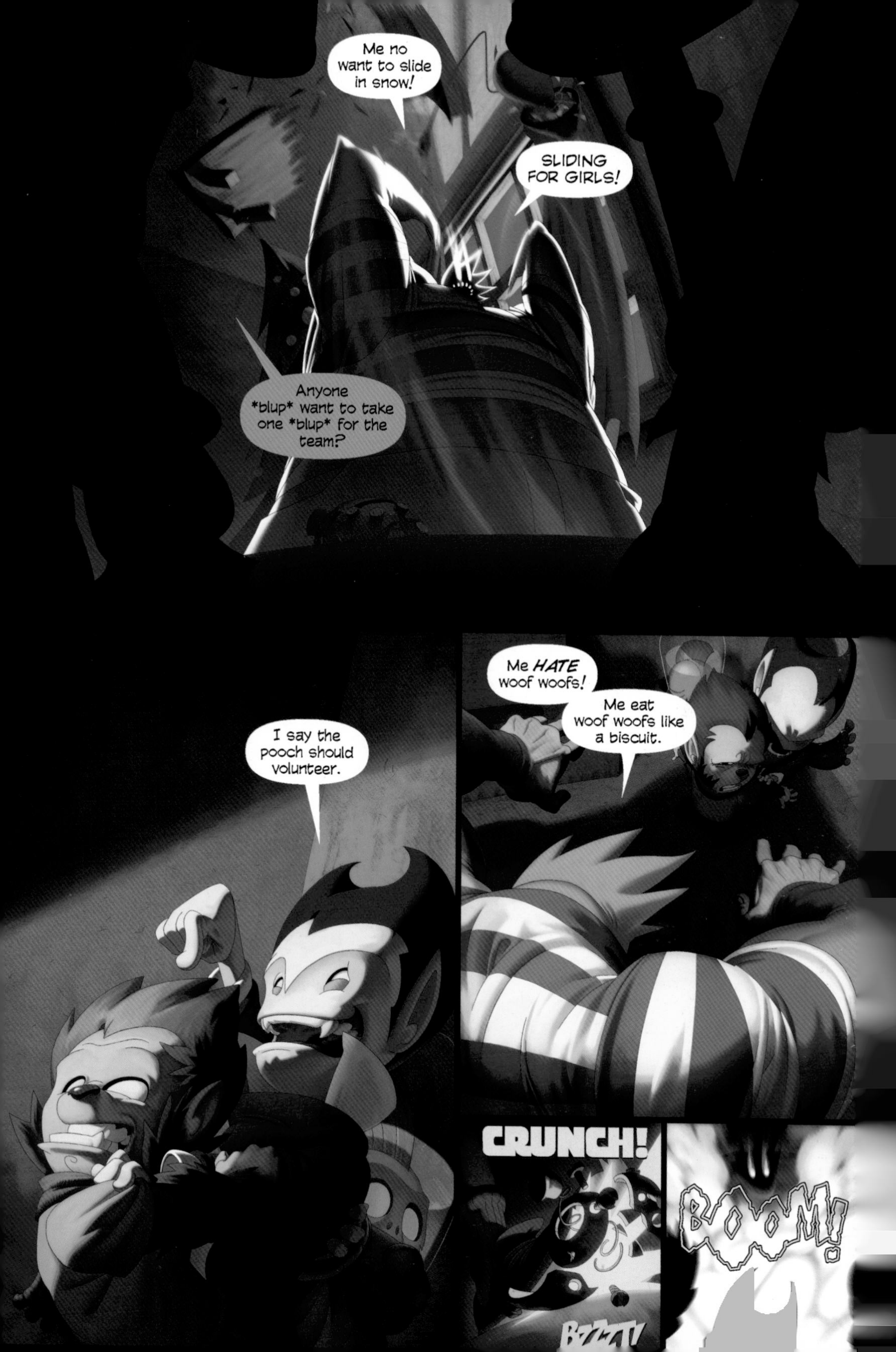
Me no want to slide in snow!
SLIDING FOR GIRLS!
Anyone *blup* want to take one *blup* for the team?
I say the pooch should volunteer.
Me HATE woof woofs!
Me eat woof woofs like a biscuit.
CRUNCH!
BZZZT!
BOOM!

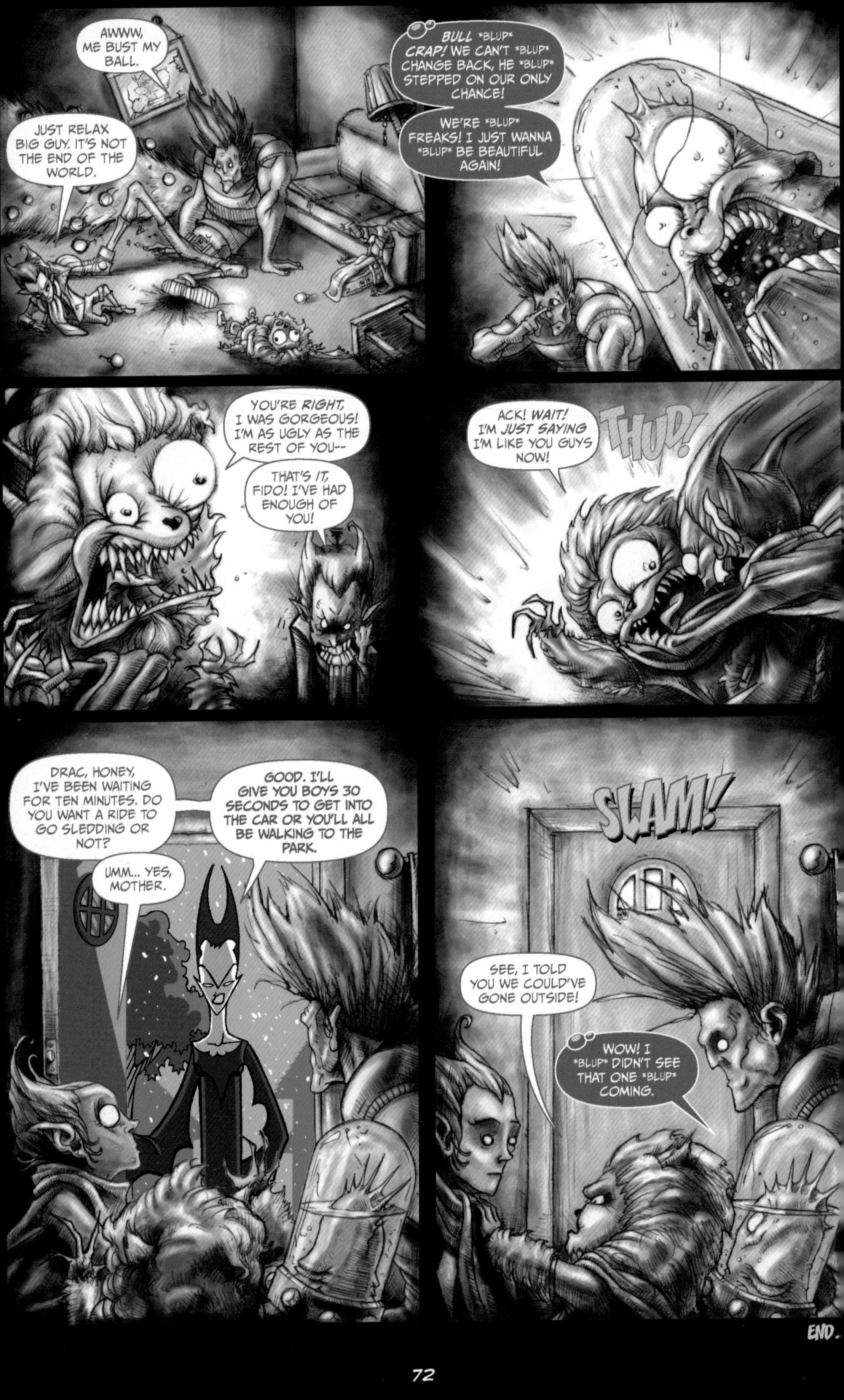
AWWW, ME BUST MY BALL.
JUST RELAX BIG GUY. IT'S NOT THE END OF THE WORLD.
BULL *BLUP* CRAP! WE CAN'T *BLUP* CHANGE BACK, HE *BLUP* STEPPED ON OUR ONLY CHANCE!
WE'RE *BLUP* FREAKS! I JUST WANNA *BLUP* BE BEAUTIFUL AGAIN!
YOU'RE RIGHT, I WAS GORGEOUS! I'M AS UGLY AS THE REST OF YOU--
THAT'S IT, FIDO! I'VE HAD ENOUGH OF YOU!
ACK! WAIT! I'M JUST SAYING I'M LIKE YOU GUYS NOW!
THUD!
DRAC, HONEY, I'VE BEEN WAITING FOR TEN MINUTES. DO YOU WANT A RIDE TO GO SLEDDING OR NOT?
UMM... YES, MOTHER.
GOOD. I'LL GIVE YOU BOYS 30 SECONDS TO GET INTO THE CAR OR YOU'LL ALL BE WALKING TO THE PARK.
SLAM!
SEE, I TOLD YOU WE COULD'VE GONE OUTSIDE!
WOW! I *BLUP* DIDN'T SEE THAT ONE *BLUP* COMING.
END.

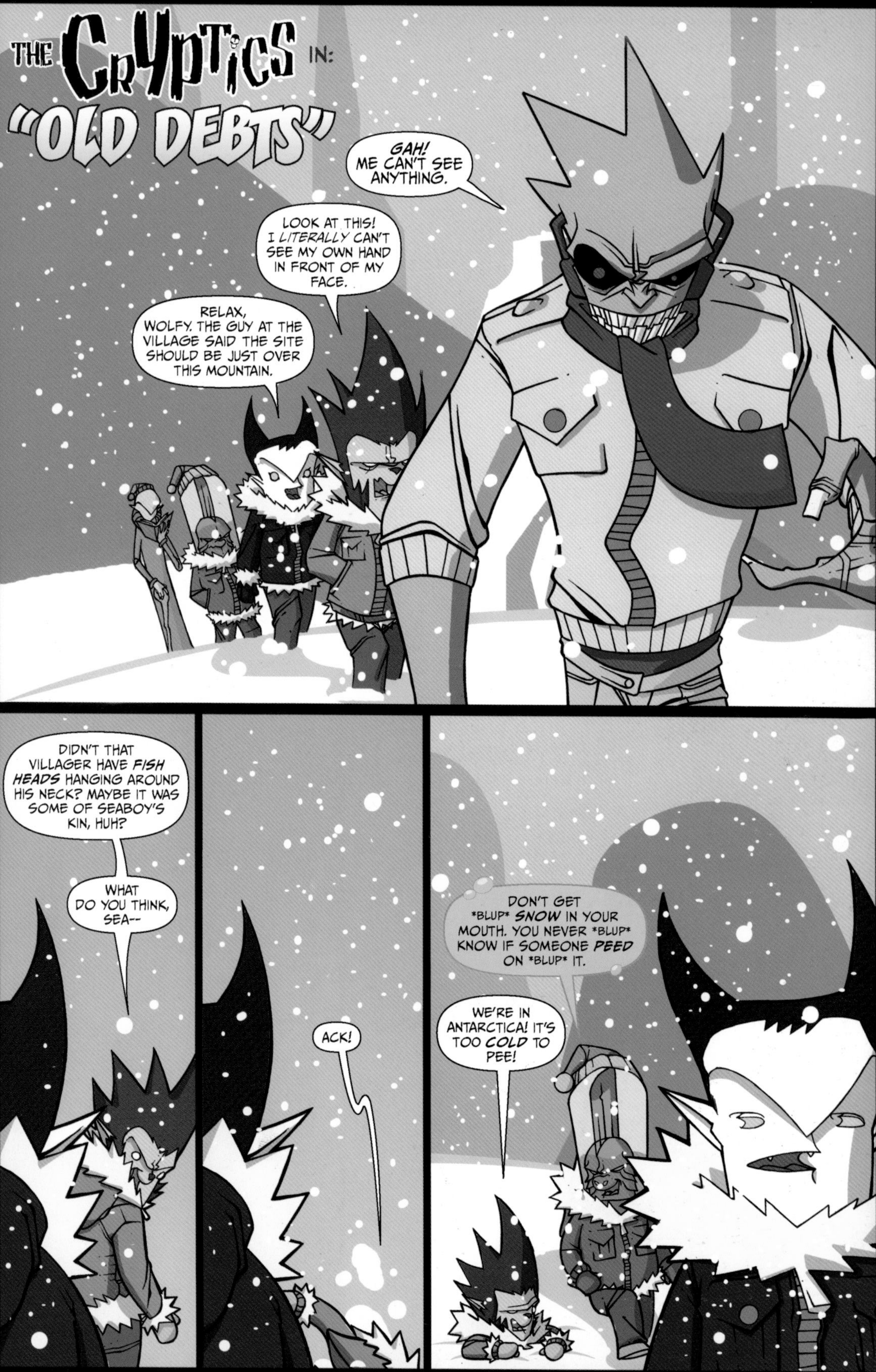
THE CRYPTICS IN:
"OLD DEBTS"
GAH! ME CAN'T SEE ANYTHING.
LOOK AT THIS! I LITERALLY CAN'T SEE MY OWN HAND IN FRONT OF MY FACE.
RELAX, WOLFY. THE GUY AT THE VILLAGE SAID THE SITE SHOULD BE JUST OVER THIS MOUNTAIN.
DIDN'T THAT VILLAGER HAVE FISH HEADS HANGING AROUND HIS NECK? MAYBE IT WAS SOME OF SEABOY'S KIN, HUH?
WHAT DO YOU THINK, SEA--
ACK!
DON'T GET *BLUP* SNOW IN YOUR MOUTH. YOU NEVER *BLUP* KNOW IF SOMEONE PEED ON *BLUP* IT.
WE'RE IN ANTARCTICA! IT'S TOO COLD TO PEE!

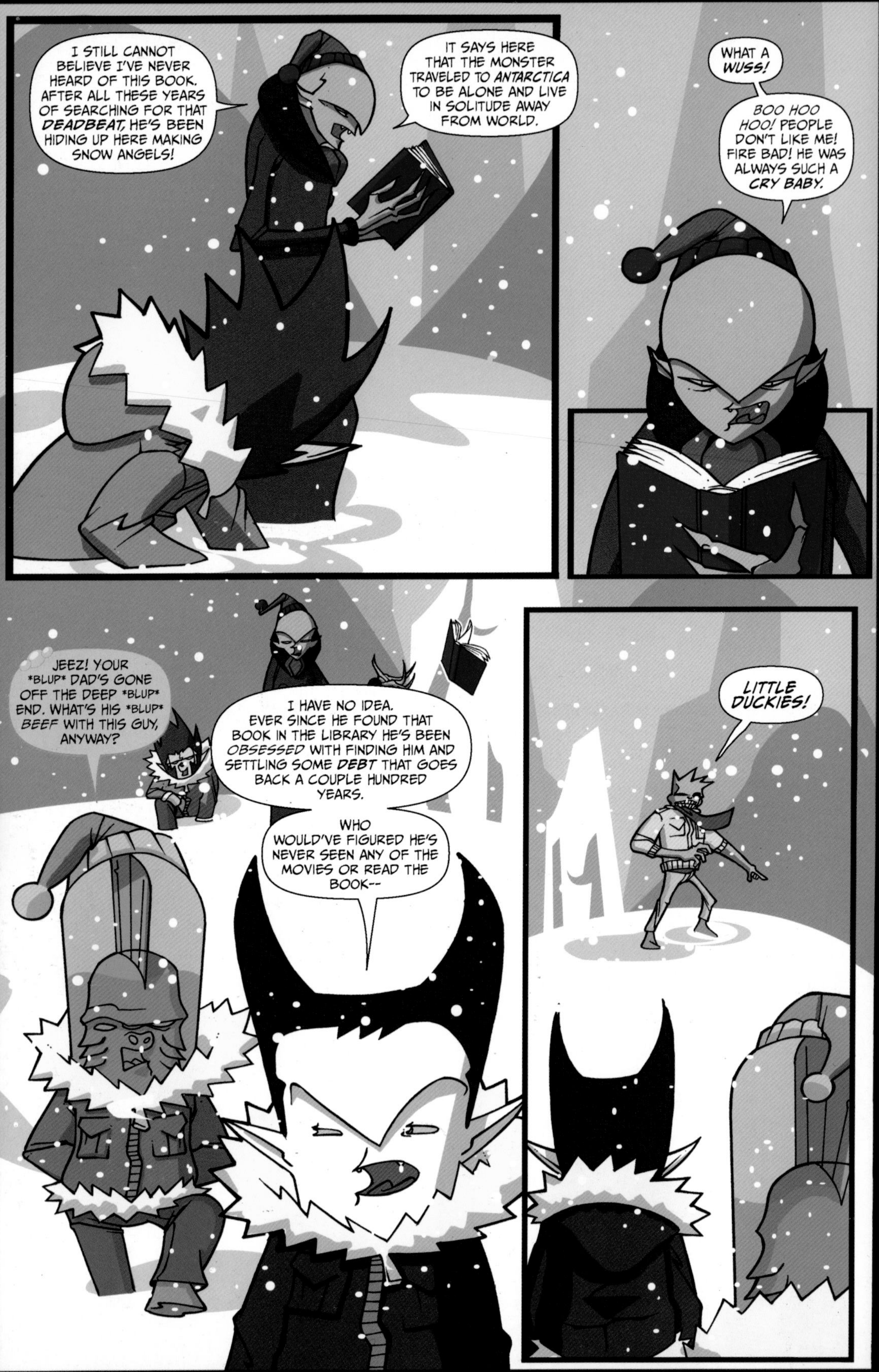
I STILL CANNOT BELIEVE I'VE NEVER HEARD OF THIS BOOK. AFTER ALL THESE YEARS OF SEARCHING FOR THAT *DEADBEAT,* HE'S BEEN HIDING UP HERE MAKING SNOW ANGELS!
IT SAYS HERE THAT THE MONSTER TRAVELED TO *ANTARCTICA* TO BE ALONE AND LIVE IN SOLITUDE AWAY FROM WORLD.
WHAT A *WUSS!*
BOO HOO HOO! PEOPLE DON'T LIKE ME! FIRE BAD! HE WAS ALWAYS SUCH A *CRY BABY.*
JEEZ! YOUR *BLUP* DAD'S GONE OFF THE DEEP *BLUP* END. WHAT'S HIS *BLUP* *BEEF* WITH THIS GUY, ANYWAY?
I HAVE NO IDEA. EVER SINCE HE FOUND THAT BOOK IN THE LIBRARY HE'S BEEN *OBSESSED* WITH FINDING HIM AND SETTLING SOME *DEBT* THAT GOES BACK A COUPLE HUNDRED YEARS.
WHO WOULD'VE FIGURED HE'S NEVER SEEN ANY OF THE MOVIES OR READ THE BOOK--
LITTLE DUCKIES!

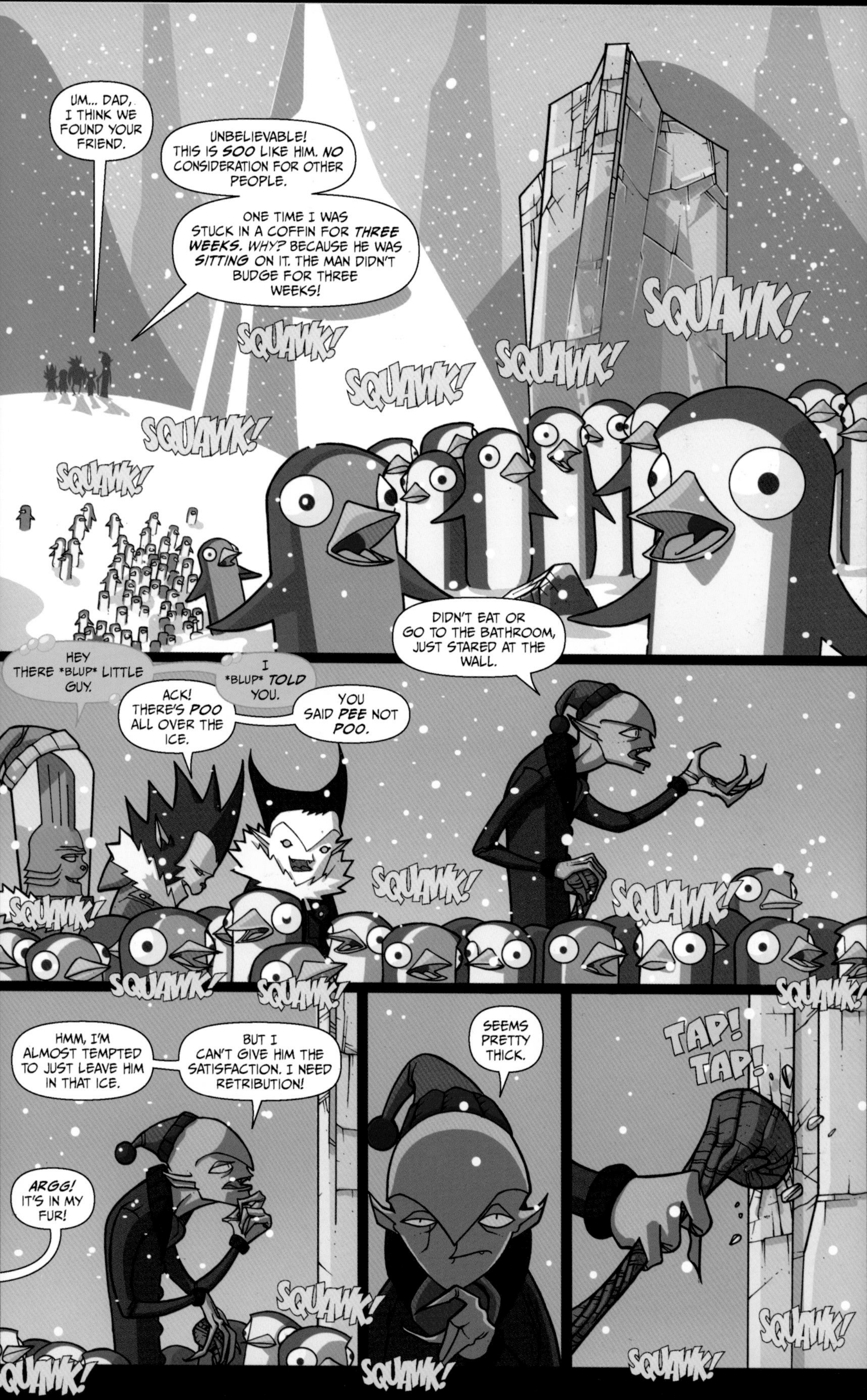

UM... DAD, I THINK WE FOUND YOUR FRIEND.
UNBELIEVABLE! THIS IS SOO LIKE HIM. NO CONSIDERATION FOR OTHER PEOPLE.
ONE TIME I WAS STUCK IN A COFFIN FOR THREE WEEKS. WHY? BECAUSE HE WAS SITTING ON IT. THE MAN DIDN'T BUDGE FOR THREE WEEKS!
SQUAWK!
SQUAWK!
SQUAWK!
SQUAWK!
SQUAWK!
SQUAWK!
DIDN'T EAT OR GO TO THE BATHROOM, JUST STARED AT THE WALL.
HEY THERE *BLUP* LITTLE GUY.
I *BLUP* TOLD YOU.
ACK! THERE'S POO ALL OVER THE ICE.
YOU SAID PEE NOT POO.
SQUAWK!
SQUAWK!
SQUAWK!
SQUAWK!
SQUAWK!
SQUAWK!
HMM, I'M ALMOST TEMPTED TO JUST LEAVE HIM IN THAT ICE.
BUT I CAN'T GIVE HIM THE SATISFACTION. I NEED RETRIBUTION!
ARGG! IT'S IN MY FUR!
SQUAWK!
SQUAWK!
SEEMS PRETTY THICK.
SQUAWK!
TAP! TAP!
SQUAWK!
SQUAWK!

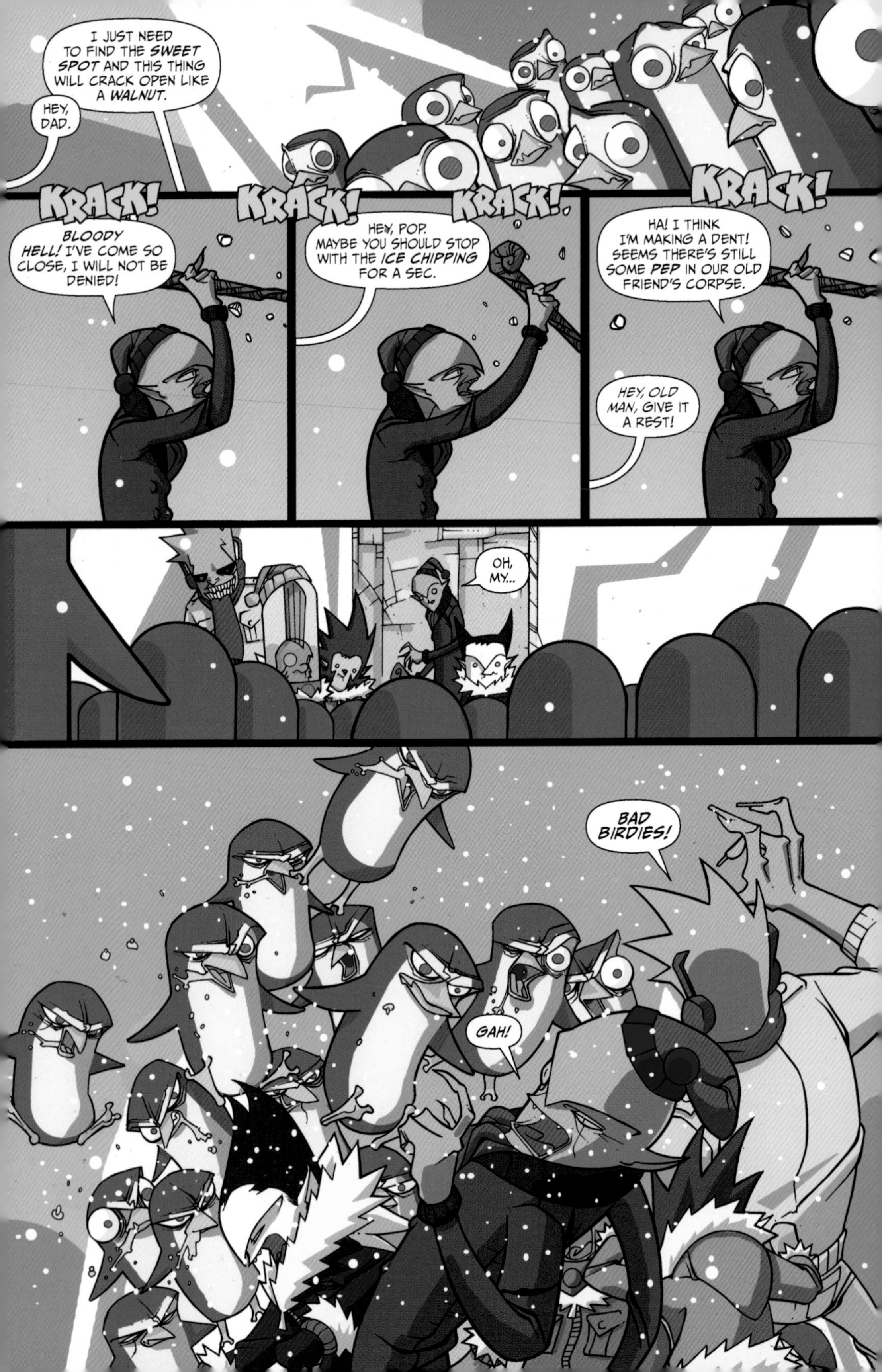
I JUST NEED TO FIND THE SWEET SPOT AND THIS THING WILL CRACK OPEN LIKE A WALNUT.
HEY, DAD.
KRACK!
BLOODY HELL! I'VE COME SO CLOSE, I WILL NOT BE DENIED!
KRACK!
HEY, POP. MAYBE YOU SHOULD STOP WITH THE ICE CHIPPING FOR A SEC.
KRACK!
KRACK!
HA! I THINK I'M MAKING A DENT! SEEMS THERE'S STILL SOME PEP IN OUR OLD FRIEND'S CORPSE.
HEY, OLD MAN, GIVE IT A REST!
OH, MY...
BAD BIRDIES!
GAH!

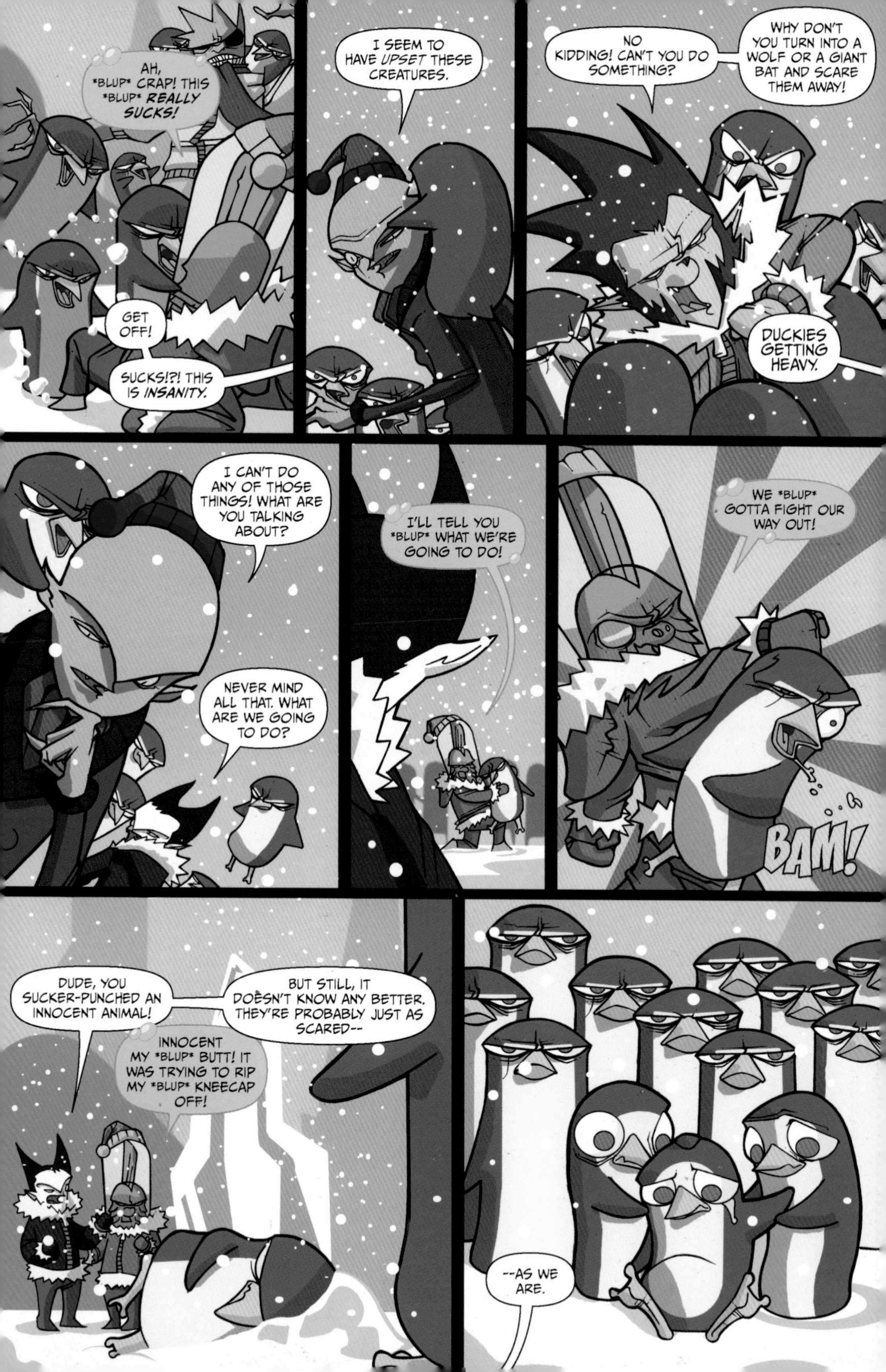
AH, *BLUP* CRAP! THIS *BLUP* REALLY SUCKS!
GET OFF!
SUCKS!?! THIS IS INSANITY.
I SEEM TO HAVE UPSET THESE CREATURES.
NO KIDDING! CAN'T YOU DO SOMETHING?
WHY DON'T YOU TURN INTO A WOLF OR A GIANT BAT AND SCARE THEM AWAY!
DUCKIES GETTING HEAVY.
I CAN'T DO ANY OF THOSE THINGS! WHAT ARE YOU TALKING ABOUT?
NEVER MIND ALL THAT. WHAT ARE WE GOING TO DO?
I'LL TELL YOU *BLUP* WHAT WE'RE GOING TO DO!
WE *BLUP* GOTTA FIGHT OUR WAY OUT!
BAM!
DUDE, YOU SUCKER-PUNCHED AN INNOCENT ANIMAL!
INNOCENT MY *BLUP* BUTT! IT WAS TRYING TO RIP MY *BLUP* KNEECAP OFF!
BUT STILL, IT DOESN'T KNOW ANY BETTER. THEY'RE PROBABLY JUST AS SCARED--
--AS WE ARE.

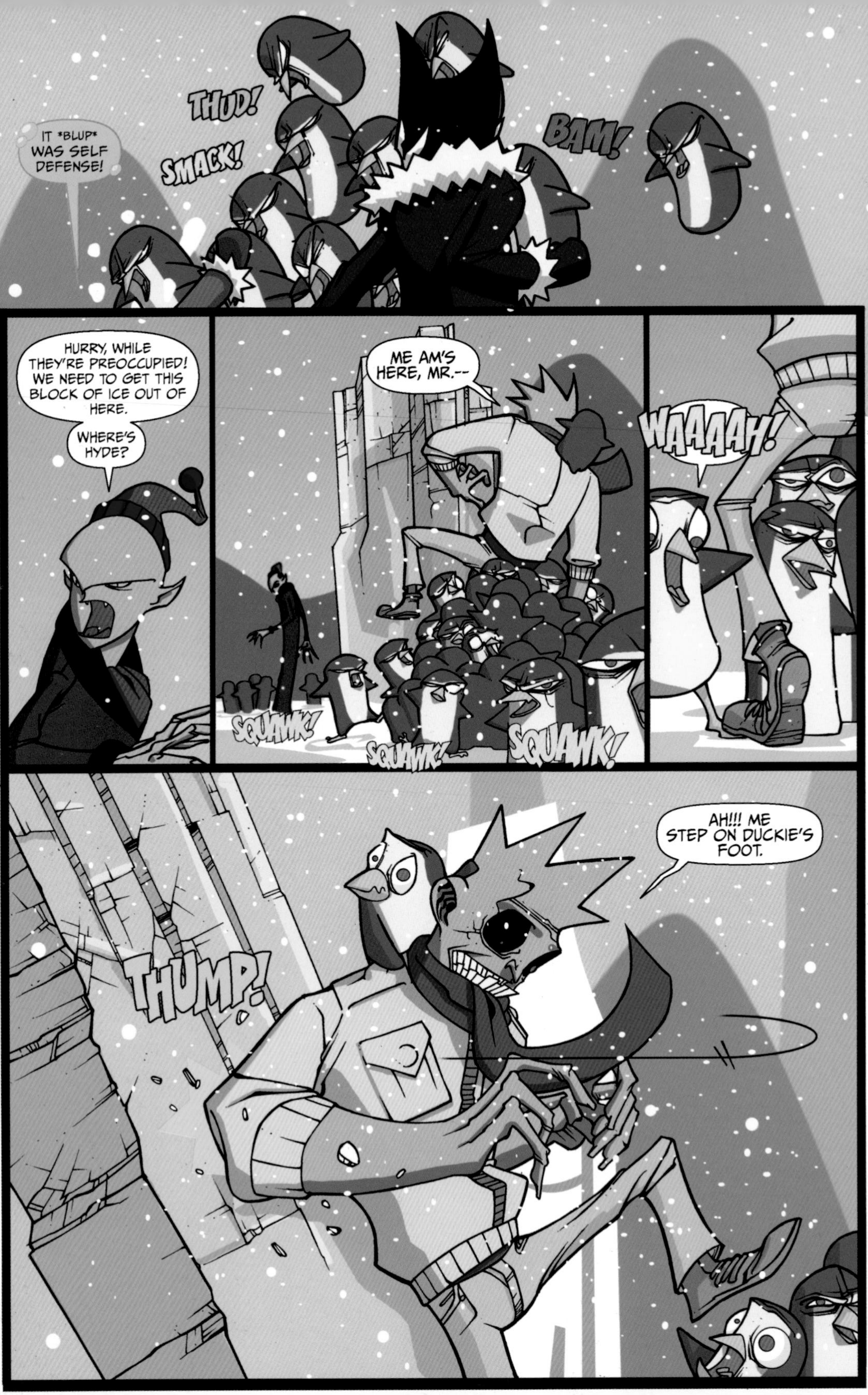
IT *BLUP* WAS SELF DEFENSE!
THUD!
SMACK!
BAM!
HURRY, WHILE THEY'RE PREOCCUPIED! WE NEED TO GET THIS BLOCK OF ICE OUT OF HERE.
WHERE'S HYDE?
ME AM'S HERE, MR.--
SQUAWK!
SQUAWK!
SQUAWK!
WAAAAH!
AH!!! ME STEP ON DUCKIE'S FOOT.
THUMP!

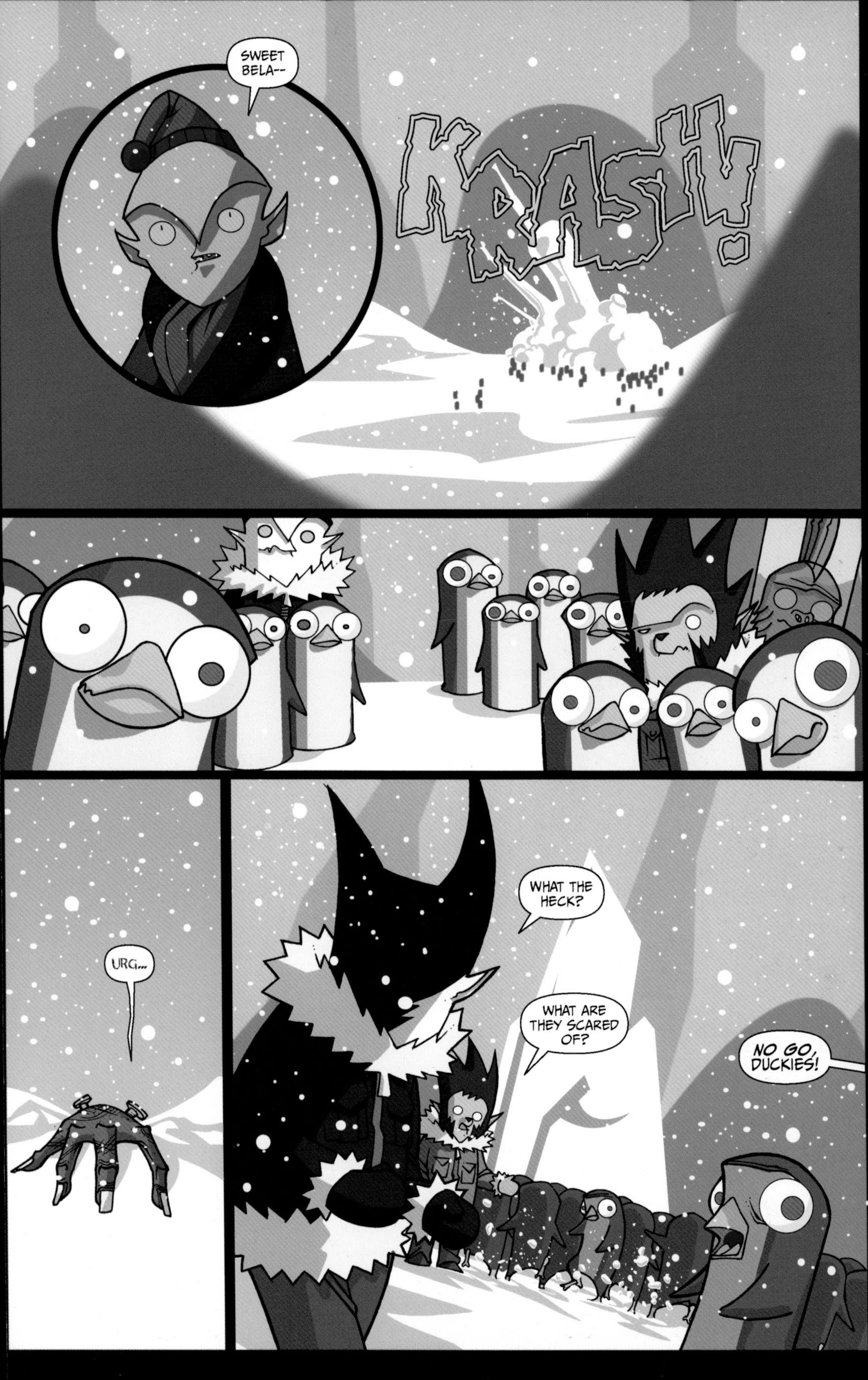
SWEET BELA--
KRASH!
URG...
WHAT THE HECK?
WHAT ARE THEY SCARED OF?
NO GO, DUCKIES!

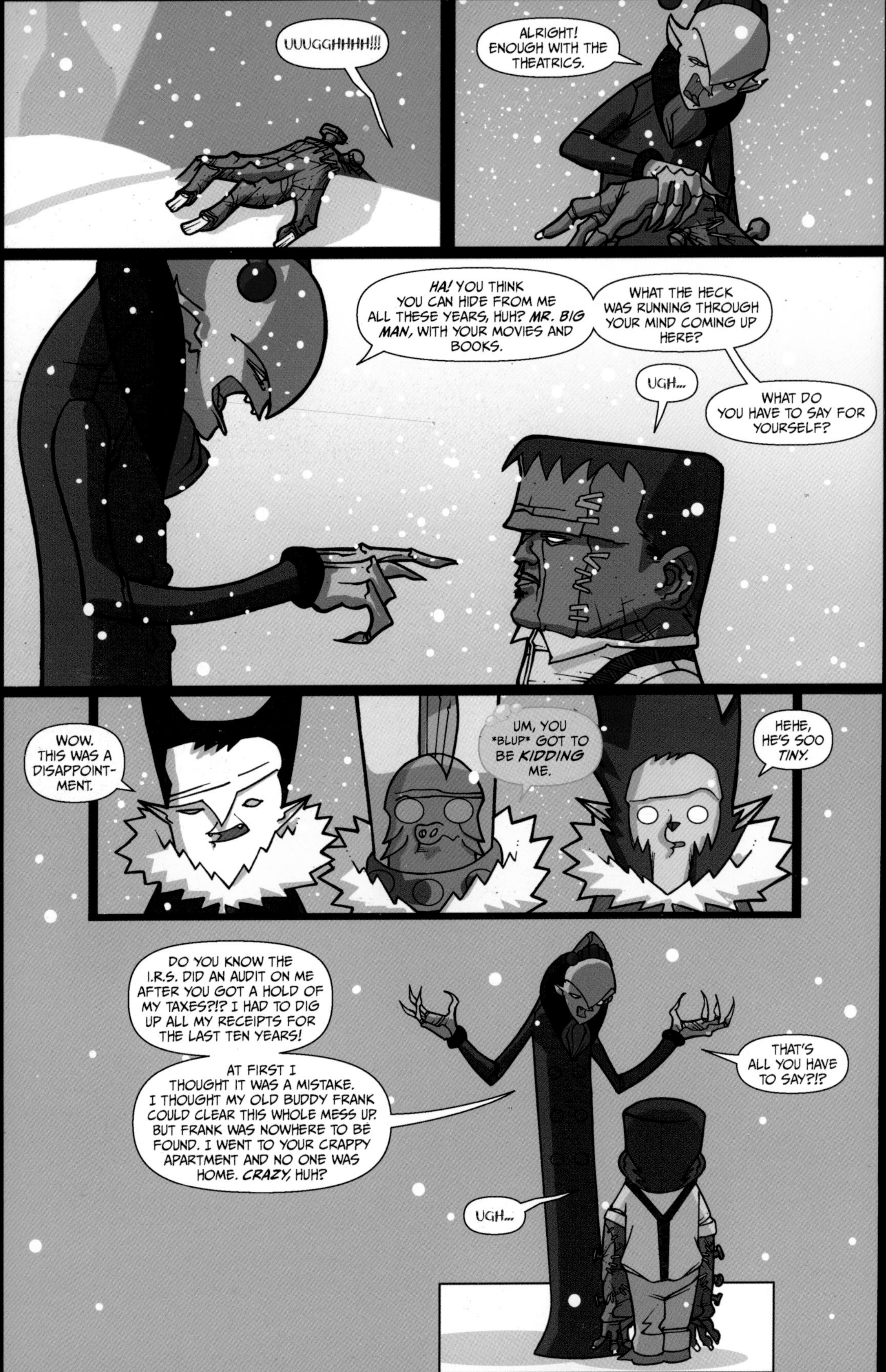
UUUGGHHHH!!!
ALRIGHT! ENOUGH WITH THE THEATRICS.
HA! YOU THINK YOU CAN HIDE FROM ME ALL THESE YEARS, HUH? MR. BIG MAN, WITH YOUR MOVIES AND BOOKS.
WHAT THE HECK WAS RUNNING THROUGH YOUR MIND COMING UP HERE?
UGH...
WHAT DO YOU HAVE TO SAY FOR YOURSELF?
WOW. THIS WAS A DISAPPOINT-MENT.
UM, YOU *BLUP* GOT TO BE KIDDING ME.
HEHE, HE'S SOO TINY.
DO YOU KNOW THE I.R.S. DID AN AUDIT ON ME AFTER YOU GOT A HOLD OF MY TAXES?!? I HAD TO DIG UP ALL MY RECEIPTS FOR THE LAST TEN YEARS!
AT FIRST I THOUGHT IT WAS A MISTAKE. I THOUGHT MY OLD BUDDY FRANK COULD CLEAR THIS WHOLE MESS UP. BUT FRANK WAS NOWHERE TO BE FOUND. I WENT TO YOUR CRAPPY APARTMENT AND NO ONE WAS HOME. CRAZY, HUH?
THAT'S ALL YOU HAVE TO SAY?!?
UGH...

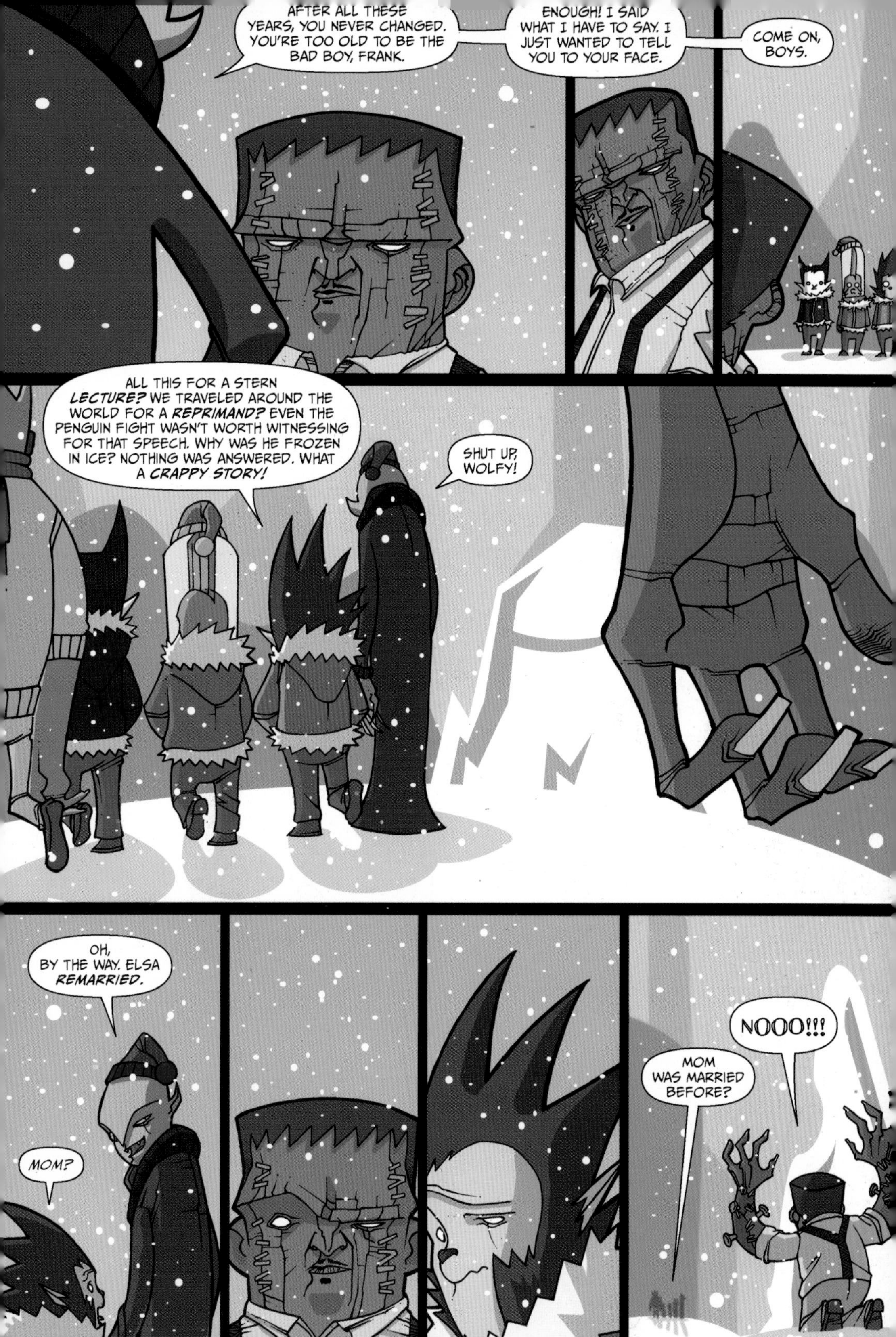

AFTER ALL THESE YEARS, YOU NEVER CHANGED. YOU'RE TOO OLD TO BE THE BAD BOY, FRANK.
ENOUGH! I SAID WHAT I HAVE TO SAY. I JUST WANTED TO TELL YOU TO YOUR FACE.
COME ON, BOYS.
ALL THIS FOR A STERN LECTURE? WE TRAVELED AROUND THE WORLD FOR A REPRIMAND? EVEN THE PENGUIN FIGHT WASN'T WORTH WITNESSING FOR THAT SPEECH. WHY WAS HE FROZEN IN ICE? NOTHING WAS ANSWERED. WHAT A CRAPPY STORY!
SHUT UP, WOLFY!
OH, BY THE WAY. ELSA REMARRIED.
MOM?
MOM WAS MARRIED BEFORE?
NOOO!!!

IMAGE GALLERY

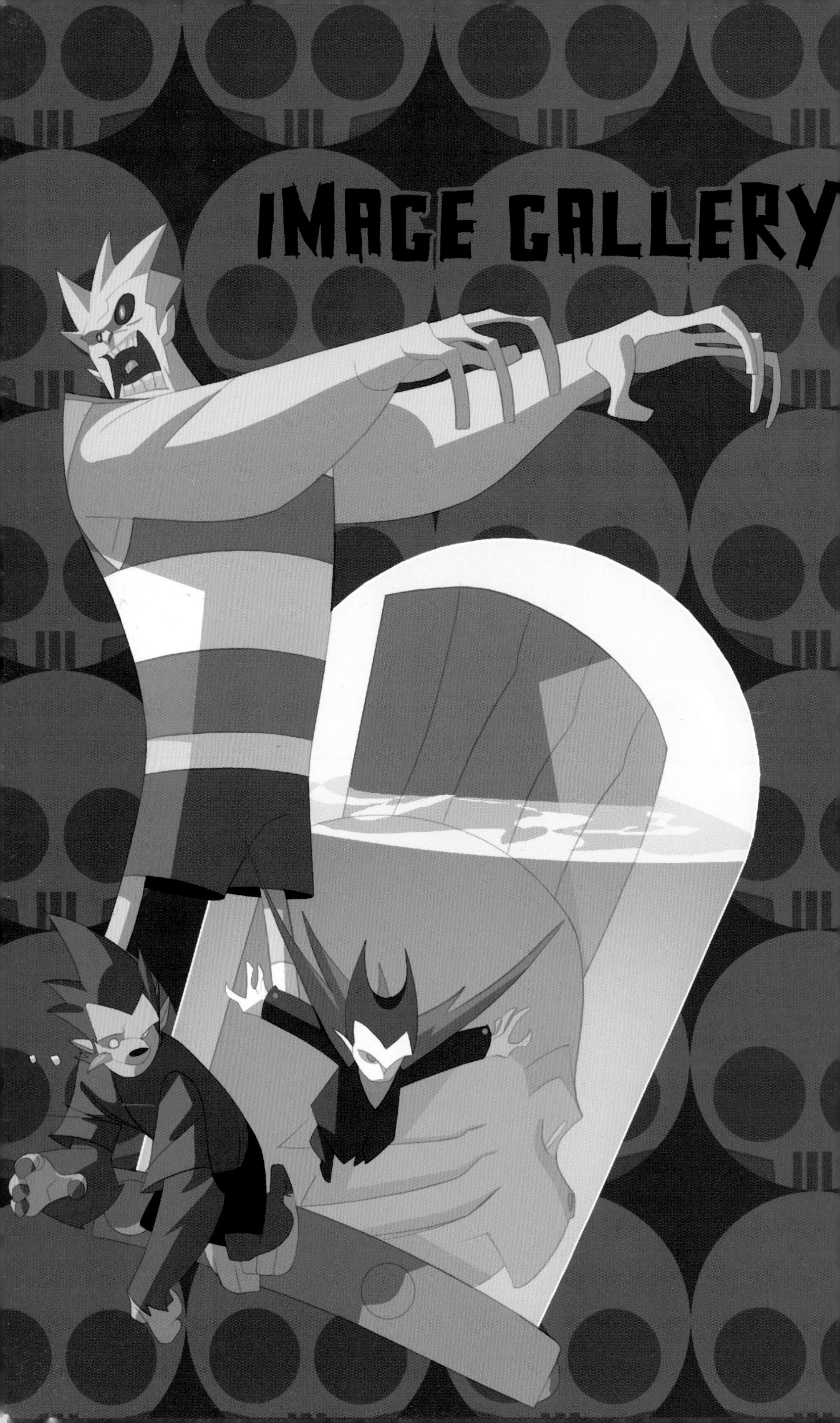

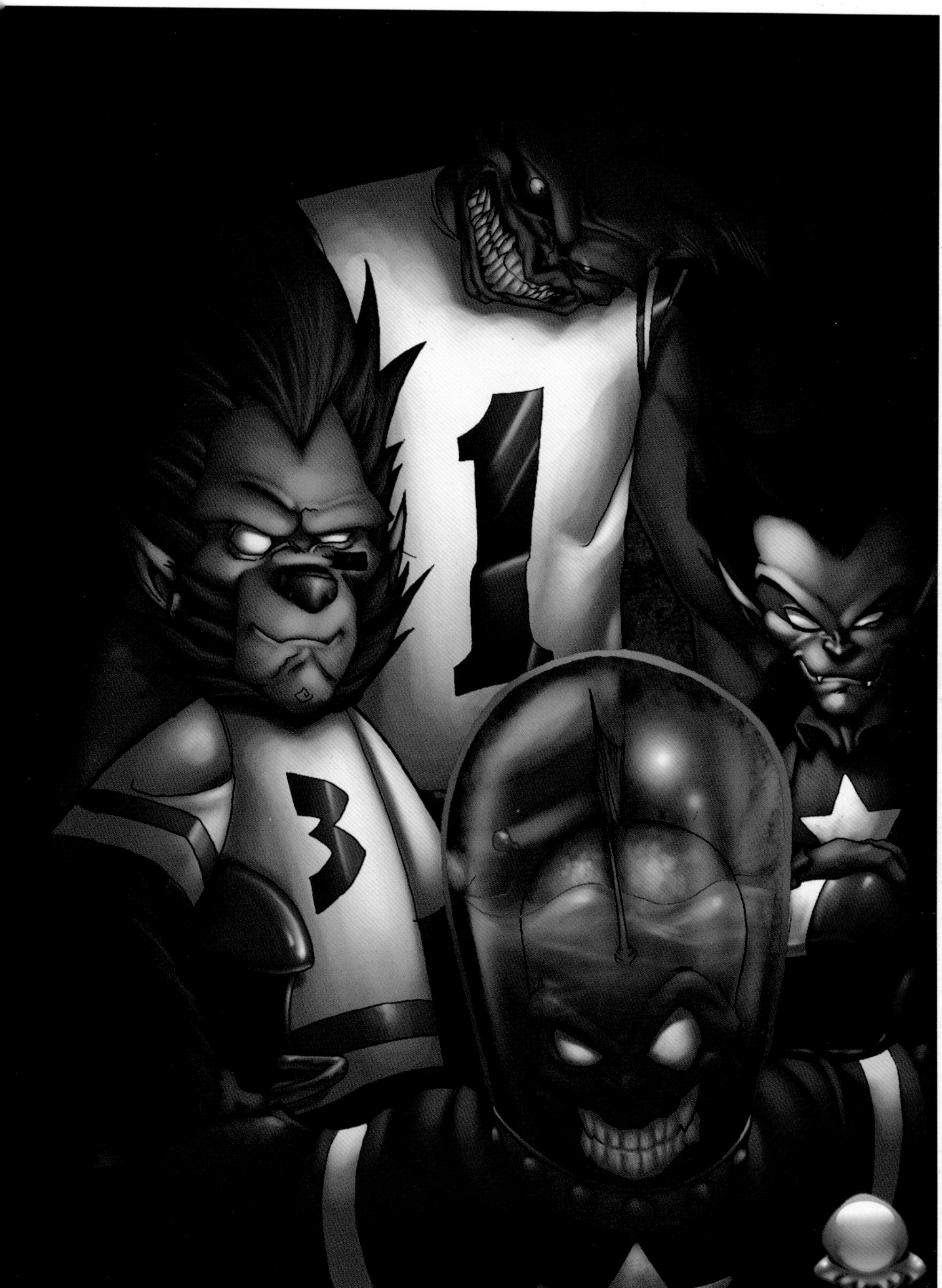

<< art and colors by Sean Galloway

art and colors by Nthinila Phumaphi ^

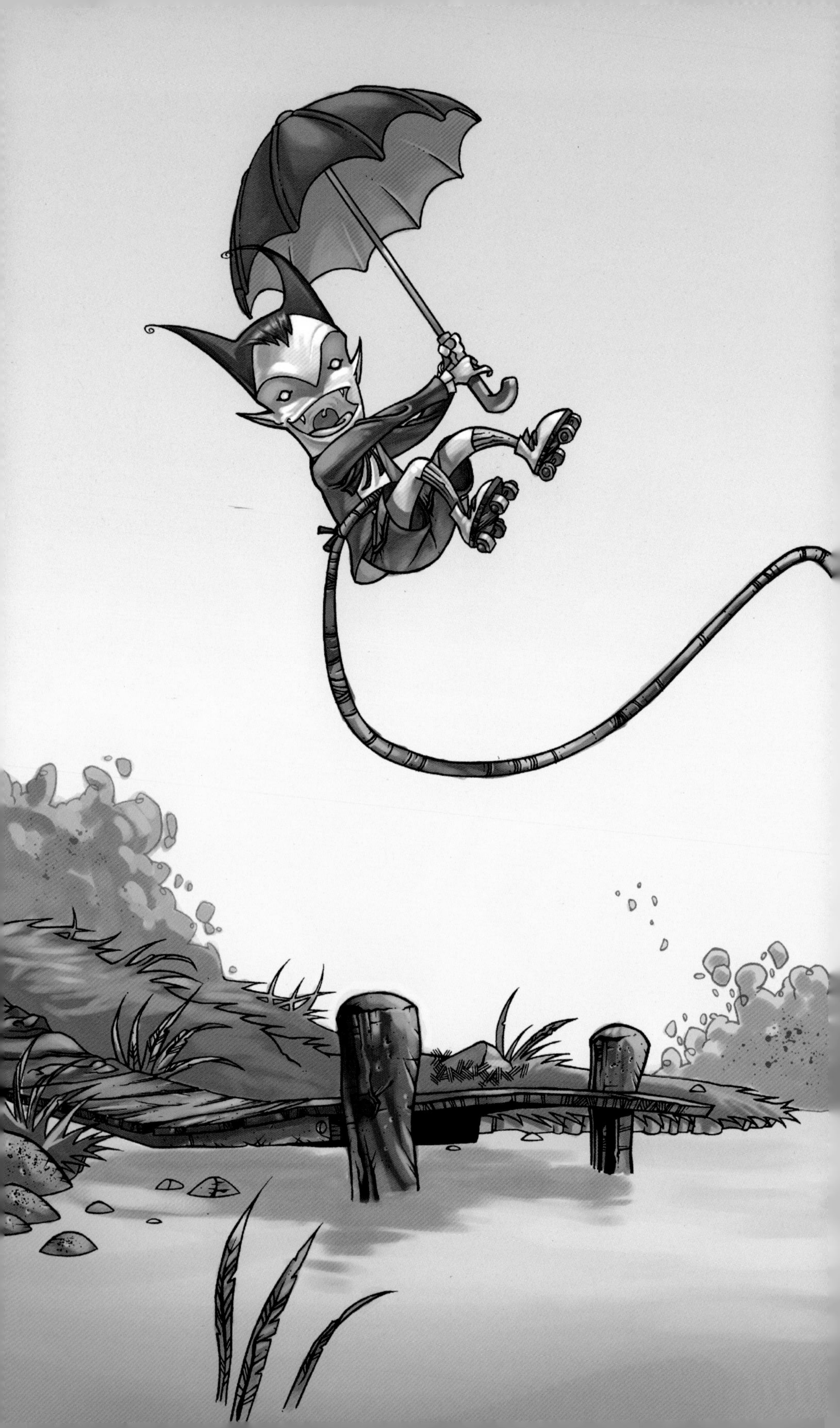

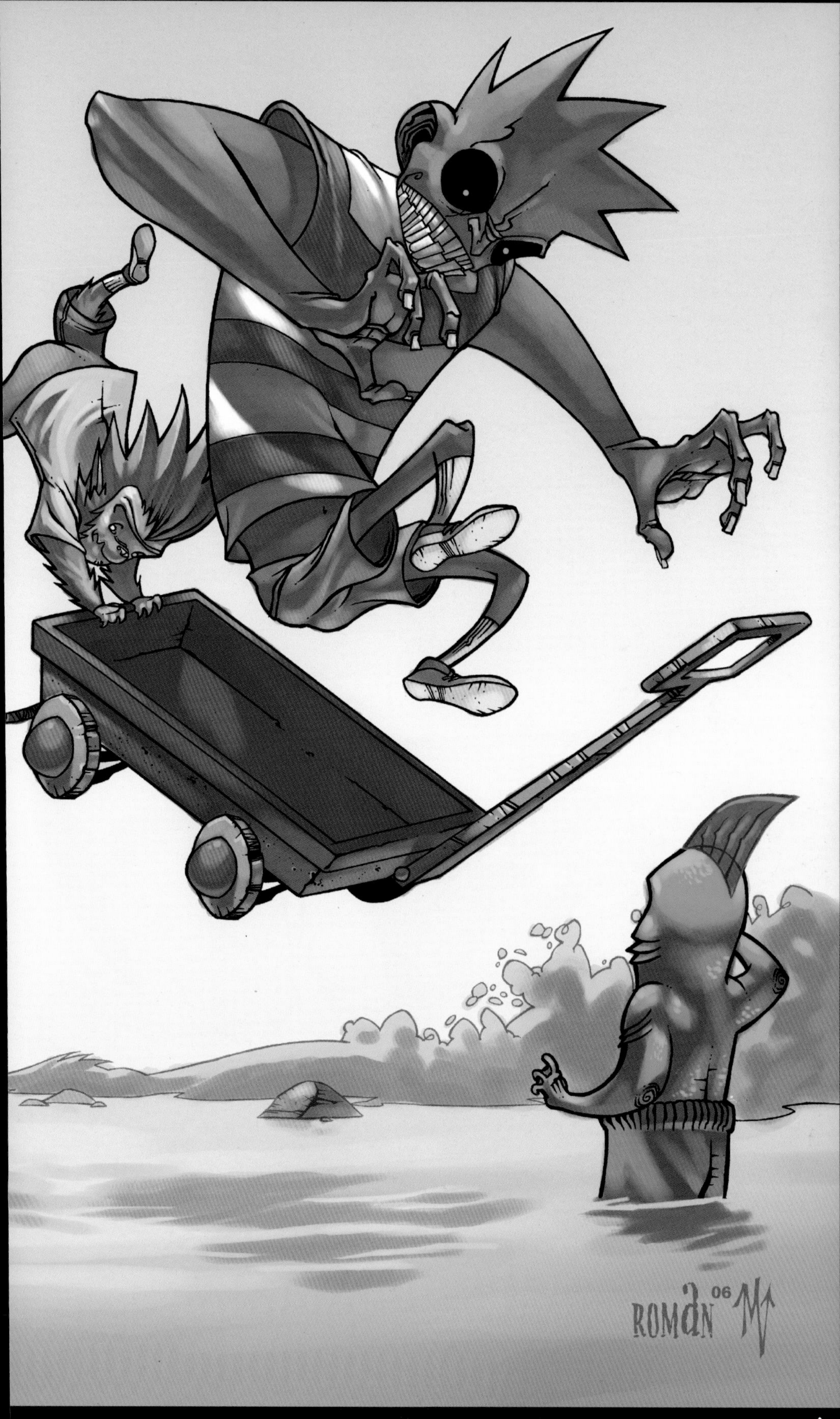
ROMAN 06

art by Benjamin Roman / colors by Jorge Molina Manzanero

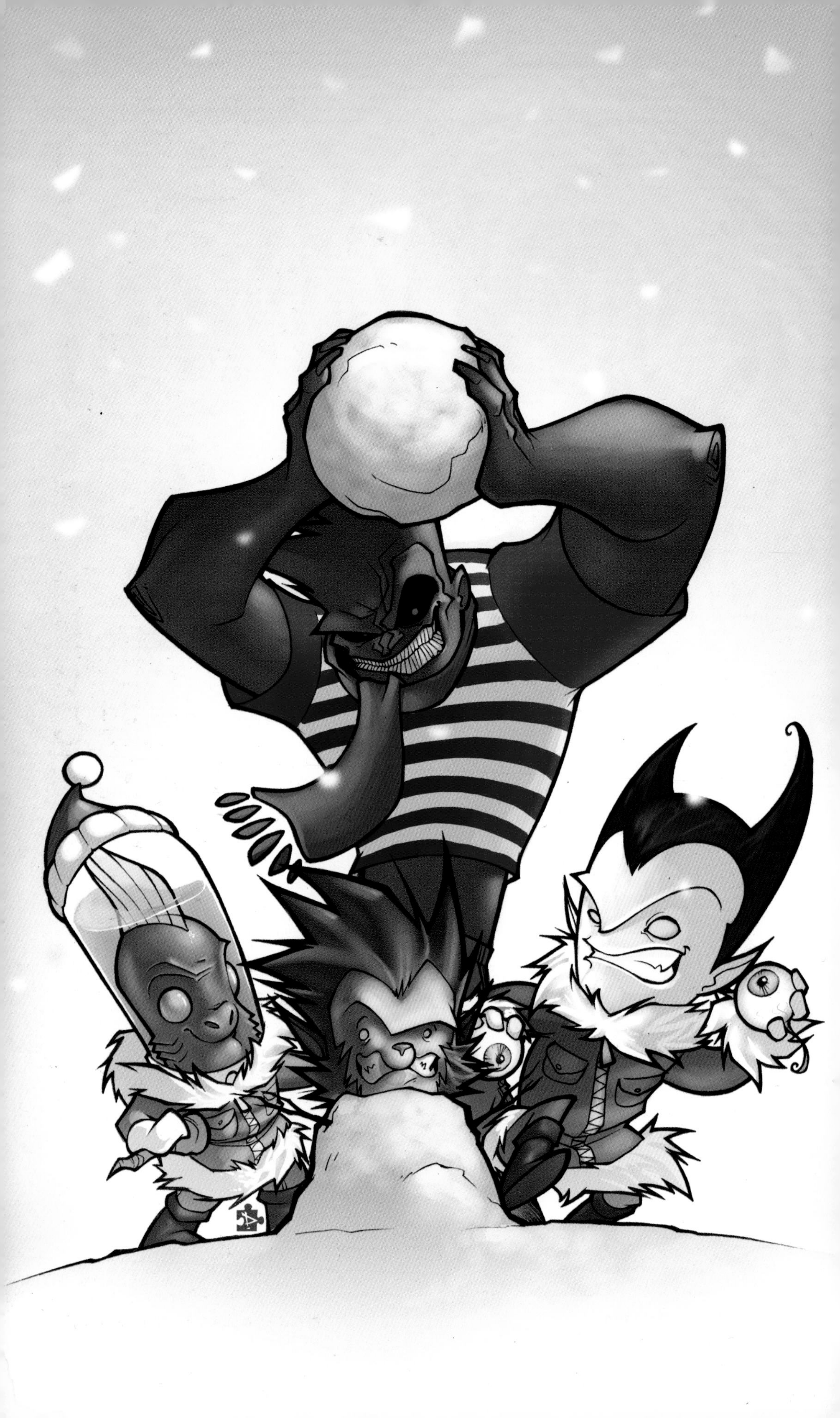

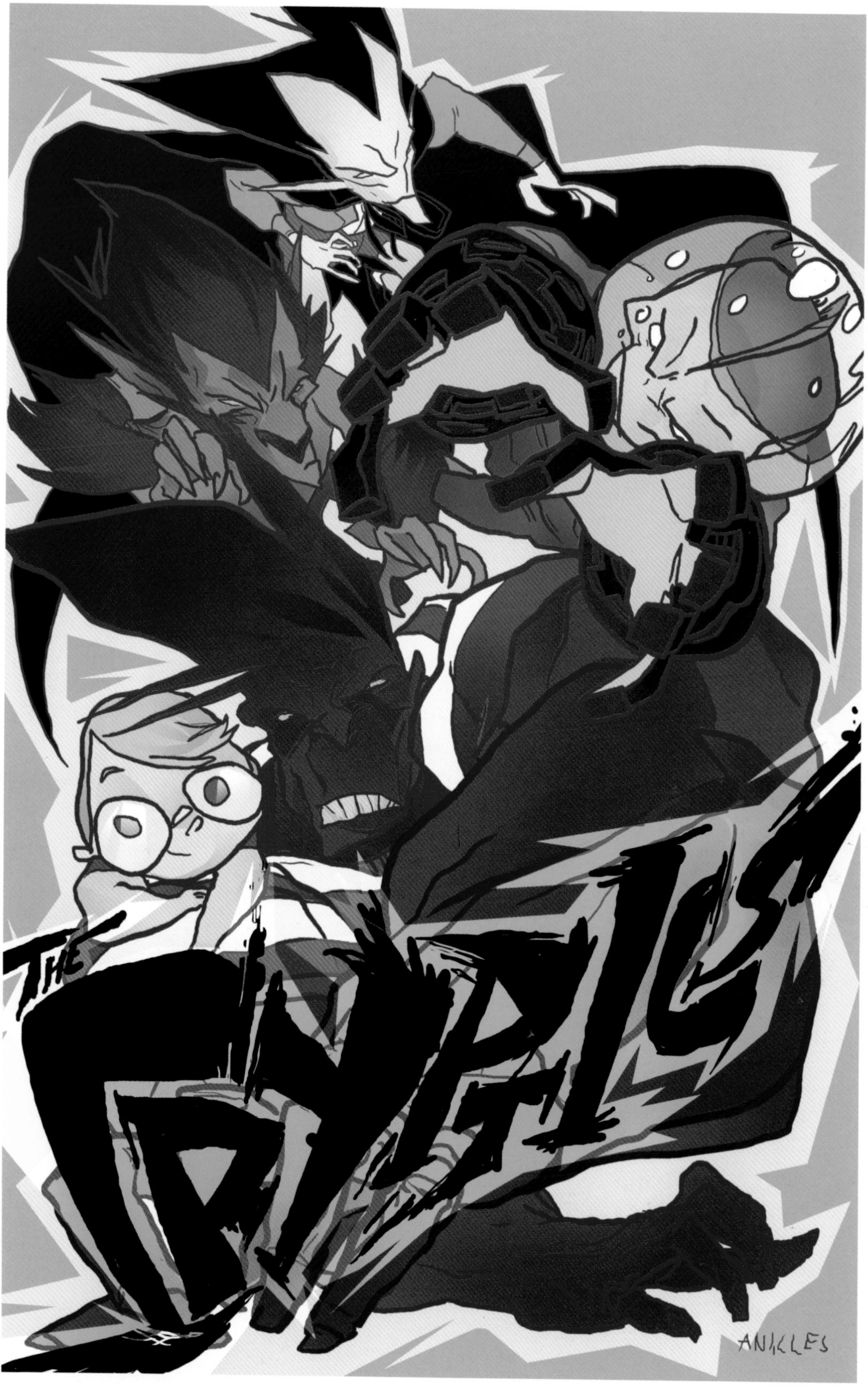
THE
ANKLES

<< art by Pedro Delgado
colors by Murfish

art and colors by Kris Anka ^

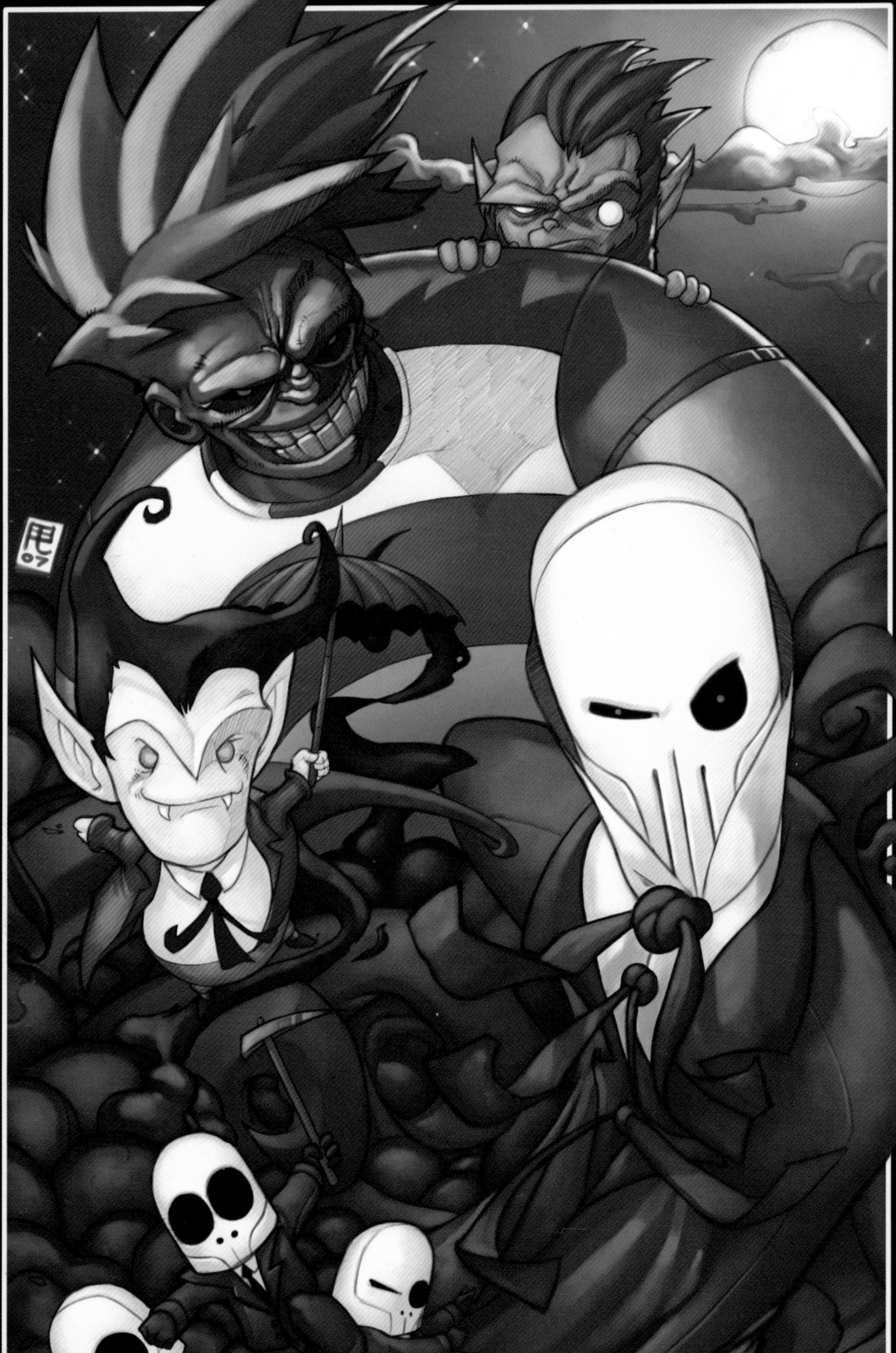

art and colors by Mario Rebuffi

art by Christopher Copeland
colors by Splashcolors

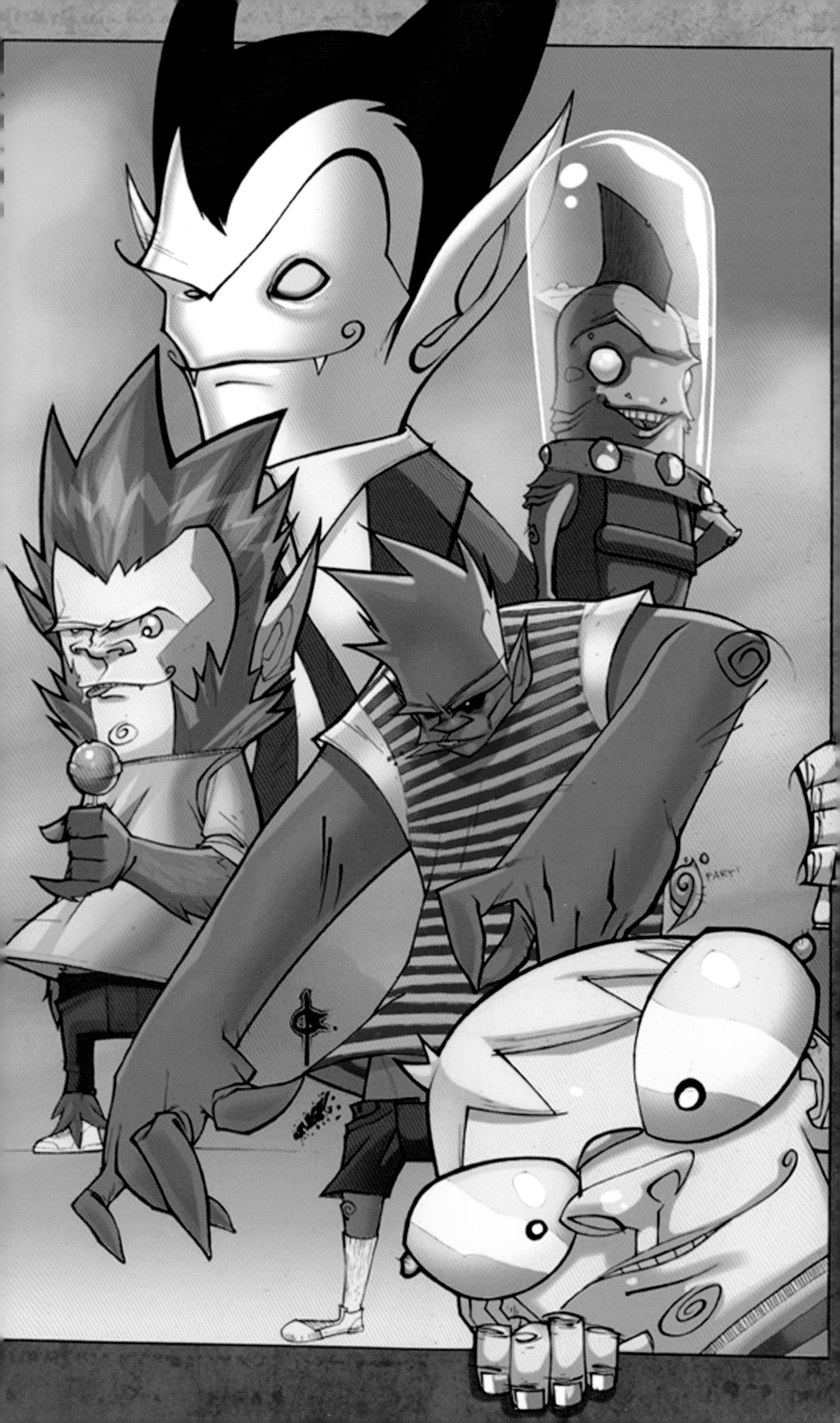

FART!

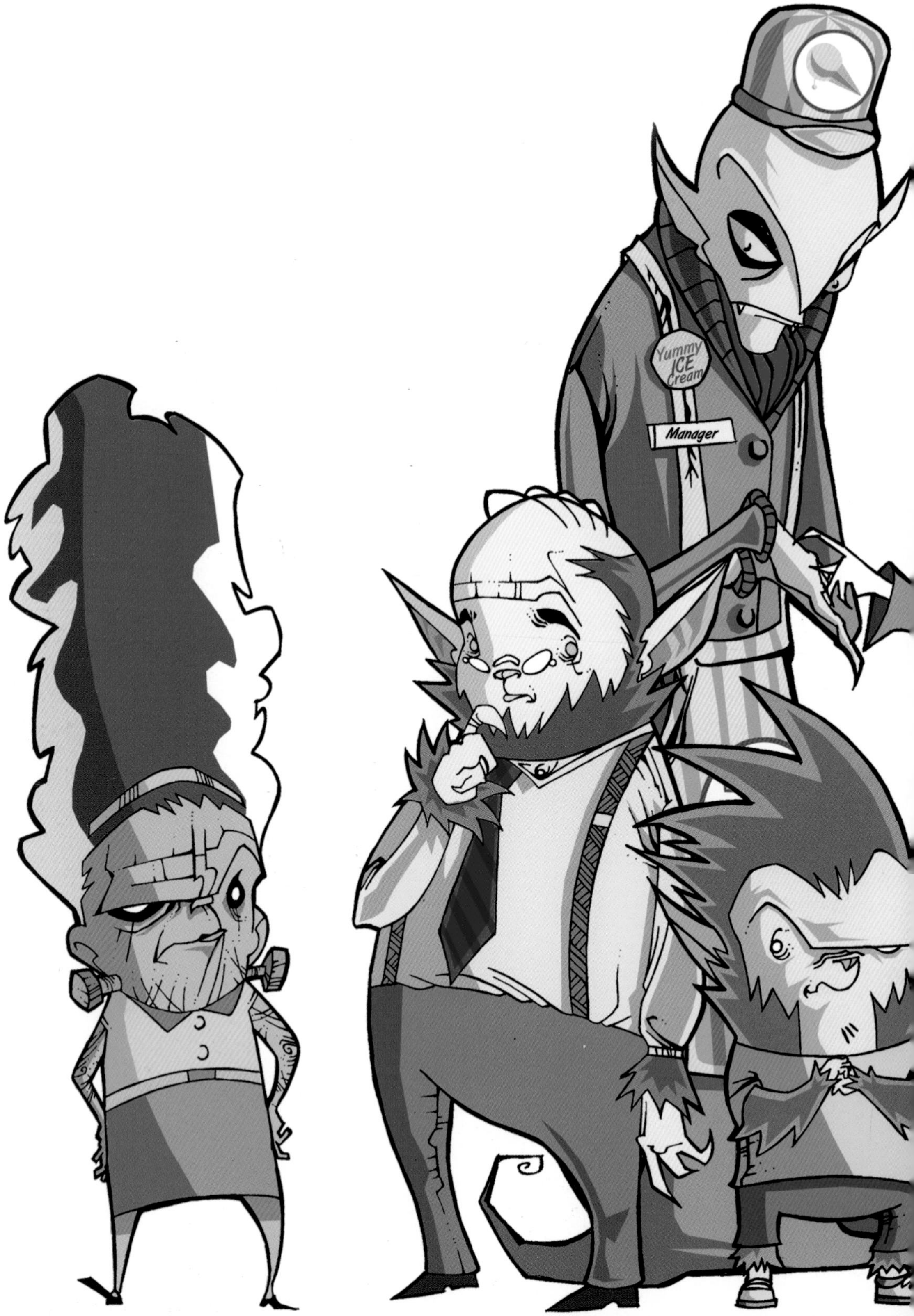

Yummy ICE Cream
Manager

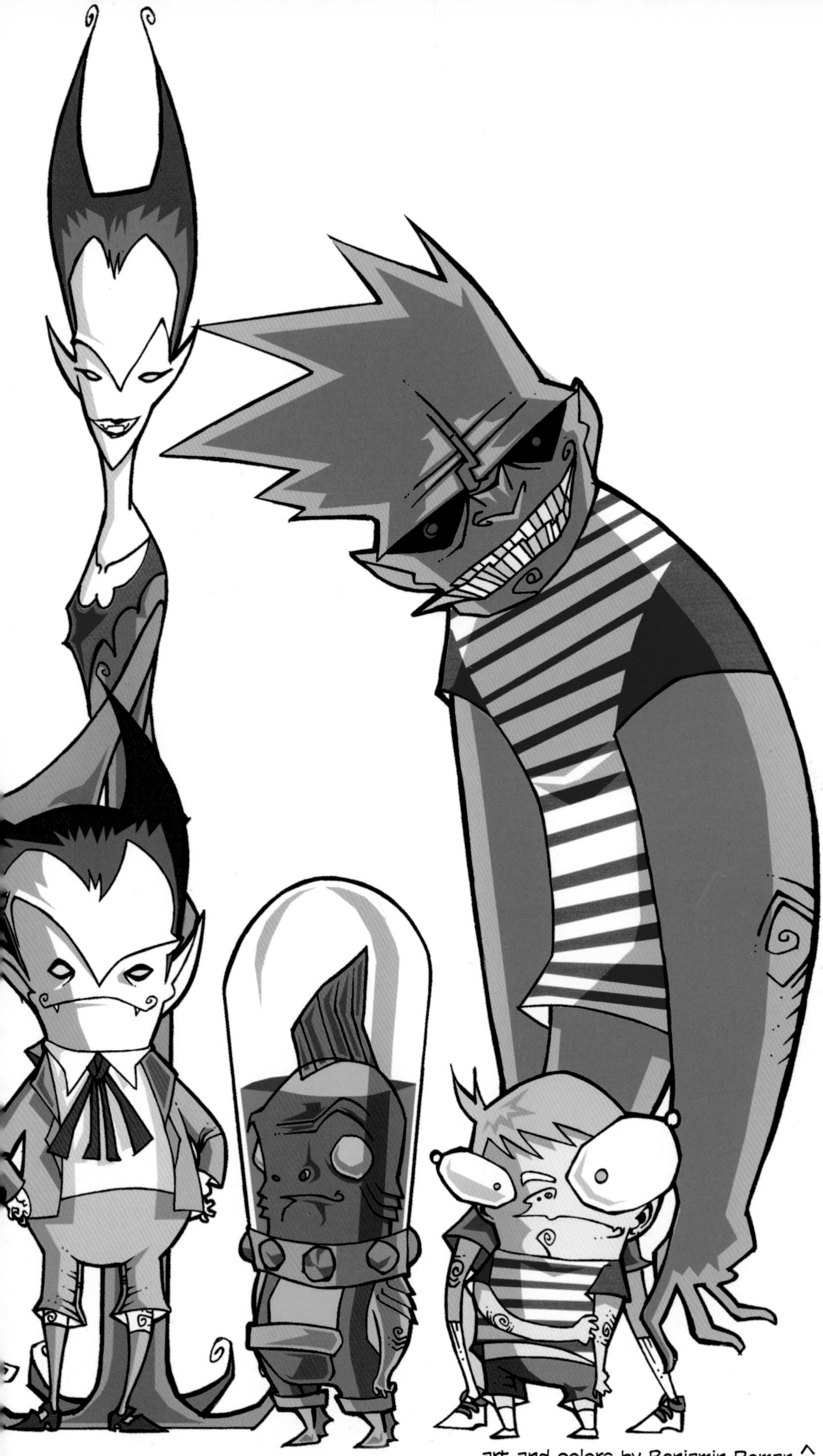

art and colors by Benjamin Roman

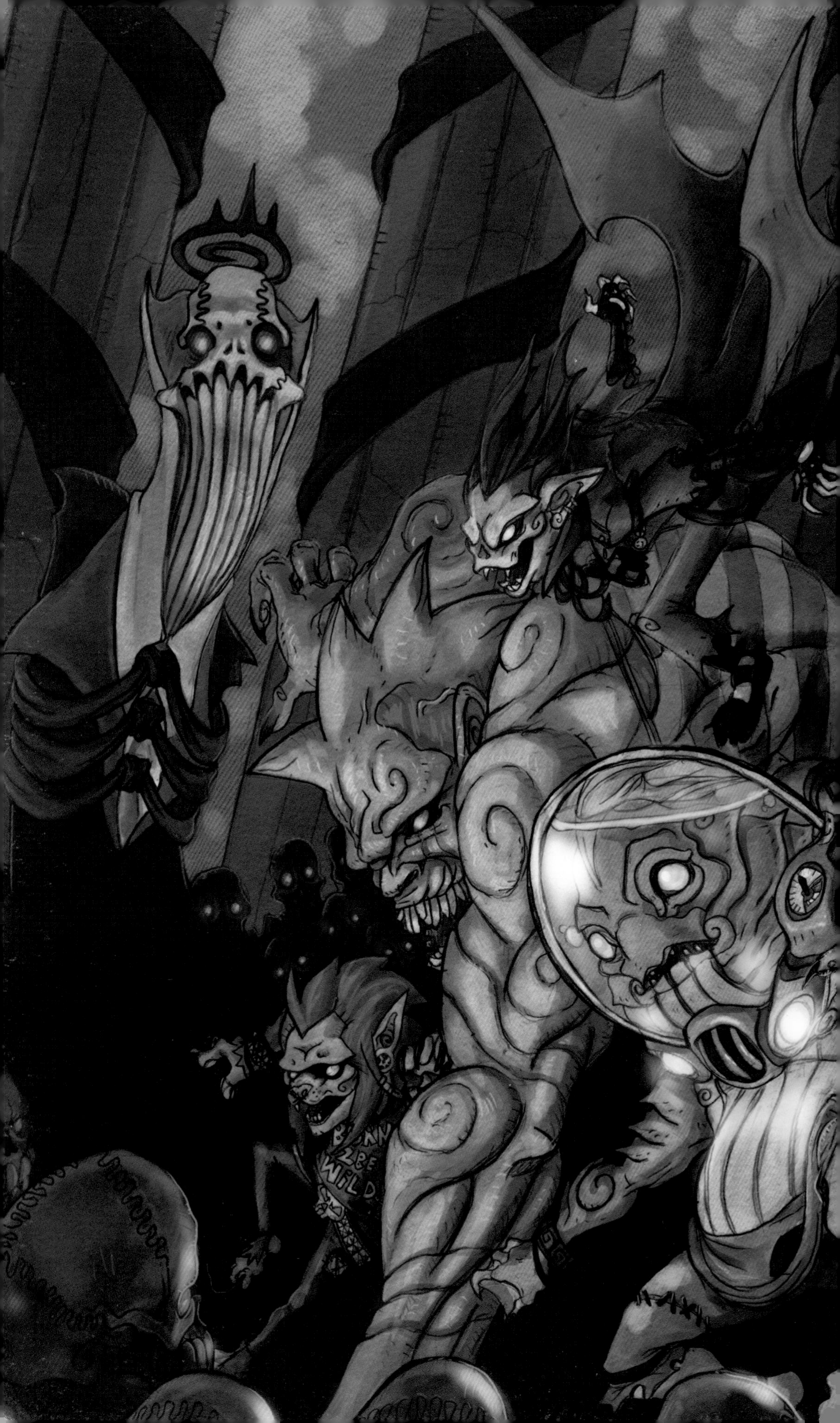
2BE
WILD

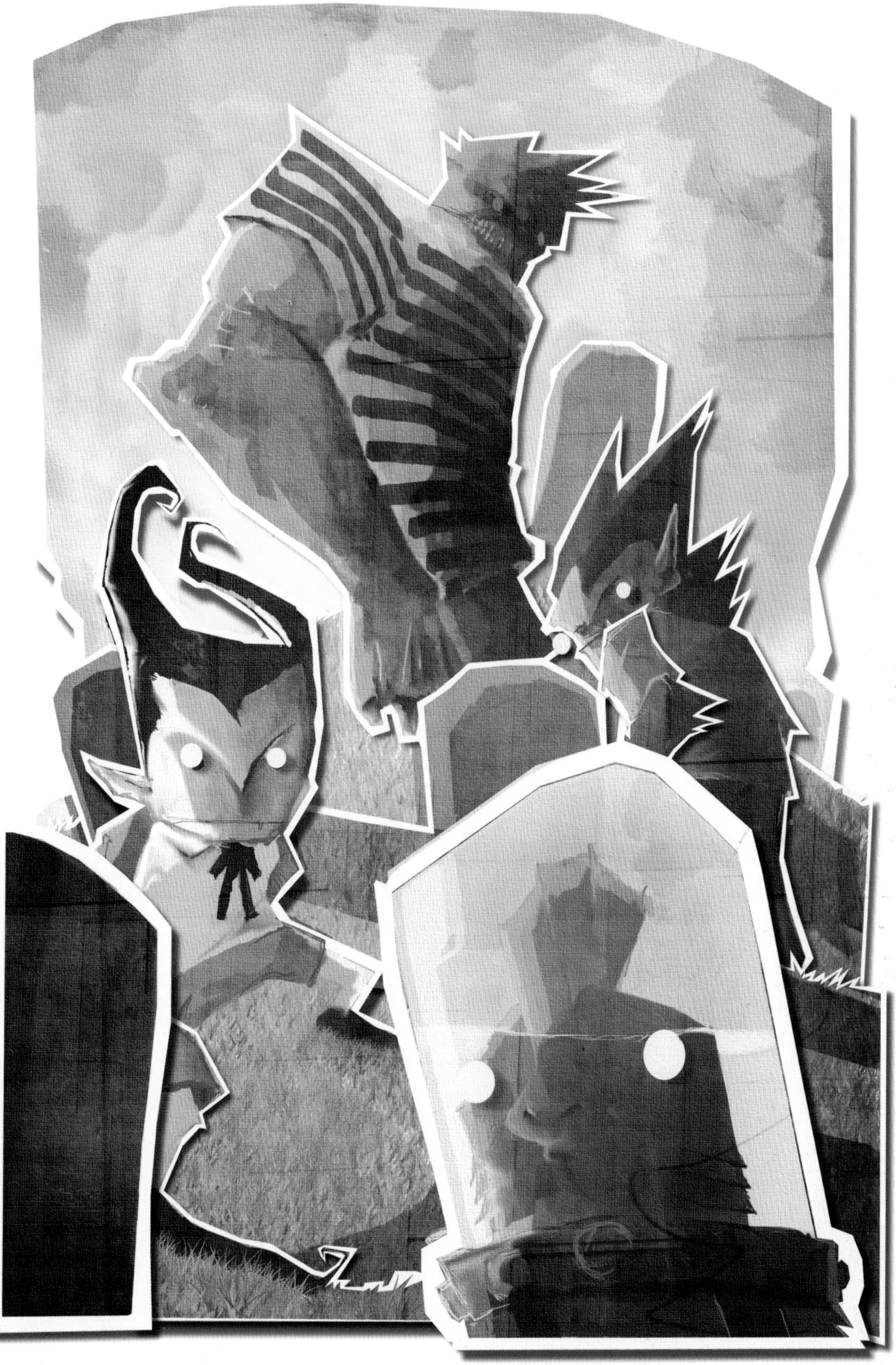

<< art and colors by Christopher Flork

art and colors by David Murdoch ^

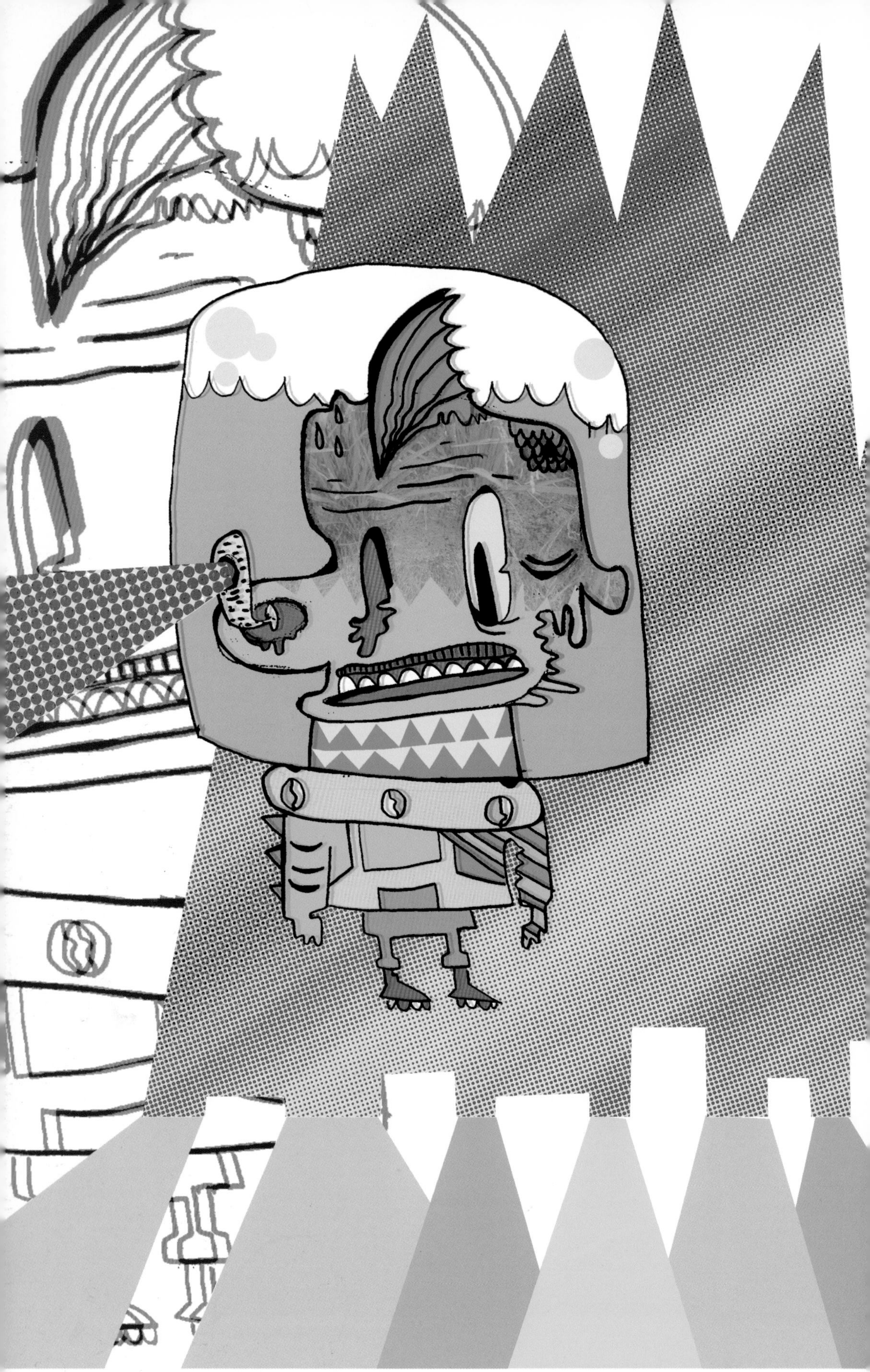

^ art and colors by Michael Skattum

art and colors by Dylan McCrae >>

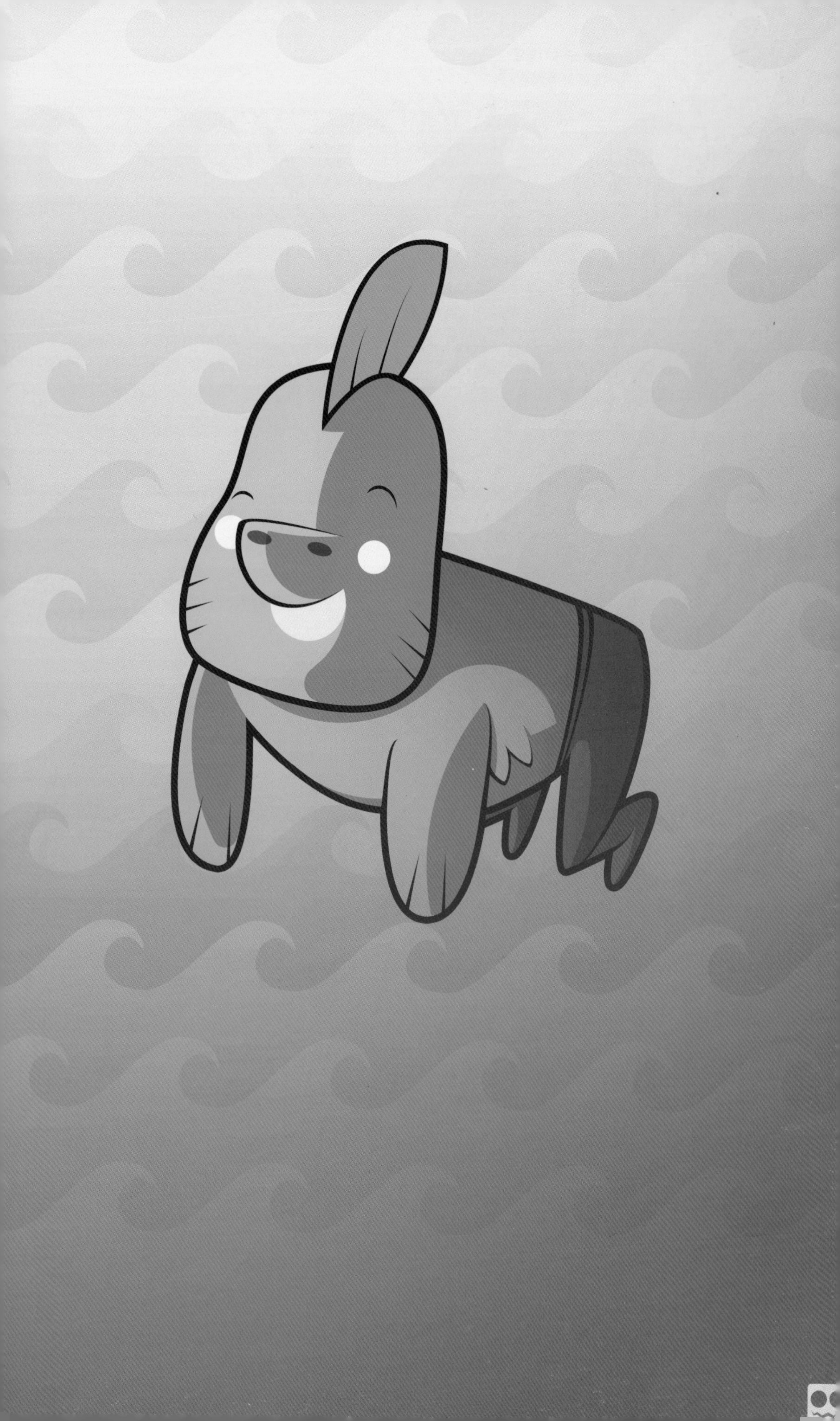

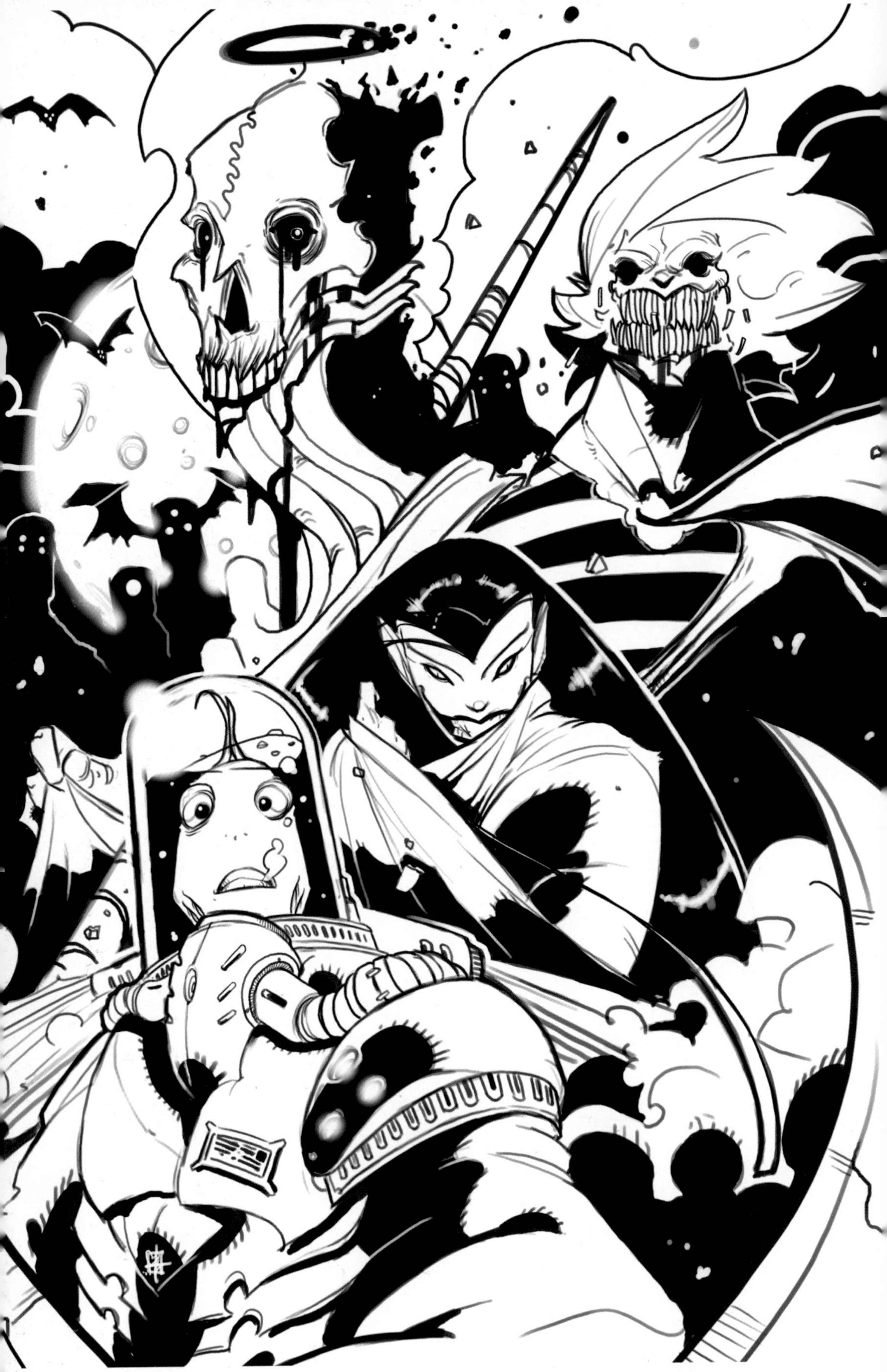

^ art by Jonah Gilbert

art and colors by Robert Iza >>

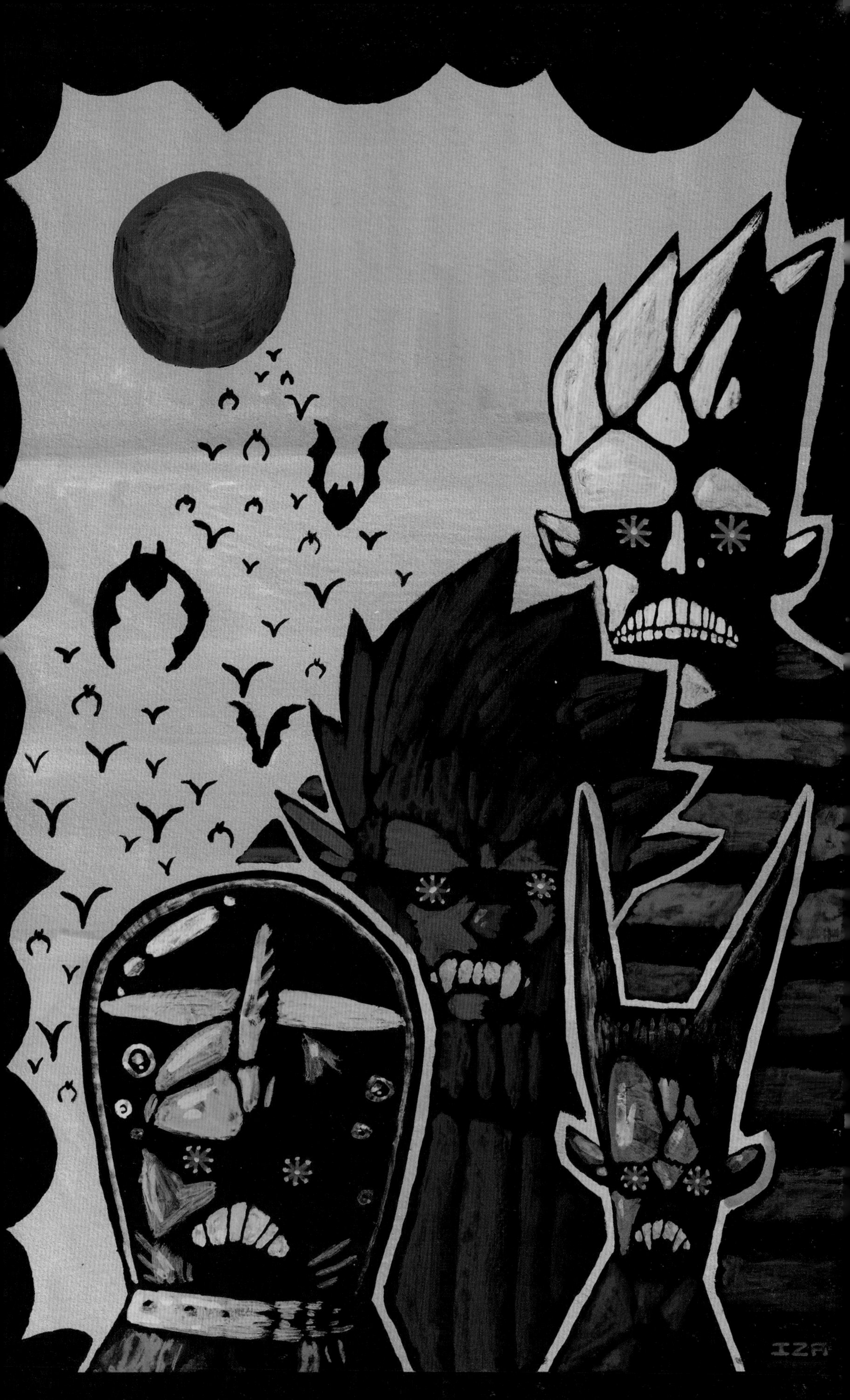
IZA

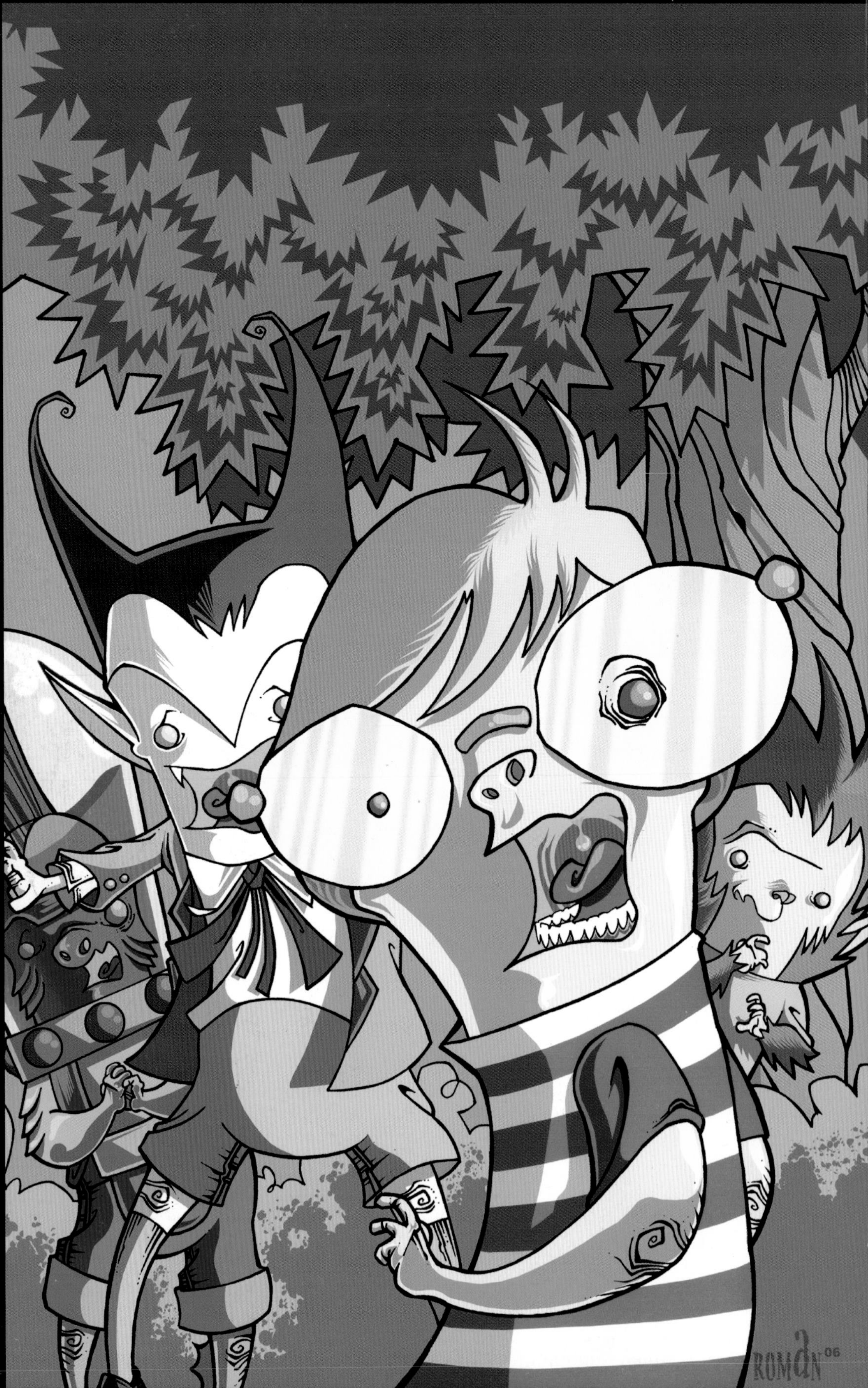
ROMAN 06

^ art and colors by Benjamin Roman

art and colors by Daniel Stone >>

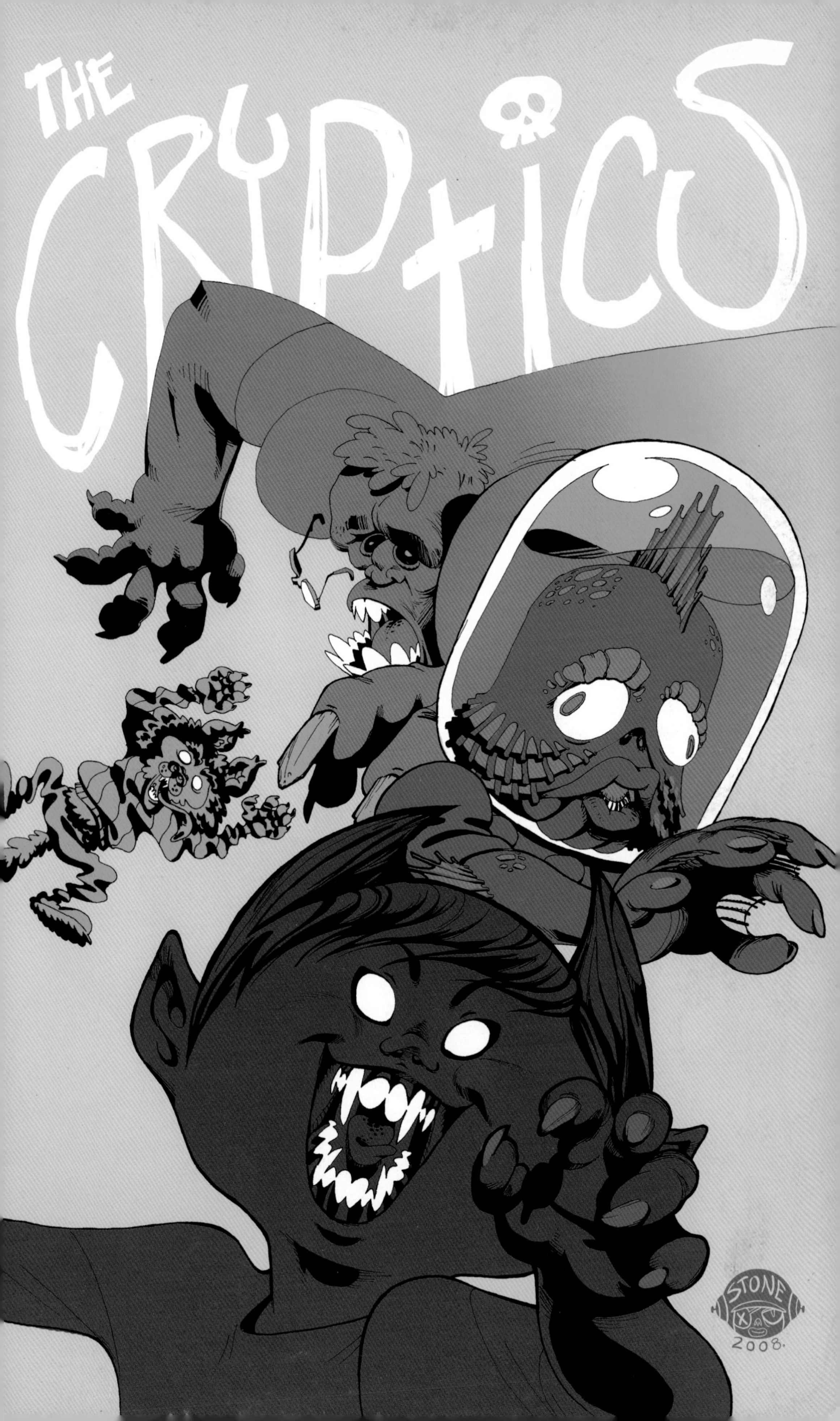
THE CRYPTICS
STONE
2008.

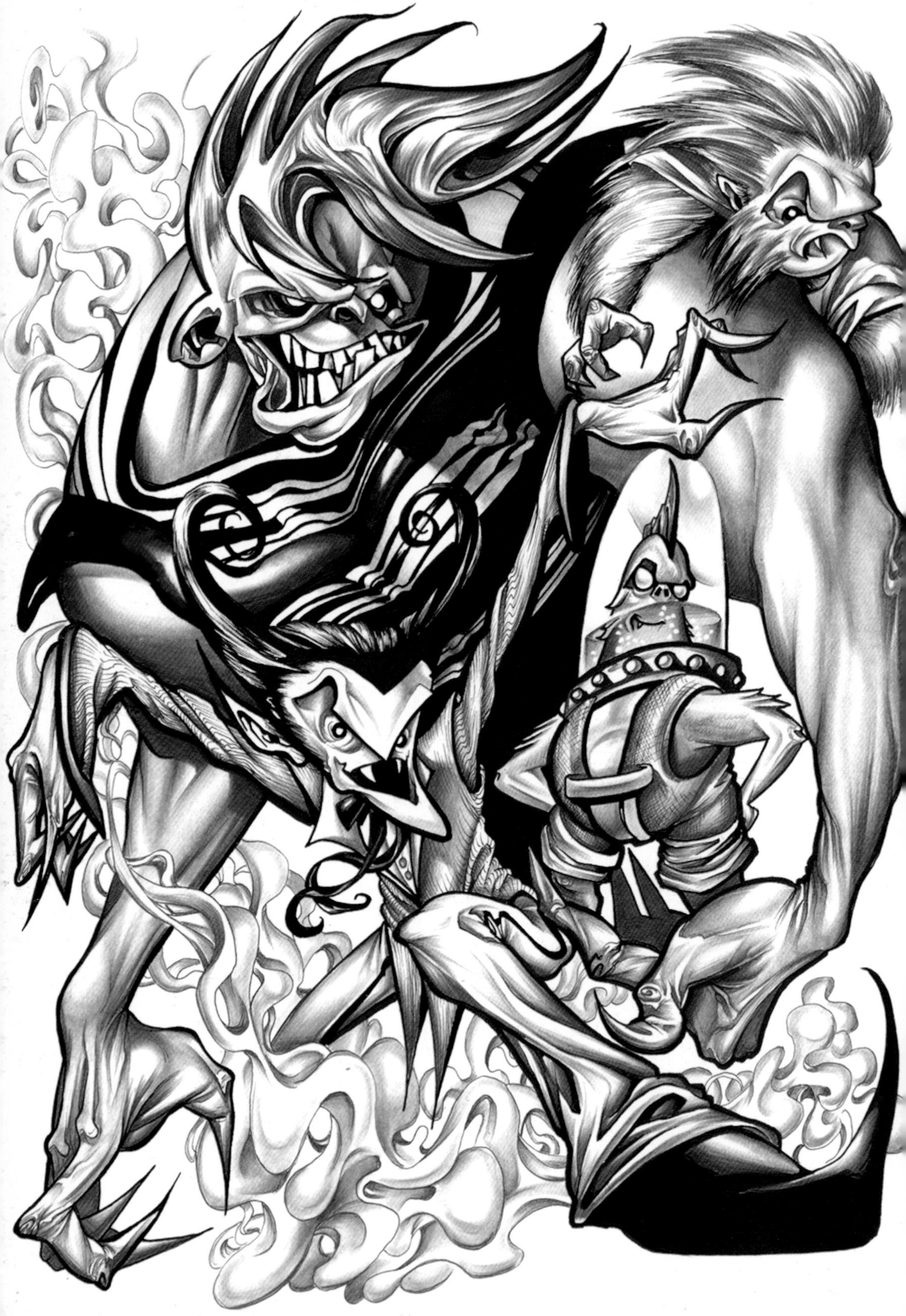

^ art by Wade Furlong

art and colors by Ryan Yee >>

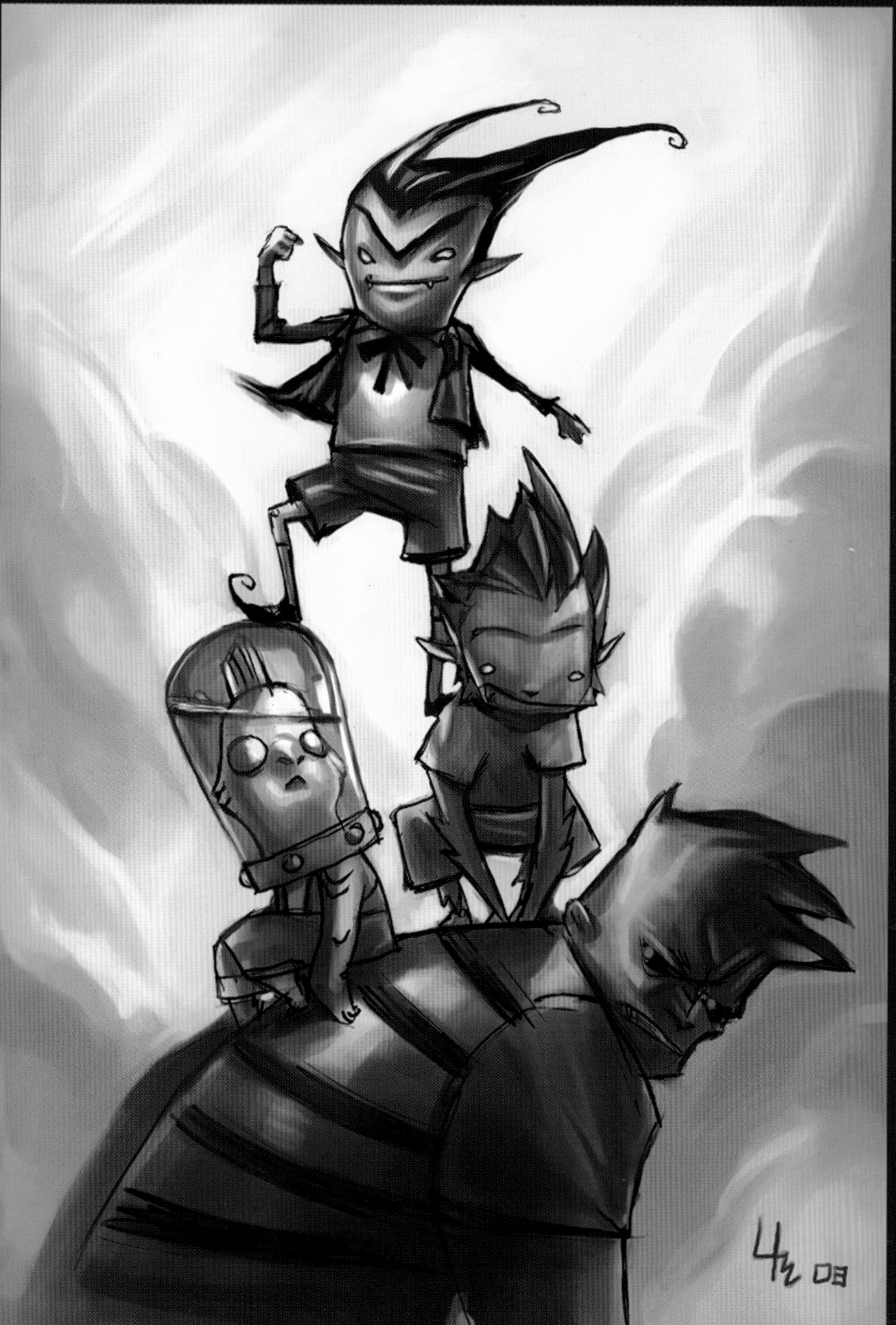

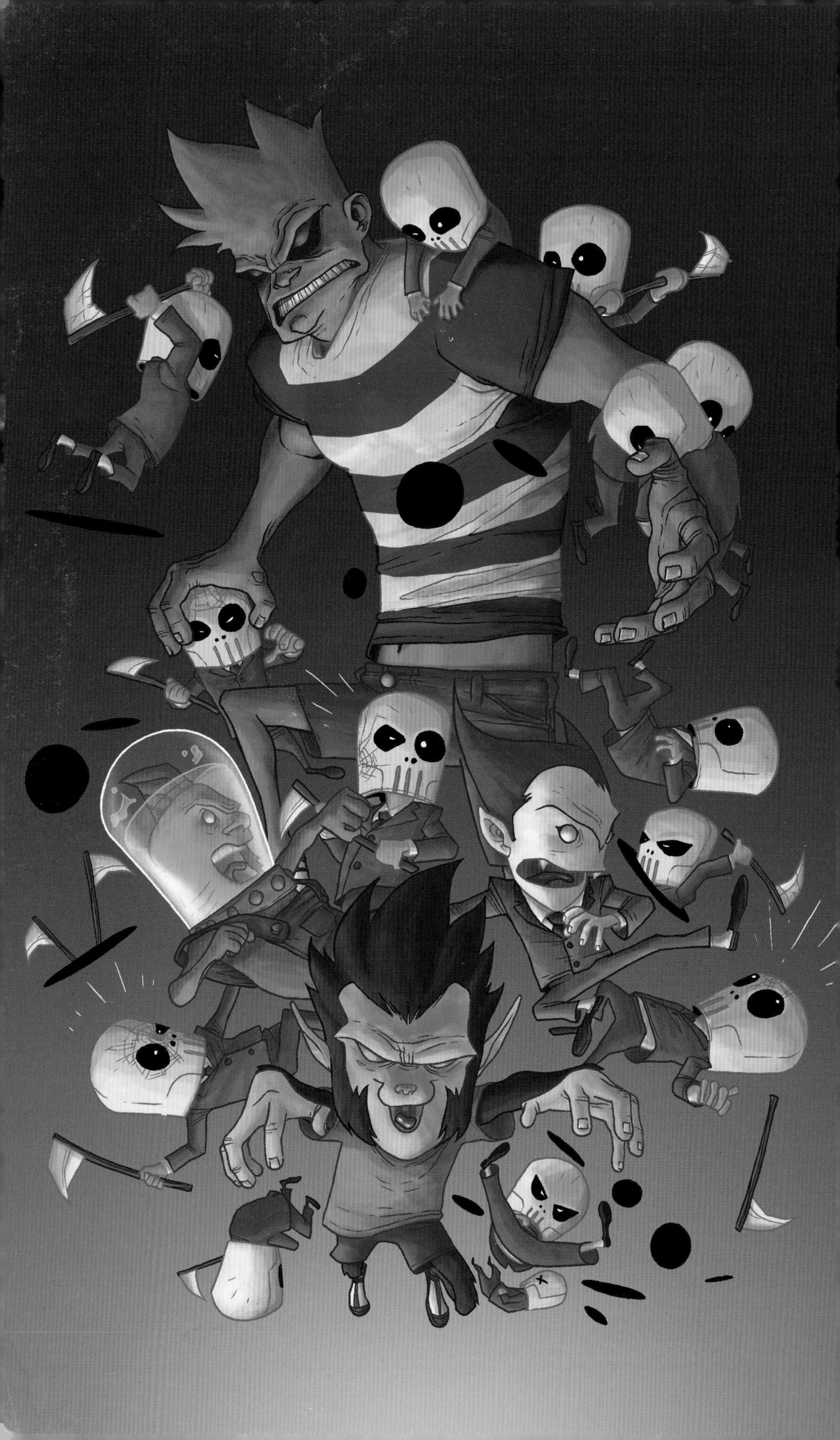

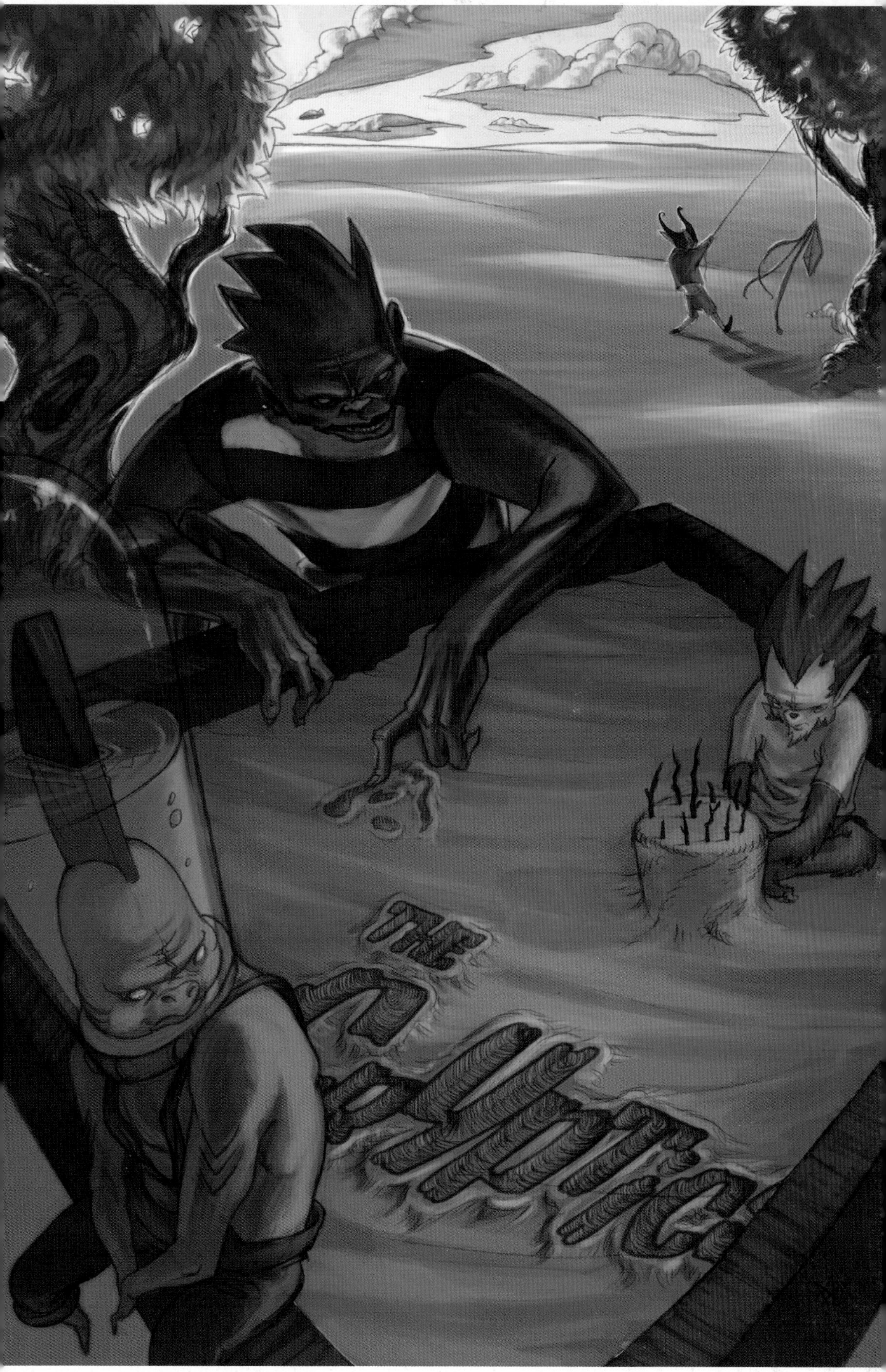
THE

<< art and colors by Jacob Baake

art and colors by Fazaad Feroze ^

art by David Igo / colors by A83 >>

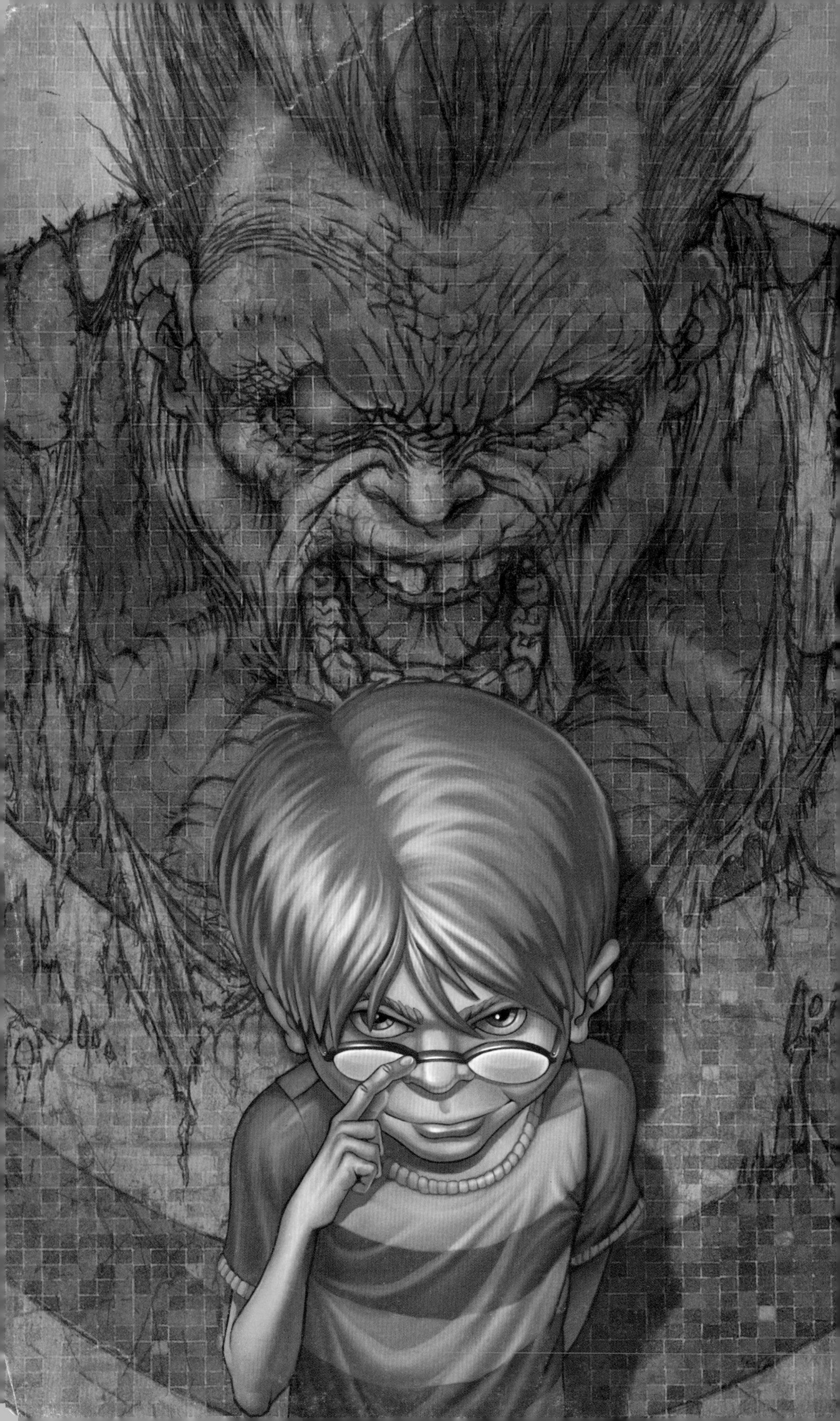